THE CLASSIC THEATRE

Volume One

Volumes II, III, and IV of THE CLASSIC THEATRE contain:

Vol. II

Vol. III

Vol. IV

THE MODERN THEATRE, Volumes I, II, III, IV, V, and VI, edited by Eric Bentley, are also available in the Anchor series.

Eric Bentley's four books on the modern theatre are available in paper backs: *The Playwright as Thinker, In Search of Theatre, The Dramatic Event, What Is Theatre?*

THE
CLASSIC THEATRE

Volume One

SIX ITALIAN PLAYS

Edited by Eric Bentley

DOUBLEDAY ANCHOR BOOKS
DOUBLEDAY & COMPANY, INC.
GARDEN CITY, NEW YORK

COVER DESIGN BY LEONARD BASKIN

TYPOGRAPHY BY EDWARD GOREY

The Anchor Books edition is the first publication of *The Classic Theatre, Volume I.*

Anchor Books edition: 1958

Library of Congress Catalog Card Number 58–12033

CONTENTS

THE MANDRAKE

Niccolò Machiavelli

English Version by
Frederick May and Eric Bentley

CHARACTERS

CALLIMACO, *a young man*

SIRO, *a servant*

MESSER NICIA CALFUCCI, LL.D.

LIGURIO, *a parasite*

SOSTRATA, *a mother*

TIMOTEO, *a friar*

A WOMAN

LUCREZIA, *wife of Messer Nicia, daughter of Sostrata*

THE TIME: *Early sixteenth century*

THE PLACE: *Florence*

PROLOGUE

Ladies and gentlemen, God bless you!
May Fate and Fortune long caress you!
(I thought I'd make a little fuss
Of you, so you'll be nice to *us*.)
Just sit quite still, don't make a sound,
And you will like us, I'll be bound.
The story's good we'll tell to you.
It happened here. What's more: it's true.
Florence we'll show you now, your home;
Tomorrow, maybe, Pisa, Rome,
The nicest towns you ever saw.
(Don't laugh so hard; you'll break your jaw.)
This right-hand door—can you all see?—
Belongs to a learnèd LL.D.
His erudition's vast: I'm told
He has Boethius down cold.
That dingy street is Lovers' Lane:
Those who fall there don't rise again.
If you don't leave us in the lurch
You'll see emerging from that church
A well-known friar (though I would not
Presume to say well known for what).
Next, you are all to get to know
A young man called Callimaco
Who lives in this next house by chance.
He is just back from Paris, France.

Callimaco is such a dandy
One look at him makes women randy.
This fellow loved unto perdition
A certain girl of good position
And played a little trick on her.
And who are we that should demur,
Good people, since on this our earth,
Of trickery there is no dearth?
(When you are tricked, fair ladies, see
That you are tricked as pleasantly.)
The mandrake of our title is
A plant with certain properties:
When women eat the root, their fate . . .
But this is to anticipate.
Our author's called . . . alas, his name
As yet is not well known to Fame.
If you should find his tale confusing,
The whole show somewhat unamusing,
He's quite a decent chap, I think,
And may well stand you to a drink.
He offers, though, for your delight
Well, what? An evil parasite . . .
A scholar who is not too bright . . .
A lover who is full of fight . . .
A friar whose moral sense is slight . . .
Is that sufficient for one night?
True, true, such antic jollity
Is nothing but frivolity.
This comedy is not profound.
I'm not so sure it's even sound.
Our author sends you his excuses.
He says life's hard, the world obtuse is,
And he most gladly would display
His gifts in any other way,
The only question is: who'd pay?
Attribute then to lack of money
His condescending to be funny.
Can he expect a warm reception?
If so, he'll be a rare exception.
This age to sour contempt is quicker,

To twisted smile, malignant snicker.
The virtues that did thrive of yore,
D'you think we'll see them any more?
Men won't devote their nights and days
To toil without their meed of praise:
Who on a plant would spend his powers
Knowing that all his lovely flowers
Would by a tempest then be tossed
Or in a fog concealed and lost?
Moreover, if you have concluded
Our man's your victim, you're deluded.
No matter for what sort you take him
You cannot nudge him, push him, shake him,
And, as for malice, he can do
Far better at the trade than you
For in the whole of Italy
Wherever reigns, not *yes*, but *sì*,
There's not a soul he would kowtow to.
The only man he'd make a bow to
Is the only V.I.P. he knows:
A man in more expensive clothes.
Backbite him if you please, but we
Must get on with his comedy
If you are to be home by three.
Don't take the play too much to heart.
If you see a monster, do not start:
Just look right through him, and he'll go.
But, wait, here comes Callimaco,
Siro his servant at his side.
These two, between them, will confide
The plot to you. Pay close attention!
The play will now unfold without my intervention.

CALLIMACO *and* SIRO

CALLIMACO. Don't go, Siro, I want to talk to you.

SIRO. I'm not going.

CALLIMACO. You must have been quite surprised by my sudden departure from Paris, and now very likely you're surprised that, having been here a month, I still haven't done anything.

SIRO. I don't deny it.

CALLIMACO. If I haven't told you already what I'm about to tell you, it's not because I don't trust you, but because it seemed best not to talk of confidential matters unless one was forced to. But now, since I shall need your help, I am going to tell you everything.

SIRO. I am your servant, and servants must never question their masters, nor pry into their affairs. But when the master volunteers information, the servant must serve him faithfully. Which is what I've done, and what I propose to do.

CALLIMACO. I know. I think you've heard me say a thousand times—but it won't hurt you to hear it the thousand and first—that when I was ten years old, my father and mother being dead, I was sent by my guardians to live in Paris, where I've been these twenty years. After ten years the Italian Wars began—as a result of King Charles's invasion of Italy, which laid waste this country—so I decided to settle in Paris and never go back to my native land. I thought I should be safer than in Italy.

SIRO. Very true.

CALLIMACO. Having sent instructions that all my possessions here, with the exception of my house, should be sold, I settled down in Paris. And I have passed the last ten years in great happiness . . .

SIRO. I know.

CALLIMACO. . . . devoting part of my time to study, part to pleasure, and part to business, and so arranging things that the three never got in each other's way. In consequence, as you know, I lived quietly, helping whoever I could, trying to injure nobody, so that, it seems to me, I came to be well thought of by everyone, be he gentleman or merchant, foreign or native, rich or poor.

SIRO. That's true, too.

CALLIMACO. But Fortune, deeming that I was *too* happy, sent to Paris a certain Cammillo Calfucci.

SIRO. I begin to guess what your trouble is.

CALLIMACO. Like the other Florentines, he was frequently invited to dine at my house, and one day, when we were gathered together, an argument started as to where the more beautiful women were to be found—Italy or France. I could have no opinion concerning Italian women—I was so little when I left the country—so Cammillo Calfucci took up the cudgels for the Italians and another Florentine defended the French. After a great deal of argument back and forth, Cammillo, in something of a temper, said that, even if Italian women in general were monsters, he had a kinswoman who could redeem her country's reputation all by herself.

SIRO. I see what you're after.

CALLIMACO. And he named Madonna Lucrezia, wife of Messer Nicia Calfucci, and so praised her beauty and sweetness of manner that he left us all amazed and aroused in me such a desire to see her that I set out for Florence, putting aside all other considerations and not bothering whether there was a war on or not. Having arrived here, I found that Madonna Lucrezia's reputation fell far short of the truth; which is quite a rare phenomenon. And I'm burning with such desire to make her mine, I hardly know what to do with myself.

SIRO. If you'd told me this when we were in Paris, I'd have known how to advise you. Now, I don't know what to say.

CALLIMACO. I'm not telling you this with a view to advice, but to get it out of my system. And so you can be ready to help when the need arises.

SIRO. I couldn't be readier. What hopes have you got?

CALLIMACO. Alas, none. Or very few. Let me explain. First, her nature is hostile to my desires. She's the quintessence of chastity. The thought of love affairs is alien to her. Then, her husband's very rich, lets himself be ruled by her in everything, and, if he's not exactly young, he's not antique either, that's clear. Again, there are no relatives or neighbors whose homes she frequents at wakes and holidays and the other pleasant occasions that young women delight in. No tradesman sets foot in her house, and she hasn't a single servant or retainer who doesn't go in fear of her. Bribery and corruption are therefore excluded.

SIRO. What are you thinking of doing, then?

CALLIMACO. No situation is so desperate that one may not continue to hope. Even if one's hopes are feeble and vain, the determination to see a thing through causes them to seem far otherwise.

SIRO. So what makes you go on hoping?

CALLIMACO. Two things. First, the simple-mindedness of Messer Nicia, who, though he holds an LL.D. from the university, is the most thickheaded and foolish man in Florence. Second, his desire, and hers, to have children. Having been married for six years without getting any, and being very rich, they're dying of their desire for a family. There's a third factor: her mother. She was a bit of a baggage when she was young; but she's rich now, and I've no idea how to deal with her.

SIRO. Since that's how matters stand, have you tried anything?

CALLIMACO. Yes. In a small way.

SIRO. Tell me.

CALLIMACO. You know Ligurio, who's always coming to eat at my house? He used to be a professional matchmaker. Now he goes around cadging dinners and suppers. Being a pleasant sort of chap, he's had no trouble becoming intimate with Messer Nicia, and leading him a dance. The old boy wouldn't invite him to dinner, it's true, but he's been lending him money from time to time. As for me, I've struck up a friendship with this Ligurio, told him of my love for Madonna Lucrezia, and he's promised to help me with all he's got.

SIRO. Take care he doesn't deceive you. These parasites don't make a habit of fidelity.

CALLIMACO. True. Nonetheless, when you place yourself in someone's hands, you place yourself in someone's hands. I've promised him a large sum of money if he succeeds, and, if he fails, a dinner and a supper. I'd never eat alone in any case.

SIRO. So what has he promised to do?

CALLIMACO. He's promised to persuade Messer Nicia to take his wife to the Baths—this May.

SIRO. What good would that do you?

CALLIMACO. What good would it do me? The place may well make a different woman out of her. In haunts like that, they do nothing but throw parties and such. And I'd be taking with me all the plausible arguments I could think up, omitting no tittle of pomp and circumstance. I'd become the bosom pal of both parties, wife and husband. Who can say what will happen? One thing leads to another. Time rules all.

SIRO. I'm quite impressed.

CALLIMACO. Ligurio left me this morning saying that he'd take this matter up with Messer Nicia and would let me know the answer.

SIRO. Here they come—together.

CALLIMACO. I'll step to one side—to be on hand for a word with Ligurio when he takes leave of the old boy. Meanwhile you go home and get on with your work. If I want you for anything I'll let you know.

SIRO. Right.

SCENE 2

MESSER NICIA *and* LIGURIO

MESSER NICIA. I think your advice is good, and I talked the matter over last night with my wife. She said she'd give me her answer today. But, to tell the truth, I'm not over-keen.

LIGURIO. Why not?

MESSER NICIA. Because I'm in a rut and I'd like to stay in it. What's more, to have to transport wife, servants, household goods, it doesn't appeal to me. Besides, I was talking yesterday evening to some doctors. One of them said I should go to San Filippo; another said Porretta; another, Villa. What a bunch of quacks! If you ask me, the medical profession doesn't know its business.

LIGURIO. What you mentioned first must be what troubles you most: you're not accustomed to lose sight of the Cupola.

MESSER NICIA. You're mistaken. When I was younger I was a victim of Wanderlust. They never held a fair at Prato but I was there. There's not a castle in the neighborhood that I haven't visited. Better yet: I've been to Pisa and Livorno. What do you think of that?

LIGURIO. Then you must have seen the Sliding Tower of Pisa?

MESSER NICIA. You mean the Leaning Tower.

LIGURIO. The Leaning Tower, of course. And at Livorno, did you see the sea?

MESSER NICIA. You know very well I did.

LIGURIO. How much bigger is it than the Arno?

MESSER NICIA. Arno! Pooh! It's four times bigger, no, more than six; you'll make me say more than seven times in a minute. Nothing but water, water, water!

LIGURIO. Well then, I'm amazed that you, who—as the saying is—have pissed your way through so much snow, should make such a fuss about going to the Baths!

MESSER NICIA. Your mother's milk is still on your lips, my child. Do you think it's a small matter to transplant an entire household? Yet my desire for children is so strong I'm ready to do anything. But have a word or two with those M.D.s. See where *they* advise me to go. Meanwhile I'll join my wife at home. I'll see you there later.

LIGURIO. Good idea.

SCENE 3

LIGURIO *and* CALLIMACO

LIGURIO. Can there be a bigger fool in the whole wide world? And how Fortune has favored him! He's rich, and his beautiful wife is well bred, virtuous, and fit to rule a kingdom. It seems to me that the proverb about marriage seldom proves true—the one that runs: "God makes men, but they find their mates for themselves." For in general we see a man of parts paired off with a shrew while a prudent woman gets a half-wit for a husband. But that fellow's half-wittedness has this much to be said for it: it gives Callimaco reason to hope. And here he is. Hey, Callimaco—lying in wait for someone?

CALLIMACO. I'd seen you with our learnèd friend, and I was waiting for you to part company with him, so I could hear what you'd done.

LIGURIO. He's a fellow of small prudence and less spirit, as you know. He doesn't want to leave Florence. However, I worked on his feelings for a while, and he told me he'd do just as I said. I believe we'll be able to move him in the right direction. Whether we can complete our project is, of course, another story.

CALLIMACO. How so?

LIGURIO. Well, as you know, all sorts of people go to these Baths, and it might be that a man would come along who'd find Madonna Lucrezia as attractive as you do. He might be richer than you. He might be more charming. So there's the danger of going to all this trouble for someone else's benefit. It is also possible that, with so many competitors for her favor, she might become the harder to attain. Or that, having got used to the idea of yielding, she might yield, not to you, but to another.

CALLIMACO. You have a point. But what am I to do? Which way am I to turn? I must try something. Something tremendous or something dangerous, something harmful or something infamous, I don't care. Better to die than to live like this! If I could sleep at night, if I could eat, if I could engage in conversation, if I could find pleasure in anything at all, I should be able to await Time's verdict more patiently. Here and now I can see no remedy. If hope is not kept alive within me by some course of action, I shall assuredly die. Faced with this prospect of Death, I am resolved to fear nothing, but adopt a course of action that is bestial, cruel, and nefarious.

LIGURIO. You mustn't talk like that! You must curb such excess of passion!

CALLIMACO. Actually, by feeding my imagination on thoughts like this, I keep myself in check—as you can see. However, it is necessary for us either to proceed with our plan for sending him to the Baths or to try some other avenue, if only that I may have a little hope to feed on. And if it can't be true hope, then let it be false, so long as it provides me with thoughts that lighten my burden of troubles!

LIGURIO. You're right. I'm for doing as you say.

CALLIMACO. Though I know that men of your sort live by cheating others, I believe you. I don't propose to fear your cheating me because, if I saw you try to, I should proceed to take advantage of the fact. And you would forfeit your right to come and go in my house, and all hope of receiving what I have promised you.

LIGURIO. Don't doubt my fidelity. Even if I had no sense of my own interests, and did not hope what I hope, well, you and I are so congenial, I'm almost as desirous as you are that you should get what you want. But enough. Messer Nicia has commissioned me to find a doctor who can say

which of the Baths it would be best for him to go to. Let
yourself be advised by me. Tell him you've studied medicine and been practicing for some time in Paris. Simple-
minded as he is, he'll believe you, and, since you're an educated man, you'll be able to treat him to a little Latin.

CALLIMACO. What good will that do us?

LIGURIO. It will enable us to send him to whichever Baths we
wish, and put into operation another plan I've thought of—
one that's more likely to succeed and takes less time.

CALLIMACO. What did you say?

LIGURIO. I say you're to take heart: if you put your trust in
me, I'll have the whole thing finished by this time tomorrow. Even if he investigates your claim to be a doctor—and
he won't—the short time at his disposal and the nature of
the case will stop him getting anywhere. By the time he
figured anything out—if he did—it'd be too late for him to
frustrate our plan.

CALLIMACO. You fill me with new life. Oh, this is too fair a
promise! You feed me with too much hope! How will you
do it?

LIGURIO. You'll find out at the proper moment. Right now
there's little enough time for action, let alone talk. Go home
and wait for me. I'll hunt up our learnèd friend. And if I
bring him along, take your cue from me, and make everything you say fit in.

CALLIMACO. I'll do as you say, though the hopes you raise
within me may, I fear, go up in smoke.

ACT II

SCENE 1

LIGURIO, MESSER NICIA, *and* SIRO

LIGURIO. As I say, I believe God expressly sent us this man that you might have your desire. His practice in Paris was extensive and successful, and you needn't be surprised that he hasn't practiced here in Florence. The reasons are, first, that he's rich, and second, that he has to return to Paris at once.

MESSER NICIA. Well, now, brother, there's an important point: I shouldn't like him to get me into an awkward situation and then leave me in it.

LIGURIO. The only thing you have to worry about is that he might not be willing to undertake your cure. If he does take you on, he won't leave you till he's seen it through.

MESSER NICIA. That part I'll leave to you, but, as for science, once I've talked with him, *I'll* tell *you* whether he knows his stuff or not. He won't sell *me* any pig in a poke!

LIGURIO. Because you're the man I know you to be, I *want* you to talk with him. And if he doesn't impress you, for presence, learning, and Latin, as someone you can trust like your dear old sainted mother, my name's not Ligurio.

MESSER NICIA. Well then, by the Holy Angel, so be it! And let's get going! Where does he live?

LIGURIO. On this square. That's his door right opposite.

MESSER NICIA. Good Fortune attend us!

LIGURIO *knocks at the door*. Here goes!

SIRO, *from within*. Who is it?

LIGURIO. Is Callimaco at home?

SIRO. Yes, he is.

MESSER NICIA. Why don't you call him *Master* Callimaco?

LIGURIO. Oh, he doesn't care about such trifles.

MESSER NICIA. Tsk, tsk, tsk. You must pay him the respect due to his profession: if he takes it amiss, so much the worse for him.

SCENE 2

CALLIMACO, MESSER NICIA, *and* LIGURIO

CALLIMACO. Who is it that wants me?

MESSER NICIA. *Bona dies, domine magister.*

CALLIMACO. *Et vobis bona, domine doctor.*

LIGURIO. What do you think?

MESSER NICIA. By the Holy Gospel, he's good!

LIGURIO. If you want me to stay, you must talk a language I understand. If not, let's part company.

CALLIMACO. What fair business brings you here?

MESSER NICIA. I wonder. I want two things that another man might run a mile to avoid. *Primo*, to give myself a lot of trouble. *Secundo*, to inflict it on someone else. I have no children, I'd like some, and, to get myself into this trouble, I've come to importune you.

CALLIMACO. It will never be less than a joy to me to give pleasure to you and to all other men of merit and virtue, nor have I practiced these many years in Paris but for the privilege of serving such as you.

MESSER NICIA. I appreciate that, and should you ever need my own professional services, I would be happy to oblige. But to return *ad rem nostram*. Have you thought which of the Baths is most likely to get my wife pregnant? I know, you see, that Ligurio here has told you—what he has told you.

CALLIMACO. Very true. But, that we may enable you to have your desire, we must know the cause of your wife's sterility. For there can be various causes. *Nam causae sterilitatis*

*sunt: aut in semine, aut in matrice, aut in strumentis
seminariis, aut in virga, aut in causa extrinseca.*

MESSER NICIA. This is the most worthy man one could hope
to find!

CALLIMACO. Alternatively, the sterility might be caused by
impotence in you. If that should be the case, there would
be no remedy.

MESSER NICIA. Impotent? Me? Hoho! Don't make me laugh!
I don't believe there's a more vigorous, virile man than me
in Florence.

CALLIMACO. Well, if that's not it, you may rest assured we'll
find a remedy.

MESSER NICIA. Would there be any remedy other than the
Baths? Because *I* don't want to go to all the inconvenience,
and my wife would be unwilling to leave Florence.

LIGURIO. Let me answer your question in the affirmative. Callimaco, being circumspect, sometimes carries circumspec-
tion to excess. Didn't you tell me you knew how to prepare
certain potions that will make a woman pregnant quite in-
fallibly?

CALLIMACO. I did. But it has not been my habit to communi-
cate that fact to strangers. They might regard me as a
charlatan.

MESSER NICIA. Don't worry about me. I'm amazed at your
abilities. There's nothing I couldn't believe you capable of.
There's nothing I wouldn't do for you!

LIGURIO. I think you ought to see a specimen of her water.

CALLIMACO. Undoubtedly. One could get nowhere without it.

LIGURIO. Call Siro, tell him to go home with Messer Nicia,
pick up the specimen, and then come back. We'll wait for
him indoors.

CALLIMACO. Siro, go with him. And if you agree, messere, you
come back too, and we'll think of a way out.

MESSER NICIA. If I agree? I shall be back like a shot. I place
more confidence in you than Hungarians do in swords!

SCENE 3

MESSER NICIA *and* SIRO

MESSER NICIA. That master of yours is a very distinguished man.

SIRO. Better than that, even.

MESSER NICIA. The King of France holds him in great esteem?

SIRO. Very great.

MESSER NICIA. And for that reason, I take it, he is glad to stay in France?

SIRO. That's my belief.

MESSER NICIA. He's quite right. The people of this city are dirty dogs. No appreciation of merit. If he were to stay, no one would trouble to look at him twice. I speak from experience. I've given it everything, learning my *hics, haecs,* and *hocs,* and, if I hadn't got a private income, I'd be having a thin time of it, I can tell you.

SIRO. Do you make a hundred ducats a year?

MESSER NICIA. Go on. I don't make a hundred *lire*. Or a hundred groats. The fact is, if you don't spend your time keeping up with the neighbors—such is Florence—you won't find a dog to bark you a civil greeting. The rest of us are good for nothing but funerals and wedding breakfasts and loafing all day on the square. But they don't bother me. I have no need of anybody. There are plenty who'd be glad to change places with me. But I shouldn't like what I've just said to get around, or someone might slap a fine on me or slug me in a dark alley.

SIRO. Don't worry, messere.

MESSER NICIA. This is my house. Wait for me here. I'll be right back.

SIRO. Go ahead.

SCENE 4

SIRO, *alone*

SIRO. If all men of learning were like that one, the rest of us
would have straw in our hair.

Gesture indicating insanity.

I'm quite sure that the wicked Ligurio and my mad master
are leading him to his downfall. And, to tell the truth, I'd
enjoy his downfall, if only we could be sure of getting away
with it. Otherwise I'm risking my neck and my master is
risking both his neck and his property. He's already turned
himself into a doctor. I just don't know what their little
plan is, or where they're heading with all this deception.
But here's Messer Nicia again, specimen in hand. You can't
help laughing at him, the old cuckoo.

SCENE 5

MESSER NICIA *and* SIRO

MESSER NICIA, *to someone in the house, evidently* LUCREZIA.
Up till now I've always done everything your way. In this
matter I want you to do things *my* way. If I'd thought that
you and I weren't going to have children, I'd rather have
married a peasant girl. Siro! Follow me. The trouble I had
getting My Lady Fool to give me this specimen! That's not
to say, of course, that she wants children less than I do. On
the contrary! But the moment I suggest anything practical,
oh, what a song and dance!

SIRO. Be patient: soft words make women do what other people want.

MESSER NICIA. Soft words! She raised the roof! Go, this instant: tell your master and Ligurio I'm here.

SIRO. Look, they're just coming out of the house.

SCENE 6

LIGURIO, CALLIMACO, *and* MESSER NICIA

LIGURIO, *aside to* CALLIMACO. Messer Nicia will be easy to persuade. The problem will be his wife. But we shall find a way to bring her round.

CALLIMACO. Have you got the specimen?

MESSER NICIA. Siro has it under his cloak.

CALLIMACO. Give it to me. Aha! Weak kidneys!

MESSER NICIA. Yes, it does look a bit turbid. Yet she only just did it.

CALLIMACO. Oh, don't let that surprise you. *Nam mulieris urinae sunt semper maiioris glossitiei et albedinis et minoris pulchritudinis quam virorum. Huius autem in caetera, causa est amplitudo canalium, mixtio eorum quae ex matrice exeunt cum urina.*

MESSER NICIA. Whores of Heaven! This man gets better all the time! He thinks of everything!

CALLIMACO. I'm afraid this woman is not properly covered at night. For that reason her urine is not of the finest quality.

MESSER NICIA. She has a good quilt over her. But she spends four hours on her knees before she gets into bed, stringing off paternosters. She's as strong as a horse when it comes to standing the cold.

CALLIMACO. Well, to cut a long story short, Messer Nicia, either you trust me or you don't. Either I am to expound a sure remedy to you or I am not. For myself, I'd let you have the remedy. Only put your trust in me, and you shall have it. And if, one year from now, your wife is not holding a child in her arms, a child of her own, I will gladly pay you two thousand ducats.

MESSER NICIA. Pray tell me what this remedy is. My only wish is to honor you in everything, and to trust you more than my father-confessor.

CALLIMACO. This, then, you must know. Nothing more surely makes a woman pregnant than getting her to drink a potion made from the root of the mandrake. This is something I have tested several times. Every time, it worked. Were that not so, the Queen of France would be childless, not to mention countless other princesses of that land.

MESSER NICIA. Is it possible?

CALLIMACO. It is exactly as I say. And Fortune must love you dearly, for she has caused me to bring to Florence all the ingredients of that potion. You could have it at once.

MESSER NICIA. When would she have to take it?

CALLIMACO. This evening after supper. The moon is well disposed. There could not be a more propitious moment.

MESSER NICIA. Well, that won't be hard to arrange. Make it up in any case. I'll see that she takes it.

CALLIMACO. There's a further consideration. The first man who has to do with her after she's taken this potion will die within the week. Nothing in this world can save him.

MESSER NICIA. Blood and guts! I won't touch the filthy stuff! You can't make me run my neck into *that* kind of noose!

CALLIMACO. Be calm. There is a remedy.

MESSER NICIA. What is it?

CALLIMACO. Arrange for someone else to sleep with her. Immediately. So that, spending the night with her, he may draw upon himself all the infection of the mandrake. After which you can lie with her without danger.

MESSER NICIA. I won't do it.

CALLIMACO. Why not?

MESSER NICIA. I don't want to make my wife a whore and myself a cuckold, that's why not.

CALLIMACO. What did you say, Messer Nicia? Is this our wise Doctor of Laws? You are not prepared to do what the King of France has done, and great lords at his court without number?

MESSER NICIA. Who on earth do you expect me to find? Who would do such a thing? If I tell him about it, he won't want to do it. If I don't tell him, I shall be guilty of treachery—which is a felony in Florence. And I don't want to get into hot water!

CALLIMACO. If that's your only trouble, I believe I can take care of it.

MESSER NICIA. How?

CALLIMACO. I'll tell you. I'll give you the potion this evening after supper. Have her drink it, then put her straight to bed. It'll be about ten o'clock. Then we'll disguise ourselves—you, Ligurio, Siro, and I—and go search the New Market, the Old Market, every street and alley. The first idle young lout that we come upon, we gag him, and, to the tune of a sound drubbing, take him into your house—and into your bedroom—in the dark. Then we put him in the bed and tell him what to do. I don't think there'll be any problem. In the morning you send the fellow packing before daybreak. Then get your wife washed and you can take your pleasure of her without the slightest risk.

MESSER NICIA. I'll go along—since you tell me that a king and princes and lords have used this method. One request, though: let's keep this secret—on account of the felony!

CALLIMACO. Who d'you think would blab?

MESSER NICIA. There's another obstacle. A tricky one, too.

CALLIMACO. What?

MESSER NICIA. We must get my wife to agree. And I don't think she ever will.

CALLIMACO. An excellent point. Personally, I would never marry in the first place unless I knew I could get the lady to see things my way.

LIGURIO. I have it!

MESSER NICIA. What?

LIGURIO. The remedy. We make use of her father-confessor.

CALLIMACO. And who'll persuade the father-confessor?

LIGURIO. You, me, and money. Our own wickedness and that of the priests.

MESSER NICIA. I'm afraid she'll refuse to talk with her father-confessor, if only to contradict her husband.

LIGURIO. There's a remedy for that too.

CALLIMACO. Tell me.

LIGURIO. Get her mother to take her to him.

MESSER NICIA. True. She trusts her mother.

LIGURIO. And I happen to know that her mother is of our way of thinking. Well, now, time's running on, and it'll soon be evening. Callimaco, go and take a little stroll, and be sure that you're at home to receive us at eight o'clock with the potion all ready. We'll go see the mother, then call on the friar, then report back to you.

CALLIMACO, *aside to* LIGURIO. Hey! Don't leave me alone!

LIGURIO. You look as if your goose were cooked.

CALLIMACO. Where am *I* supposed to put myself?

LIGURIO. Here, there, everywhere. Up this street and down the next. Florence is such a big city.

CALLIMACO. I'm dead.

ACT III

SCENE 1

SOSTRATA, MESSER NICIA, *and* LIGURIO

SOSTRATA. I have always heard it said that it is the part of the prudent man to choose the lesser of two evils. If this is the only way you can have children, you must take it —provided it in no way offends against conscience.

MESSER NICIA. That's right.

LIGURIO. You will go and see your daughter, and Messer Nicia and I will call on her confessor, Friar Timoteo. We'll tell him how things stand, so that you won't have to. Then you'll hear what *he* has to say.

SOSTRATA. Very good. You take that street there. I'll go see Lucrezia and, come what may, I'll take her to talk with Friar Timoteo.

SCENE 2

MESSER NICIA *and* LIGURIO

MESSER NICIA. You're probably surprised, Ligurio, that we have to go all round the world to persuade my wife? You wouldn't be—if you knew the whole story.

LIGURIO. I imagine it's because all women are suspicious.

MESSER NICIA. It's not that. She used to be the sweetest person in the world, and the easiest to manage. But one of her neighbors told her that, if she made a vow to attend first Mass at the Chapel of the Servites for forty mornings

in a row, she would become pregnant. She made the vow
and went to the chapel about twenty times. Well, you know
how it is, one of those frisky friars started pestering her.
Naturally, she refused to go back. It's a sad state of affairs
when the very people who ought to be setting a good example turn out like that. Am I right?

LIGURIO. Right, by Satan!

MESSER NICIA. From that day to this she's gone around with
her ears pricked like a hare. Suggest anything at all, and
she kicks up a fuss.

LIGURIO. My surprise is gone. But that vow—how did she go
about fulfilling it?

MESSER NICIA. She got a dispensation.

LIGURIO. Good. Now let me have twenty-five ducats if you
have them. Affairs of this kind cost money. One must make
friends with the friar and give him hopes of better things
to come.

MESSER NICIA. Here you are, then. I'm not worried. I'll get
it back in other ways.

LIGURIO. These friars are smart. Shrewd. Which stands to reason, since they know both their own sins and everyone else's.
If you're not wise to their ways, you can easily get gypped,
and not know how to make them do what you want. So
don't spoil everything by talking to him. A man like you,
who spends the whole day in his study, knows all about
his books, but can't cope with mundane matters.

Aside.

This fellow is such a fool, I'm afraid he'll spoil everything.

MESSER NICIA. Tell me what you want me to do.

LIGURIO. Leave the talking to me. Don't say a word unless I
give the signal.

MESSER NICIA. I'm happy to do as you say. What signal will
you give?

LIGURIO. I shall wink—and bite my lip. No, no. Let's try something else. How long is it since you last spoke with Friar
Timoteo?

MESSER NICIA. Over ten years.

LIGURIO. Good. I'll tell him that you've gone deaf and can't answer him: you needn't say a word unless we shout.

MESSER NICIA. I'll do that.

LIGURIO. And don't be upset if I say something that doesn't seem to fit. Everything contributes to the final result.

MESSER NICIA. When the time comes!

SCENE 3

TIMOTEO *and* A WOMAN

TIMOTEO. If you wish to make confession, I shall accede to your wish.

THE WOMAN. Not today. Someone's expecting me. It's enough if I worked some of it out of my system just standing here. Have you said those masses to Our Lady?

TIMOTEO. Yes, madonna.

THE WOMAN. Here, take this florin. Every Monday for the next two months I want you to say the Mass for the Dead for my husband's soul. He was a terrible man, but then there's the call of the flesh. I get a bit of the old feeling whenever I think of him. Do you think he's in Purgatory?

TIMOTEO. Undoubtedly.

THE WOMAN. I'm not so sure. You know what he did to me —and not just once either. I used to complain about it to you. I got as far over in bed as I could, but he was so importunate. Ugh, Lord Above!

TIMOTEO. Don't worry. God's clemency is great. If a man lack not the will, he shall not lack the time for repentance.

THE WOMAN. Do you think the Turks will invade Italy this year?

TIMOTEO. If you don't say your prayers, yes.

THE WOMAN. Glory be! Lord preserve us from the Turks and all their deviltries! All that impaling they go in for—it scares the life out of me! But there's a woman with a piece of

linen for me—in the church yonder. I must let her know I'm
here. Good day.

TIMOTEO. God be with you.

SCENE 4

TIMOTEO, MESSER NICIA, *and* LIGURIO

TIMOTEO. Women are the most charitable creatures, and the
most trying. The man who shuns them avoids the trials, but
also goes without their services; while the man who accepts
them gets both the services and the trials. Well, it's the old
truth, you can't have honey without flies. What are you
about, my worthy friends? Can that be Messer Nicia?

LIGURIO. You'll have to shout. He's got so deaf, he can't hear
a word.

TIMOTEO. You're welcome, messere.

LIGURIO. Louder!

TIMOTEO. Welcome!!

MESSER NICIA. Pleased to see you, Father!

TIMOTEO. What are you about?

MESSER NICIA. Oh, nicely, thanks.

LIGURIO. You'd better talk to me, Father. If you want *him* to
hear, you'll have to shout till the whole square resounds
with it.

TIMOTEO. What do you want with me?

LIGURIO. Messer Nicia here and another worthy man—I'll tell
you about *him* later—are charged with the distribution of
several hundred ducats as alms.

MESSER NICIA. Blood and guts!

LIGURIO, *aside.* Hold your tongue, damn you. We shan't need
that much.

Aloud.

Don't be surprised at anything he might say, Father, he

can't hear a thing. Every now and again he *thinks* he hears something and replies with an irrelevant remark.

TIMOTEO. Pray continue. Let him say what he likes.

LIGURIO. I've got some of the money with me now. They've chosen you as the person to distribute it.

TIMOTEO. I'll be very glad to.

LIGURIO. But first, you must help us. A strange thing has happened to Messer Nicia. Only you *can* help us. It concerns the honor of his house.

TIMOTEO. What is it?

LIGURIO. I don't know if you've met Messer Nicia's nephew, Cammillo Calfucci?

TIMOTEO. Yes, I have.

LIGURIO. Well, a year ago, he went to Paris on business, and, as his wife was dead, he left his daughter, who was of marriageable age, in the care of a convent which shall be nameless.

TIMOTEO. What happened?

LIGURIO. What happened? Just this. As a result of the nuns' carelessness or her own featherheadedness, she now finds herself four months pregnant. If things can't very discreetly be put to rights, Messer Nicia, the nuns, the girl, Cammillo, and the house of Calfucci will all be dishonored together. Now Messer Nicia values his honor so highly and is so sensitive to scandal that—if the whole thing can be prevented from leaking out—he will give three hundred ducats for the love of God.

MESSER NICIA. There's a story for you!

LIGURIO, *aside*. Quiet!

Aloud.

And he wants to put the matter in your hands. Only you and the mother superior can set things to rights.

TIMOTEO. How?

LIGURIO. You can persuade the mother superior to give the girl a potion. To make her miscarry.

TIMOTEO. This is something that requires a little thinking over.

LIGURIO. Think over all the good that will result. You'll be preserving the honor of the convent, the girl, and all her relatives. You'll be restoring a daughter to her father. You'll be giving satisfaction to Messer Nicia here and all *his* relatives. And you'll be able to distribute alms to the tune of three hundred ducats. While, on the other hand, the only harm you do is to a piece of unborn flesh that knows neither sense nor sensation and might miscarry anyhow in any number of ways. I believe in the greatest good of the greatest number. Always do what benefits the greatest number!

TIMOTEO. So be it, in God's name! You shall have your way! May all be done for the good Lord's sake and in Holy Charity's name! Give me the name of the convent, give me the potion, and, if you agree, the money you mentioned, that we may start to do good!

LIGURIO. There's a man of God for you! Just what I expected. Here's the first installment.

Gives him money.

The convent is called . . . Oh, but wait. There's a woman in the church signaling to me. I'll be right back. Don't leave, Messer Nicia. I've a couple of things to say to this woman.

SCENE 5

TIMOTEO *and* MESSER NICIA

TIMOTEO. How many months gone is she?

MESSER NICIA. I'm amazed!

TIMOTEO. I said: How many months gone is she?

MESSER NICIA. God blast him where he stands!

TIMOTEO. Why?

MESSER NICIA. So that he'll get hurt, that's why!

TIMOTEO. I seem to have landed in mud right up to my neck. Of these fellows I've got to deal with, one is crazy, and the other's deaf as a post. One runs away and the other hears nothing. But if they're trying to put one over on me, I'll beat them at that game any day of the week. But look, Ligurio is back.

SCENE 6

LIGURIO, TIMOTEO, *and* MESSER NICIA

LIGURIO. Keep quiet, messere! Oh, Father, I have wonderful news!

TIMOTEO. What is it?

LIGURIO. That woman I just spoke to told me the girl has had a miscarriage.

TIMOTEO. Good! This money will go into the general fund.

LIGURIO. What did you say?

TIMOTEO. I said you've more reason than ever to distribute alms.

LIGURIO. The alms are yours for the asking. But now you'll have to do something else for Messer Nicia.

TIMOTEO. Such as what?

LIGURIO. Something less burdensome, less scandalous, more acceptable to us, more profitable to you.

TIMOTEO. What is it? I'm with you all the way. We've been growing so intimate, there's nothing I wouldn't do for you.

LIGURIO. I'll tell you all about it in church. Just the two of us. Messer Nicia will be so kind as to wait for us. We'll be back in a trice.

MESSER NICIA. As the hangman said to his victim.

TIMOTEO. Let us go.

SCENE 7

MESSER NICIA, *alone*

MESSER NICIA. Is it day or night? Do I wake or dream? Am I drunk? I haven't touched a drop all day and I can't make head or tail of these carryings-on. We've got something to tell Friar Timoteo, so he tells him something else. Then he wanted me to pretend to be deaf. I'd have had to stop my ears up as if there were Sirens around if I wasn't to hear the mad things he was saying. God only knows what he had in mind. I find myself twenty-five ducats the poorer, not a word has been said about my affair, and now they leave me looking like a stuffed dummy. But look, they're back. If they haven't been talking of *my* affair, they're going to catch it.

SCENE 8

TIMOTEO, LIGURIO, *and* MESSER NICIA

TIMOTEO. Get your womenfolk to come and see me. I know what I have to do. And if only my authority prevail we shall conclude this alliance tonight.

LIGURIO. Messer Nicia, Friar Timoteo is ready to do everything we ask. It's for you to see that the ladies come and see him.

MESSER NICIA. You make a new man of me. Will it be a boy?

LIGURIO. A boy.

MESSER NICIA. I weep for sheer tenderness!

TIMOTEO. Go into the church. I'll wait for the ladies here. Keep to one side, so they don't see you. As soon as they're gone, I'll tell you what they said.

SCENE 9

TIMOTEO, *alone*

TIMOTEO. I wish I knew who's being taken in by whom. This scoundrel Ligurio came with that first story just to try me out. If I hadn't consented to do what he asked, he wouldn't have told me what he's now let out and revealed their plot for nothing. That first story was neither here nor there. So I myself have been taken in! And yet the cheat is not against my interests. Messer Nicia and Callimaco are rich, and both of them, for different reasons, will have to spend some of their riches. It is fitting that the affair should be kept secret: that's as important to them as it is to me. Whatever happens, I have no regrets. It's true there are going to be difficulties. Madonna Lucrezia is a good woman and nobody's fool. But I'll get at her through her goodness. Women are pretty brainless, anyhow. A woman need only put one word after another, and she's considered a genius. In the kingdom of the blind, the one-eyed man is King. Here she comes with her mother, a real shrew who will help me make the daughter do as I want.

SCENE 10

SOSTRATA *and* LUCREZIA

SOSTRATA. I believe you believe me, daughter, when I tell you that no one in the world holds your honor more dear than I, and that I would never advise you to do anything that wasn't right. As I've told you over and again, if Friar Timoteo says that something shouldn't weigh on your conscience, don't give it a thought—go ahead and do it.

LUCREZIA. I've always feared that Messer Nicia's desire to have children might cause him to make some blunder. That's why, when he talked to me about anything, I always felt suspicious and doubtful, particularly since that business at the Chapel of the Servites. But of all the things he's tried, this seems the strangest. To have to submit my body to such an outrage! To be the cause of a man's death by such an outrage! If I were the only woman left alive, and the world depended on me for the continuance of the human race, even then I don't see how I could agree to it.

SOSTRATA. There's not much *I* can say to you, daughter. You'll be talking with the friar: see what he says, and then do as he tells you. As I tell you. As everyone that loves you tells you.

LUCREZIA. This is torture. I'm breaking out in a sweat.

SCENE 11

TIMOTEO, LUCREZIA, *and* SOSTRATA

TIMOTEO. Welcome, ladies. I know what you want to hear about: Messer Nicia has already talked to me. As a matter of fact I've been poring over my books two hours and more, studying up on the subject. My researches have yielded many things, both general and particular, that support our case.

LUCREZIA. Are you serious? You're not laughing at me?

TIMOTEO. Ah, Madonna Lucrezia, this is no laughing matter! Don't you know me better than that?

LUCREZIA. I know you, Father. But this seems to me the strangest thing ever.

TIMOTEO. I believe you, madonna: but I would not have you continue to talk so. There are many things which, at a distance, seem terrible, unbearable, strange, but which, when you come close, are found to be human, bearable, familiar. That's why they say that fear can be greater than the thing feared. This is a case in point.

LUCREZIA. I pray God it is!

TIMOTEO. To return to what I was saying before. As far as conscience is concerned, you must pay attention to this general truth: when it is a question of a certain good and a doubtful evil, one must never forego the good from fear of the evil. Here we have a certain good—that you will become pregnant—that you will win a soul for the Lord God. The uncertain evil is that whoever lies with you after you've taken the potion will die. In some cases the man does not

die. But, since there's an element of doubt, it is best that
Messer Nicia should not run the risk. As to the act itself,
to call it a sin is mere moonshine, for it is not the body that
sins, it is the will. The real sin would be to act contrary to
your husband's wishes, and you will be acting in accordance
with them. It would be a sin to take pleasure in the act,
but you *won't* be taking pleasure in it. Besides, what one
should always think of is the end in view. What are your
proper aims? To fill a seat in Paradise and to make your
husband happy. Now the Bible says that the daughters of
Lot, believing that they were the only surviving women in
the world, consorted with their father. Their intention being
good, they were not sinning.

LUCREZIA. What are you persuading me to do, Father?

SOSTRATA. Let yourself *be* persuaded, daughter. Can't you
see that a childless woman has no home? Her husband dies,
and she's no better than a lost dog. Everyone abandons her.

TIMOTEO. Madonna, I swear to you, by this consecrated
breast, that to yield to your husband's wishes in this matter
need weigh on your conscience no more than eating meat
on Fridays. A little holy water will wash the sin away.

LUCREZIA. Where are you leading me, Father?

TIMOTEO. To such things as will ever cause you to pray to
God on my behalf, and will bring you greater joy next year
than this.

SOSTRATA. She'll do what you want. I'll put her to bed tonight
myself. What are you frightened of, crybaby? I know fifty
women in this city who'd thank God for the opportunity.

LUCREZIA. I consent. But I do not believe that I shall live to
see tomorrow.

TIMOTEO. Have no fear, my daughter. I shall pray to God for
you. I shall call upon the Archangel Raphael to be with
you. Go then, make haste. Prepare yourself for this mystery. Evening is upon us.

SOSTRATA. Peace be with you, Father.

LUCREZIA. God and Our Lady help me, and keep me from
harm!

SCENE 12

TIMOTEO, LIGURIO, *and* MESSER NICIA

TIMOTEO. Oh, Ligurio, come out here!

LIGURIO. How is it going?

TIMOTEO. Well. They've gone home, prepared to do everything. There'll be no hitch: her mother's going to stay with her. She'll put her to bed herself.

MESSER NICIA. Is that the truth?

TIMOTEO. Oh! So you've been cured of your deafness?

LIGURIO. St. Clement has granted him that boon.

TIMOTEO. Then you must set an *ex voto* on the altar to publicize the event and enable me to share in the proceeds.

MESSER NICIA. We're getting off the subject. Will my wife make a fuss about doing what I want?

TIMOTEO. No, I tell you.

MESSER NICIA. I'm the happiest man alive.

TIMOTEO. I can well believe it. You'll soon be the father of a fine boy. Let childless men go hang!

LIGURIO. Then go to your prayers, Father. If we need anything else, we'll come for you. You, messere, go to her and keep her steadfast in this resolve. I'll go see Master Callimaco and have him send you the potion. Arrange things so that I can see you at seven o'clock and settle what's to be done at ten.

MESSER NICIA. Well said. Good-by!

TIMOTEO. God be with you.

ACT IV

SCENE 1

CALLIMACO, *alone*

CALLIMACO. I'd very much like to know what those fellows have done. Shall I ever see Ligurio again? It's the eleventh hour, after all, maybe even the twelfth. What anguish I've had to suffer! What anguish I'm still suffering! It's very true that Nature and Fortune keep man's account in balance: there's nothing good befalls but that it's made up for by something bad. The more my hopes have grown, the more my fears have grown. Unhappy that I am! Can I go on living amid such afflictions? Tormented by hopes and fears like these? I am a ship rocked by opposing winds, and the nearer she gets to the harbor, the more she has to fear. Messer Nicia's simple-mindedness gives me grounds for hope; the foresight and resolution of Lucrezia give me cause for fear. No respite, no peace anywhere! From time to time I try to regain my self-control. I take myself to task for my raging passion. I say to myself: "What are you doing? Are you mad? If you possess her, what then? You'll see what a mistake you've made. You'll repent all the trouble and thought that you lavished on the affair. Don't you know how little good a man discovers in the things that he desires, compared with what he thought he would discover? Look at it another way. The worst that can befall you is that you will die and go to hell. Many a man has died before you, a large number of worthy men have gone to hell, are *you* ashamed to go there? Look Fate in the face. Fly from evil—or, if you cannot fly from it, bear it like a man, don't grovel and prostrate yourself before it like a woman!" That is how I cheer myself up! But it doesn't last very long. The desire to be with her at least once comes at me from all points of the compass. It shoots through me from top to toe and changes my whole being. My legs tremble, my bowels melt, my heart is pounding fit to burst, my arms hang limp, my tongue falls mute, my eyes are dazed, my head swims. If I could only find Ligurio I'd have someone to pour out my woes to. Here he comes now—in a hurry, too. The news he brings will either grant me a few more moments of life or kill me.

SCENE 2

LIGURIO *and* CALLIMACO

LIGURIO. I've never been more eager to find Callimaco, and I've never found it harder to find him. If it had been bad news that I was bringing, I'd have found him right away. I've been to his house, out into the square, down to the market, along the Pancone degli Spini, up to the Torna-quinci Loggia, and not found him. These young lovers have quicksilver under their feet, they can't stand still.

LIGURIO *is wandering all over the place.*

CALLIMACO. Why do I hold back? Why not give him a shout? He looks rather pleased with himself. Ligurio! Ligurio!

LIGURIO. Callimaco! Where have you been?

CALLIMACO. What's the news?

LIGURIO. Good.

CALLIMACO. Really good?

LIGURIO. The best.

CALLIMACO. Lucrezia is willing?

LIGURIO. Yes.

CALLIMACO. Friar Timoteo did the necessary?

LIGURIO. He did.

CALLIMACO. Blessèd Friar Timoteo! I shall pray for him all the rest of my life!

LIGURIO. That's a good one! As if God's Grace were for evil as well as good! The friar will need more than prayers.

CALLIMACO. Such as what?

LIGURIO. Money.

CALLIMACO. We'll give him some. How much have you promised him?

LIGURIO. Three hundred ducats.

CALLIMACO. Excellent.

LIGURIO. And Messer Nicia came up with twenty-five.

CALLIMACO. Why on . . . ?

LIGURIO. Suffice it that he did.

CALLIMACO. And what did Lucrezia's mother do?

LIGURIO. Almost everything. The moment she knew her daughter was going to have such a pleasant night—and without sin—she went to work on Lucrezia, pleading, commanding, reassuring, everything. She got her over to Friar Timoteo's place, continuing the good work till she gave her consent.

CALLIMACO. God, what have I done to deserve such a boon? I could die for joy!

LIGURIO. What sort of man *is* this? Whether for joy or sorrow, he's determined to die! Did you get the potion ready?

CALLIMACO. Yes, I did.

LIGURIO. What'll you send him?

CALLIMACO. A glass of hippocras. Just the thing to settle the stomach and cheer the brain. Oh dear, oh dear, oh dear! I am undone!

LIGURIO. What's the matter? What can it be?

CALLIMACO. There's no remedy now.

LIGURIO. What the devil's the matter with you?

CALLIMACO. We're getting nowhere! I'm locked in a fiery furnace!

LIGURIO. Why? Why won't you tell me? What's the matter? Take your hands from your face!

CALLIMACO. Don't you remember I told Messer Nicia that you, he, Siro, and I would catch somebody to put in bed with his wife?

LIGURIO. What of it?

CALLIMACO. What of it? If I'm with you, I can't be the man that's caught! And if I'm not with you, he'll see through the deception!

LIGURIO. True. But can't we find a remedy?

CALLIMACO. I don't see how.

LIGURIO. Yes, we can.

CALLIMACO. What?

LIGURIO. Let me think it over for a moment.

CALLIMACO. So that's it! If you're still at the thinking stage, my goose *is* cooked.

LIGURIO. I have it!

CALLIMACO. What?

LIGURIO. The friar. He's brought us this far. He can bring us the whole way.

CALLIMACO. How?

LIGURIO. We must all wear disguises. I'll have the friar wear a disguise, then get him to change his voice, his features, his clothes, and then tell Messer Nicia that he's you. He'll believe me.

CALLIMACO. I like that. But where do I come in?

LIGURIO. I'm counting on you to put a tattered old cloak on, then to come round the corner of his house, lute in hand, singing a little song.

CALLIMACO. With my face showing?

LIGURIO. Yes. If *you* wore a mask he'd smell a rat.

CALLIMACO. He'll recognize me.

LIGURIO. No, he won't. I want you to grimace, twist your face up, open your mouth, grind your teeth together. Close one eye. Go on, try it!

CALLIMACO. Like this?

LIGURIO. No.

CALLIMACO. Like *this?*

LIGURIO. Not enough.

CALLIMACO. This way?

LIGURIO. Yes, yes, keep that. And I have a false nose at home. I'd like you to stick that on.

CALLIMACO. All right. Then what?

LIGURIO. As soon as you appear at the corner, we'll be there. We'll snatch the lute from you, grab hold of you, twirl you round and round, take you into the house, put you into the bed. The rest you'll have to do for yourself.

CALLIMACO. The thing is to get there.

LIGURIO. You'll get there. But as to how you're to get there again, *you* must solve that one.

CALLIMACO. How?

LIGURIO. Possess her tonight, and, before you leave, let her know how things stand, reveal the deception. Let her see how much love you bear her, tell her you adore her. Tell her she can be your friend without loss of reputation or your foe *with* loss of reputation. It's inconceivable that she wouldn't want to co-operate. On the contrary, she won't want this night to be the only one.

CALLIMACO. Do you believe that?

LIGURIO. I'm certain of it. But don't let's waste any more time. It's eight o'clock already. Call Siro and send the potion to Messer Nicia. Then wait for me at home. I'll collect Friar Timoteo, see that he gets into disguise, and bring him back here. Then we'll dig out Messer Nicia, then do what's left to do.

CALLIMACO. That sounds good. Get going.

SCENE 3

CALLIMACO *and* SIRO

CALLIMACO. Hey, Siro!

SIRO. Sir?

CALLIMACO. Come here.

SIRO. Here I am.

CALLIMACO. Get the silver goblet from my bedroom closet. Cover it with a cloth. Bring it here. And be sure you don't spill the stuff on the way over.

SIRO, *going.* I'll do that.

CALLIMACO. That fellow's been with me ten years now, and he's always served me faithfully. I believe I can trust him even in this affair. And, although I've not said a word to him about this deception, he's guessed what's afoot, for he's quite a rascal, and he's falling in, I see, with my plans.

SIRO, *returning.* Here it is.

CALLIMACO. Good. Now go to Messer Nicia's house, and tell him this is the medicine that his wife is to take right after supper. And the sooner supper is, the better it'll work. Tell him that we'll be at the corner, in due order, at the time he's to meet us there. And hurry.

SIRO. Right.

CALLIMACO. One moment. Listen. If he wants you to wait for him, wait, and come back here with him. If he *doesn't* want you to wait, come right back as soon as you've given him this—and the message.

SIRO. Yes, sir.

SCENE 4

CALLIMACO, *alone*

CALLIMACO. Here I stand, waiting for Ligurio to come back with Friar Timoteo. And the man who said that waiting is the hardest part spoke true. I'm wasting away at the rate of ten pounds an hour, thinking where I am now and where I may be two hours hence and fearing lest something should happen to upset my plan. For, if anything did, this would be my last night on earth. I should either throw myself in the Arno, or hang myself, or fling myself out of the window, or stab myself on her doorstep. But isn't that Ligurio? And there's someone with him with a hunchback and a

limp. That'll be the friar in disguise, I'll swear. These friars!
Know one, and you know the lot! Who's the fellow that's
joined them? It looks like Siro. He must have finished his
errand at Messer Nicia's. It's him all right. I'll wait here
for them. Then—to business!

SCENE 5

SIRO, LIGURIO, TIMOTEO,
in disguise, and CALLIMACO

SIRO. Who's that you've got with you, Ligurio?

LIGURIO. A very worthy man.

SIRO. Is he lame, or shamming?

LIGURIO. Mind your own business.

SIRO. Oh, he looks like a regular scoundrel.

LIGURIO. For God's sake, be quiet, you'll spoil everything!
Where's Callimaco?

CALLIMACO. Here. Welcome!

LIGURIO. Oh, Callimaco, give a word of warning to this lunatic
Siro. He's said a thousand crazy things already.

CALLIMACO. Listen, Siro. This evening you must do everything
Ligurio says. When he tells you to do something, it is I
who am telling you to do it. And everything you see, feel,
hear, and smell you're to keep strictly to yourself. That's if
you value my honor, my wealth, my life, and your own
best interests.

SIRO. I'll do as you say.

CALLIMACO. Did you give the goblet to Messer Nicia?

SIRO. Yes, sir.

CALLIMACO. What did he say?

SIRO. That everything was now in order, and that he'd go
ahead.

TIMOTEO. Is this Callimaco?

CALLIMACO. At your service. Let's agree on the terms of the

transaction: you may dispose of me and mine as of yourself.

TIMOTEO. So I have heard and, believing every word of it, I have agreed to do what I should never have done for any other man in the world.

CALLIMACO. Your labor shall not be in vain.

TIMOTEO. It will be enough to possess your favor.

LIGURIO. An end to all this hanky-panky! We'll get into our disguises, Siro. Callimaco, you come with us, and make your preparations. Friar Timoteo will wait for us here. We'll be right back and then dig out Messer Nicia.

CALLIMACO. Good idea. Let's go.

TIMOTEO. I'll wait for you.

SCENE 6

TIMOTEO, *alone*

TIMOTEO. It's true what they say: "Bad company will lead a man to the gallows." And a man often comes to grief by being too easygoing and goodhearted, not by being too wicked. God knows, *I* never thought of doing anybody any harm. I stayed in my cell, said my office, tended my flock, until that devil Ligurio turned up, and made me dip my finger in this transgression. I then had to follow with my arm, and finally it was total immersion. I still have no idea where I'll end up. I comfort myself with this thought: when something involves a large number of people, a large number of people have to be extremely careful. But here's Ligurio with that servant.

SCENE 7

TIMOTEO, LIGURIO, *and* SIRO

TIMOTEO. Welcome back!

LIGURIO. Do we look all right?

TIMOTEO. More than all right.

LIGURIO. Only Messer Nicia is missing. Let's walk toward his house. It's after nine. Let's go.

SIRO. Who is that opening his door? Is it his servant?

LIGURIO. No, it's the man himself. Ha! Ha! Ha!

SIRO. You find it funny?

LIGURIO. Who wouldn't? Just look at him—wearing some kind of jerkin that doesn't even cover his arse. And what the devil has he got on his head? It looks like one of those silly hoods that canons wear. And—lower down—a smallsword! Ha! Ha! Ha! And he's muttering God knows what under his breath. Let's stand to one side and hear his tale of woe about his wife and what she's been doing to him.

SCENE 8

MESSER NICIA, *in disguise*

MESSER NICIA. The way that loony wife of mine has been carrying on! She sent the maidservant to her mother's house and the manservant to our country house. I applaud her for that—but not for making such a fuss before she'd get into the bed. "I don't want to!" "What is it I'm to do?" "What are you making me do?" "Woe is me!" "Mother, Mother!" And if "Mother, Mother" hadn't given her a tongue-lashing, she'd never have got into that bed. I hope she catches a fever that goes from bad to worse! I like my women finicky, it's true. But not that finicky! She's made my head swim, the bird brain! Oh, these women! They drive you crazy, you tell 'em so, and they come back at you with: "What have I done now? What's eating you this time?" Oh, well. Soon—very soon now—we shall be seeing a little action around here. And I intend to see it with both hands, so to speak. I'm doing all right, aren't I? Look at me now: taller, younger, slimmer. . . . At this rate I could get me a woman without even paying for the privilege. But where have the others got to?

SCENE 9

LIGURIO, MESSER NICIA, TIMOTEO,
and SIRO

LIGURIO. Good evening, messere.

MESSER NICIA. Oooh! Hey! Oooh!

LIGURIO. Don't be afraid, it's only us.

MESSER NICIA. Oh! You're all here! If I hadn't recognized you,
I'd have run you through with this sword! You're Ligurio,
aren't you? And you're Siro! Hm? And the other one's your
master. Eh?

LIGURIO. Yes, messere.

MESSER NICIA. Let me have a look! Oh, he's well disguised!
His own mother wouldn't know him!

LIGURIO. I had him put a couple of nuts in his mouth, so nobody can recognize his voice.

MESSER NICIA. You're stupid.

LIGURIO. Why?

MESSER NICIA. Why didn't you tell me sooner? Then *I* could
have put nuts in my mouth. You know how important it is
that nobody should recognize our voices!

LIGURIO. Here you are then. Put this in your mouth!

MESSER NICIA. What is it?

LIGURIO. A ball of wax.

MESSER NICIA. Give it here. . . . Ca, pu, ca, coo, co, cu, cu,
spu . . . A pox take you, you murdering hound!

LIGURIO. Oh, forgive me! I must have got them mixed up.

MESSER NICIA. Ca, ca, pu, pu . . . What, what was it?

LIGURIO. Bitter aloes.

MESSER NICIA. Damn you, Ligurio! Master Callimaco, do you
stand by and say nothing?

TIMOTEO. I'm very angry with Ligurio.

MESSER NICIA. You *have* disguised your voice! That's *good!*

LIGURIO. Don't let's waste any more time here. I'll take over the duties of captain and give the army the order of the day. Callimaco will take the right horn of the crescent; I'll take the left. Messer Nicia will be in between us. Siro will bring up the rear and back up any of our forces that yield ground. The password shall be St. Cuckoo.

MESSER NICIA. Who's St. Cuckoo?

LIGURIO. He's the most venerated saint in all France. Let's go. Let's prepare our ambush at this corner. Listen! I hear a lute.

MESSER NICIA. That's our man. What shall we do?

LIGURIO. We'll send a scout forward to find out who he is. On hearing his report, we decide what action to take.

MESSER NICIA. Who'll go?

LIGURIO. You go, Siro! You know what to do. Observe, study the situation, return at the double, report.

SIRO. Right.

MESSER NICIA. I hope we don't make some terrible mistake. Suppose it's a cripple or a sickly old man, we'd have to repeat the performance tomorrow night!

LIGURIO. Don't worry: Siro's a reliable fellow. And here he comes. What have you found, Siro?

SIRO. The loveliest piece of man you ever saw and still on the right side of twenty-five! He's alone—walking along in a tattered old cloak playing a lute.

MESSER NICIA. It's a stroke of luck, if what you say is true, but be sure of what you say, it'll be your fault if anything goes wrong.

SIRO. He's just like I said.

LIGURIO. Let's wait for him to turn this corner, then pounce!

MESSER NICIA. Come over here, Master Callimaco. You *are* quiet this evening. Here he comes.

SCENE 10

CALLIMACO, LIGURIO, MESSER NICIA, TIMOTEO, *and* SIRO

CALLIMACO, *singing*.

Since Fortune keeps me from thy bed
Mayst thou find the Devil there instead!

LIGURIO. Hold him! Tightly now! Hand over that lute!

CALLIMACO. Help! What have I done?

MESSER NICIA. You'll soon see! Put something over his head. Gag him.

LIGURIO. Twirl him around!

MESSER NICIA. Give him another twirl! And another! Now pop him into the house.

TIMOTEO. Messer Nicia, I'm going to take a rest. I've got a splitting headache. I won't come back in the morning unless you need me.

MESSER NICIA. No, of course, Master Callimaco, don't bother. We can take care of this.

SCENE 11

TIMOTEO, *alone*

TIMOTEO. Now they're safely in the house, I'll be off to the monastery. And you, spectators, don't be impatient with us, for none of us will take time out to sleep tonight—so the action of the play won't be interrupted. I'll be saying my office. Ligurio and Siro will be having supper, since they haven't eaten all day. Messer Nicia will be pacing the floor like a cat on hot bricks till the suspense is over. And, as for Callimaco and Madonna Lucrezia, if I were he and you were she, do you think we'd sleep tonight?

ACT V

SCENE 1

TIMOTEO, *alone*

TIMOTEO. I've not been able to shut my eyes all night, so great was my desire to know how Callimaco and the others were getting on. While waiting I've been killing time in various ways: I said Matins, read a life of one of the Holy Fathers, went into church and relit a lamp that had gone out, changed the veil on a Madonna that works miracles. How many times have I told those friars to keep her clean! And then they're surprised that people aren't devout any more! I can remember the time when there were five hundred *ex votos*. Today there aren't twenty. It's our own fault. We haven't known how to keep up her reputation. Every evening after Compline we used to have a procession in there. We used to sing Lauds there every Saturday. We were always making vows, so there were always fresh *ex votos* on the altar. We used to comfort our confessees and get *them* to make offerings to her. Now none of this is done, and they're surprised that the life's gone out of it all! Oh, the dim-wittedness of my brothers in Christ! But I hear a rumpus in Messer Nicia's house. By my faith, there they are! They're shoving their prisoner out of the house. I'm just in time. They certainly took ages getting him out. It's daybreak already. I'll stay and listen without letting them see me.

SCENE 2

MESSER NICIA, CALLIMACO, LIGURIO, *and* SIRO

MESSER NICIA. You take this side, and I'll take the other. Siro, you take him by his cloak from behind.

CALLIMACO. Don't hurt me!

LIGURIO. Don't worry! Just get moving!

MESSER NICIA. Don't let's go any further!

LIGURIO. You're right. Let's let him go. Let's give him a couple of turns, so that he won't know which house he came out of. Round with him, Siro!

SIRO. Here we go!

MESSER NICIA. One more!

SIRO. There you are!

CALLIMACO. My lute!

LIGURIO. Be off, you scoundrel! And if I ever hear you breathe a word about this, I'll slit your windpipe for you!

MESSER NICIA. He's gone. Now let's go and get these disguises off. And we must all be seen out of doors bright and early so that it shan't appear that we've been up all night.

LIGURIO. Correct.

MESSER NICIA. You and Siro, go find Master Callimaco and tell him all went well.

LIGURIO. But what can we tell him? We don't know a thing. As you know, when we got into the house we went straight down to the cellar and started drinking. You and your mother-in-law were still at grips with him when we left you. We didn't see you again till just now when you brought us to throw him out.

MESSER NICIA. That's true. Oh, I've got some fine things to tell you. My wife was in bed in the dark. Sostrata was waiting for me by the fire. I got up there with the said young fellow and, to leave nothing to chance, I took him into a small room off the big room, where the lamp casts a very faint light—he could hardly see my face.

LIGURIO. Wisely done.

MESSER NICIA. I made him undress. When he boggled, I turned on him and showed him my teeth like a dog. He couldn't get out of his clothes fast enough. Finally he was naked. He'd got quite an ugly mug. His nose was tremendous. His mouth was sort of twisted. But you never saw such fine skin. White, soft, smooth. As for the rest, don't ask.

LIGURIO. No good *talking* of that sort of stuff. You had to see it.

MESSER NICIA. You're not making fun of me? Well, since I had my hands in the dough, so to speak, I decided to go through with it, and find out if the fellow was hale and hearty. For if he had the pox, where would I be then, hm?

LIGURIO. Oh, you're right.

MESSER NICIA. As soon as I saw he was healthy I dragged him to the bedroom, put him into bed, and, before I left, stuck in both hands to feel how things were going. I'm not a man to take a firefly for a lantern.

LIGURIO. How prudently you've managed this affair!

MESSER NICIA. Having made this checkup, I left the room, bolted the door, and went to join my mother-in-law by the fire—where we spent the whole night talking.

LIGURIO. What about?

MESSER NICIA. About how foolish Lucrezia had been, and about how much better it would have been if she'd given in without shilly-shallying. Then we talked about the baby. I felt as if I held him in my arms already, dear little chap! Then I heard it striking seven and, fearing that day might be breaking any minute, back I went to the bedroom. Now what would you say if I told you that I just couldn't wake the scoundrel up?

LIGURIO. I can well believe it.

MESSER NICIA. He'd enjoyed his anointing. Finally I got him up, called you, and we whisked him out of the house.

LIGURIO. Things *have* gone well.

MESSER NICIA. Now what will you say if I tell you I'm sorry?

LIGURIO. About what?

MESSER NICIA. About that young man. To have to die so soon! That this night should cost him so dear!

LIGURIO. That's *his* problem. Don't you have your own worries?

MESSER NICIA. You're right. But it will seem a thousand years before I see Master Callimaco and share my joy with him.

LIGURIO. He'll be out and about within the hour. But it's broad daylight now. We'll go and get these things off. What will you do?

MESSER NICIA. I'll go home too and put on my best clothes. I'll have them get my wife up and washed. Then I'll see that she goes to church to receive a blessing on this night's work. I'd like you and Callimaco to be there. And we should talk to the friar and thank and reward him for his good offices.

LIGURIO. An excellent notion. Let's do that.

SCENE 3

TIMOTEO, *alone*

TIMOTEO. I heard what they were saying, and liked it. What a stupid fellow this Messer Nicia is! It was the conclusion they came to that pleased me most. And since they'll be coming to see me, I won't stay here, I'll wait for them in church, where my merchandise will have a greater value. But who's coming out of that house? It looks like Ligurio, and the man with him must be Callimaco. I don't want them to find me here, for the reason I just gave. After all, if they don't come and see me, there's always time for me to go and see them.

SCENE 4

CALLIMACO *and* LIGURIO

CALLIMACO. As I've already told you, my dear Ligurio, I didn't begin to be happy till past three o'clock this morning, because, though I *had* had a lot of pleasure, I hadn't really enjoyed it. But then I revealed to her who I was, and made her appreciate the love I bore her, and went on to tell her how easily—because of her husband's simple-mindedness—we should be able to live together in happiness without the slightest scandal. I finished by promising her that whenever it pleased God to translate her husband I should take her as my wife. She thought this over and having, among other things, tasted the difference between my performance and Nicia's, between, that is, the kisses of a young lover and those of an old husband, she said to me, after heaving several sighs:

"Since your guile, my husband's folly, the simple-mindedness of my mother, and the wickedness of my father-confessor have led me to do what I should never have done of my own free will, I must judge it to be Heaven that willed it so, and I cannot find it in myself to refuse what Heaven wishes me to accept. In consequence, I take you for my lord, my master, and my guide. You are my father, my defender, my love and sovereign good, and what my husband wanted on *one* night I want him to have forever. So make friends with him, and go to church this morning, and then come and have dinner with us. You shall come and go as you please, and we shall be able to meet at any time without arousing the least suspicion."

When I heard these words I was ravished by their sweetness. I couldn't tell her more than a fraction of what I wished to say in reply. I'm the happiest and most contented man that ever walked this earth, and if neither Death nor Time take my happiness from me, the saints themselves shall call me blessèd!

LIGURIO. I am delighted to hear of all your good fortune. Everything's worked out just as I said it would. But where do we go from here?

CALLIMACO. We walk in the direction of the church, because I promised her I'd be there. She'll be coming with her mother and Messer Nicia.

LIGURIO. I can hear their door opening. Yes, it's the ladies, and the learnèd doctor's bringing up the rear.

CALLIMACO. Let's go into the church and wait for them there.

SCENE 5

MESSER NICIA, LUCREZIA, *and* SOSTRATA

MESSER NICIA. Lucrezia, it is my belief that we should do things in a God-fearing manner, not foolishly.

LUCREZIA. Why, what is there to do now?

MESSER NICIA. There! The answers she gives me! She's getting quite cocky!

SOSTRATA. You mustn't be so surprised: she's a little bit changed.

LUCREZIA. What are you getting at?

MESSER NICIA. I meant that it would be best for me to go on ahead and have a word with Friar Timoteo. I want to tell him to meet us at the church door, so he can confer the blessing on you. Why, this morning, it's as if you'd been reborn!

LUCREZIA. Then why don't you get moving?

MESSER NICIA. You're saucy this morning! Last night you seemed half dead!

LUCREZIA. I have you to thank, haven't I?

SOSTRATA. Go and find Friar Timoteo. But there's no need: he's just coming out of church.

MESSER NICIA. So he is.

SCENE 6

TIMOTEO, MESSER NICIA, LUCREZIA,
CALLIMACO, LIGURIO, *and* SOSTRATA

TIMOTEO. Callimaco and Ligurio told me that Messer Nicia and the ladies are on the way to church, so I've come out.

MESSER NICIA. *Bona dies,* Father!

TIMOTEO. Welcome! And Heaven's blessing upon you, madonna! May God give you a fine baby boy!

LUCREZIA. May God so will it!

TIMOTEO. You may rely on that: He *will* so will it!

MESSER NICIA. Is it Ligurio and Master Callimaco that I see there in church?

TIMOTEO. Yes, messere.

MESSER NICIA. Invite them over.

TIMOTEO. Come, sirs!

CALLIMACO. God save you!

MESSER NICIA. Master Callimaco, give my wife here your hand.

CALLIMACO. Willingly.

MESSER NICIA. Lucrezia, when we have a staff to support our old age, we shall owe it to this man.

LUCREZIA. I hold him dear. May he be a good friend of the family!

MESSER NICIA. Heaven bless you! I should like him and Ligurio to come and dine with us this morning.

LUCREZIA. By all means.

MESSER NICIA. And I should like to give them the key to the downstairs room off the loggia, so that they can come and go when they like. For they have no women at home. They must live like beasts.

CALLIMACO. I accept, and I'll use it whenever the occasion arises.

TIMOTEO. Am I to have the money for the almsgiving?

MESSER NICIA. You are, *domine:* I shall be sending you some today.

LIGURIO. Does no one remember poor old Siro?

MESSER NICIA. He only has to ask, I'm at his service. Lucrezia, how much shall I give the friar for his blessing?

LUCREZIA. Give him ten groats.

MESSER NICIA. God Almighty! *He nearly chokes.*

TIMOTEO. Madonna Sostrata, you seem to have taken on a new lease of life!

SOSTRATA. Who wouldn't be happy today?

TIMOTEO. Let us enter the church and say the customary prayers. After the service, go dine at your leisure. As for you, spectators, don't wait for us to come out again. The service is long, and I shall stay in church, and they'll go off home through the side door. Farewell!

SONGS

The following songs were added for the 1526 performance at Modena. The prince in the "Song to be sung before the Play" is Francesco Guicciardini who was present.

1

Song to be sung before the Play
by a Chorus of Nymphs and Shepherds

Since life is brief
And many are the pains
That living, striving man sustains,
We idly masticate the years
And batten on our own desires.
He who shuns pleasure and retires
To live with troubles and with tears
Is ignorant still
Of the deceits that fill
This world of ours, knows not
That men are misbegot
Or else by Fortune quite forgot.

Fleeing this misery,
In solitude
We choose to live
By sorrow unpursued,
In festal joys,
Fair nymphs and happy boys.
We bring our harmony
To celebrate this holiday
And honor you who come to see the play.

We also come, attracted
By the name of your great prince and mine
In whom, reflected,
We see the countenance divine.

Prosperity
Security
Felicity
—You know them.
Give thanks to him to whom you owe them!

2

(*After Act I*)

Who makes no trial of your mighty power,
O Love, it is in vain he seeks to know
The highest blessing Heaven can bestow.
He'll never learn how in the selfsame hour
A human being can both live and die,
Or in a flash from good to evil fly.
Never shall he be able to discover
How man more than himself can love another,
How hope and fear can freeze the blood, how gods above
And men are frightened by the arms you bear, O Love.

3

(*After Act II*)

The happiest of men we now shall sing
Who, being a fool, can believe anything.
Ambition drives him not
And fear deprives him not
Though these are things that ever made men grieve.
The learnèd Messer Nicia would believe
A donkey capable of aviation—
Such is his eagerness for procreation.*
All other goods he consigns to the fire
And fills his mind with a single desire.

* Anti-anachronists can substitute: "A donkey could take leave
of earth and fly / Such is his eagerness for progeny." But the
Prologue contains an allusion to V.I.P.s.

4
(After Act III)

Deception's sweet when carried through
To the belovèd end in view:
It cures all ills
Sweetens all bitter pills.
Then hail to thee
Great Remedy!
To erring men thou showest
The straight and narrow way,
And as thou knowest
How to make people blithe and gay
Love is thy debtor.
With a phrase, a word, a letter,
O Deception, thou canst quell
Poison, magic stone, or spell!

5
(After Act IV)

Nocturnal hours so still! O night
That lovers' company doth bless!
By thee alone (such is thy might)
The human soul finds happiness.
Lovers, in their exertions hard,
Only in thee find due reward.
O happy hours! In your name
Each frozen heart bursts into flame!

RUZZANTE RETURNS
FROM THE WARS

[IL REDUCE]

Angelo Beolco

English Version by
Angela Ingold and Theodore Hoffman

CHARACTERS

RUZZANTE[*]

MENATO

GNUA

GNUA'S PROTECTOR[**]

The scene is a street or one of the smaller squares of Venice, looking out onto a canal.

[*] Beolco usually signed himself *Ruzante*. Modern practice, however, is to use the form *Ruzzante*.

[**] Ruzzante's assailant, Gnua's lover, is not mentioned in the original cast of characters.

RUZZANTE, *alone*

RUZZANTE. Well, here I am at last! In Venice! The place I've
been yearning for worse than a spindle-shanked, empty-
bellied old mare yearns for the sweet green grass! What I
need is a rest, a chance to build up my muscles, and to get
back to my wife, Gnua. She's living here now. To hell with
war, and battlefields, and soldiers! You won't catch me on
any battlefields again! I've had enough of those drums beating in my ears. No more trumpets! No more call to arms!
And no more getting scared to death! Because when I hear
them sound off that call to arms I feel just like a thrush
trapped in the hunter's hand. No more muskets going bang!
No more artillery blasting! They're not going to get me
again, and if they do it'll be in the backside. No, sir, you're
not going to catch me scrounging around, ducking arrows.
I'm going to get a good night's sleep, and cheer up my belly
with a square meal, for a change. Sure as God, there were
times when they didn't give you the right to shit in comfort!
Well, glory be to St. Mark, here I am, safe and sound! I
made damn good time getting here, too. Bet I made sixty
miles a day. It only took me three days to get here from
Cremona. Bah! It isn't as far as they claim it is. Forty miles
from Cremona to Brescia? Poppycock! It's not even eighteen. Thirty from Brescia to Peschiera? Thirty? Huh! The
devil it is! More like sixteen. And from Peschiera here? How
much is that? I did it in a day! Why, the falcon isn't born

yet that can fly as fast as I've walked. Take my word for it, my legs are shot. But I'm not what you'd really call tired. It was fear kept me moving, and desire that guided my footsteps. I hope to God it's just my shoes that are battered. Let's take a look. There, what'd I tell you? Ream my guts, it looks like the sole's ripped right off one, doesn't it? That's what *I* got out of the war! Sure as God, I couldn't have walked further if the enemy was charging up my backside. Yes, a fat mess I got out of it! Well, I suppose I can pick up another pair somewhere. That's how I got these. Lifted them off some hayseed on the battlefield. To tell the truth, it's not a bad place for a little shoplifting, the battlefield— if you weren't scared stiff all the time. A pox on property! Here I am, safe and sound, and I can hardly believe it. Hey, suppose I'm just dreaming all this! That'd be a blow! What do you mean, dreaming? Didn't I get on board that ship at Fusina? I'm me, ain't I? Sure as God, I am. Didn't I dedicate myself to the Holy Virgin as a good little footslogging soldier? Well, that's one little vow I'm taking back. But suppose I'm not really me? Suppose I got killed in combat? So, now I'm a ghost! Oh, that'd be a great one! But, uh, uh! Ghosts don't get hungry. I'm me, all right. Me, myself, and I'm alive. Now if I only knew where to locate my Gnua. Or my old neighbor, Menato. He's come to live in Venice, too. Won't my wife be terrified of me now? I'd better show her what a brave old hellcat I've become. Well, I am brave. Didn't I manage to escape from the teeth of those dogs back there? Menato'll ask me about the fighting, and pox take me if I don't shoot him a line. Hey, I honest and truly declare that's him over there. Yes, it honest and truly is! Hey, good neighbor Menato! It is you, isn't it, Menato? It's me! Ruzzante! Your old friend, Ruzzante!

MENATO. Good God, can it be you, good neighbor Ruzzante? Who in the world could recognize you? Why you're so beat up and skinny that anyone'd think you were a half-baked skeleton. I couldn't have told you from a hole in the ground. But, you're welcome!

RUZZANTE. So I don't look so hot, eh? Well, if you'd been where I've been, my friend . . .

MENATO. Did you come straight from the front? Have you been sick? Or in prison? You look awful, absolutely awful, good neighbor Ruzzante. You've got a nasty look about you, a treacherous, hanging look. I don't like to say it, my friend, but I've seen at least a hundred characters strung up by the neck who didn't look half as treacherous as you do! Now I'm not saying that you are—you understand that, don't you?—I'm not saying that you look like a rogue or a scoundrel. You get what I mean, don't you? I mean that you look unkempt, and grubby—and all beat up. You sure as God must have had a narrow escape from those dogs!

RUZZANTE. Good neighbor Menato, those cuirasses—it's those metal breastplates that make a man look so treacherous. The heavier they are, the more they strip the flesh off you. And what's more, in the army you can't drink when you want to. And the trouble getting something to eat!

In a very affected manner.

Ah, if only you had been through what I have been through. . . .

MENATO. A pox on your fancy talk, good neighbor Ruzzante! Hoo! Have you been picking up that la-di-da Florentine stuff those Brisighelli spout?

RUZZANTE. Well, good neighbor Menato, when you move around the world a bit, you do pick up a few things. After all, I have spent quite some time with the Brisighelli from Urbino. And talked to them just like that! Now, if I were to speak French to you, you wouldn't understand a word. But fear'd teach it to you in a day! Oh, they're a high and mighty lot of bastards! They say to you: "Villan cuchin," "Pallyard," "Par la song Dew," "I'll cut your throat for you, and eat it!"

MENATO. A pox on them! That's what I say! I get that bit about cutting your throat and eating it, Ruzzante, but I don't get the rest of those words. Tell me, what do they mean?

RUZZANTE. Gladly. "Villan" means "Hayseed," see? "Cuchin" means "Cuckold," "Pallyard" means "House made of straw," "Par la song Dew" means "For the love of God!"

MENATO. They lie in their throats! Those are fighting words and it costs plenty to try them on us!

RUZZANTE. You said it! I wish their chiefs were all strung up. Like this!

MENATO. Hey, Ruzzante? That cape you're wearing hangs down below your jacket!

RUZZANTE. I filched it from a hayseed out there. I was feeling the cold. Pox on them, the sly, miserly yokels! For a couple of cents they'd cheerfully watch you freeze to death.

MENATO. Do you know what, Ruzzante? I believe that since you've become a soldier you've stopped being a villein yourself.

RUZZANTE. No, good neighbor Menato, what I mean is, you see, what I mean is that they don't accept you in the same friendly way us Paduans do. Villeins for them are people who are up to villainy, not just people who live in the country.

MENATO. God Almighty, Ruzzante, what's that you stink of?

RUZZANTE. Stink? Huh? What stink? The smell of hay is nothing to turn your nose up at! I've been sleeping on hay, in a tent, for the last four months. And, believe me, the bed didn't give me the least bit of trouble.

MENATO. Wait a minute, Ruzzante! What's that? Looks like an insect to me, only it hasn't got any wings.

RUZZANTE. Pooh! A louse? Why, in camp, if you didn't brush the bread crumbs off you, they grew legs and a head and turned into lice. And the wine! You'd no sooner get it down than your blood would start fermenting! Because it's out to get you! You get a bile inside you, which throws out nasty scabs. Scurvy sets in. A mangy itch. And nice crusty sores all over your body!

MENATO. Well, I can see that you've got your full share of them, good neighbor Ruzzante. You're covered with them! So I guess you didn't lay your hands on as much plunder as you thought you would, eh?

RUZZANTE. No, I didn't get a thing, either in my hands or my knapsack. And, damn me, Menato, if I didn't come close to eating my weapons.

MENATO. Good God! What did you say? You got so ravenous you ate iron?

RUZZANTE. Good neighbor Menato, if you had been through what I have been through, you'd learn to eat iron too, plus any old clothes that came your way. I sold mine at an inn, so I could get something to eat. Besides that, I was broke.

MENATO. But didn't you manage to pick up anything when you took prisoners?

RUZZANTE. Good God, Menato! I never wanted to hurt anybody. Why should I take any prisoners? What good would they do me? Oh no, what I did was to try to capture a cow or a mare. But I never had any luck.

MENATO. You know, good neighbor Ruzzante, you've got a pretty beat-up look for a brave soldier. Who'd believe you ever went to war? Why I thought you'd come back with a scarred face, or a leg missing, maybe an arm, or blind in one eye. Oh well, why talk about it? You've had luck! But I must say you certainly don't look much like a hell-raising soldier.

RUZZANTE. You don't need a scarred face, or a missing leg, to be one hell of a soldier. Now, you don't really think that I—me, Ruzzante?—that I'd be scared of four of them chasing me, just because they had scars on their faces? Why couldn't I break their legs for them anyway? But, they'd be too scared to move. And they'd get the itch from me anyhow—the itch to run away.

MENATO. Ruzzante, I've got a sneaking suspicion that you don't want to go back to the war. Am I right? Have I guessed it?

RUZZANTE. Well, now, good neighbor Menato, how can I explain it? If the pay was good to begin with—if they paid you regularly every month, instead of stretching those months out into half years—well, then I might consider going back.

MENATO. And you were so hot for it when you left. How you've changed!

RUZZANTE. Ah, neighbor, if you had been through what I have been through!

MENATO. You must have been scared stiff? Got a bellyful of it, eh?

RUZZANTE. No, all I mean is that rustling up the old rub-a-dub is no lead-pipe cinch.

MENATO. What do you mean, "rustling up the old rub-a-dub"? Huh, Ruzzante? Sounds like double talk to me.

RUZZANTE. Oh, that's the way we talk in the army. "Rub-a-dub" means "grub"—you know, *victuals*. Just like "Passing the ford" means "Gifts from the Lord"—which is to say, to have a great victory over your enemy.

MENATO. Strumpety-dumpety! I'd have thought "rub-a-dub" meant the washtub. And as for "crossing the ford," why, I'd have thought that's what you do through water when there's no bridge. Ah, what things they've taught you, Ruzzante. And did you get to take part in a real skirmish, Ruzzante, huh?

RUZZANTE. Huh! Not me! Not a single one! Not that I was scared, understand, *or* off sick, *or* just keeping out of trouble, mind you. It's just that when our men met the enemy they turned tail. Anyhow, the ones up front did. I was in the rear, naturally. I was a corporal, in charge of a squad. I *had* to stay in the rear. Well, the line up front would suddenly turn tail and come charging back, helter-skelter, so there wasn't much sense in me doing anything different, no matter how much courage I had. I ask you, good neighbor Menato, what chance would I have, one man against the whole enemy? No sir, I ran as fast as my legs would carry me. I was wearing my sword, that beauty I once showed you, but I ripped it off, even though it was worth three crowns.

MENATO. Well, why the devil did you run away?

RUZZANTE. Listen, Menato, if you'd been in *my* shoes! Let me tell you, that's no place for fog-brained numskulls or for stupid horsing around. Look! When I couldn't run any more I threw the sword away and slipped into the enemy's ranks. Why did I throw the sword away? Because they don't use the same type weapons we do, that's why! I didn't want them to recognize me. And, anyhow, if they did— well, you ought to understand, my friend, no one goes and clobbers an unarmed man. You sort of feel sorry for him. It brings out the pity in you.

MENATO. I get what you mean. But what about the cross on your shield? Didn't they see that?

RUZZANTE. Well, I'll tell you. My shield just happened to have a red cross on one side and a white cross on the other. So I simply turned it around. How's that for an idea? As I was saying, the battlefield's no place for fog-brained numskulls. And even if I do say it myself—and who shouldn't— I'm a pretty shrewd character. When our side counterattacked I just turned that shield around again. And do you know what? After a while, whenever we'd get into action, I'd do a little tail-turning myself. So, you see . . . ?

MENATO. Yes, I get it. You were always figuring which way to run.

RUZZANTE. Exactly. Not because I wanted to run *away*. It was just that I wanted to keep my skin in one piece, that's all. And, like I say, what can one man do against a whole horde of them?

MENATO. Tell me the truth, Ruzzante. When you got mixed up in one of those skirmishes, didn't you find something deep down inside you saying: "I wish I was safe at home!"? Come on, just between ourselves. You can speak freely with me.

RUZZANTE. Ah, my friend, if you had been through what I have been through, you'd have had that thought a thousand times over. Can you imagine what it's like being over there in that foreign land? You don't know a soul. You don't know where to go. And the only thing to look at is hordes of men shouting: "Kill 'em! Kill 'em! Give 'em hell!" Cannon balls and bullets and arrows are whistling through the air. You turn around and there's one of your buddies lying dead. Killed! And there's somebody at your elbow trying to do the same for you. You try to sneak out of it all, and there you are, right in the middle of the enemy. And you never even realize when you turn tail that you're likely to get a bullet in your back. Let me tell you, it takes real courage to duck out of a mess like that. Can you guess how many times I pretended to be dead? Letting a whole squadron of cavalry pass over me? Nothing could have made me budge! They could have piled Mount Venda on top of me! I'm just telling you the simple truth about the whole mess. And, believe me, that's why I say that any man who can save his skin in a spot like that is nothing more or less than a hero!

MENATO. But, damn it all, Ruzzante, couldn't you have slipped into a hollow tree trunk, or climbed an oak, or burrowed behind a hedge when you wanted to? Why run?

RUZZANTE. For God's sake! Certainly not, Menato! The truth of the matter is—well, it's not that I didn't think of it, or that I was afraid to, but I just didn't feel it was safe to stop! Why, I'd rather run ten miles anywhere than stay put when I'm in danger! If you'd been in my place, Menato, you'd have prayed for wings once or twice. Now, wait till you hear this one! One time we got into a battle, and as I was tailing off, one of our men on a horse rode by and his horse's hoof caught my foot and ripped my shoe off. Do you think I stopped to put it on again? Not on your life! I was in too much of a hurry! And I finished that little adventure with the sole of my foot in shreds, because we were hightailing it over a lot of stony ground in some God-forsaken wilderness. But, believe me, I wouldn't have stopped to pick up an eye if I'd lost one. So don't give me any of that stuff about hiding somewhere. If you want to talk about something, talk about running away, running till there's not a bit of breath left in you. And don't think that you can afford the time to take a shit while you're on the run like that. Oh no! What happens is that your body gets moving so fast that you do it in your pants, and you don't give it a second thought. How about Prince Antenor, the one who fought so bravely at Troy? Didn't he dive into a river to get away, even though he saw plenty of men drowning in it? And he ran all the way to Padua to get away from it all. No, sir, you've got to keep running until there's not a breath left in you, that's all there is to it! It's not worth while trying to be a hero. And, you know, I'm not afraid of anyone. I'll take on four men any time. But when there's a whole army running away, why, Roland himself would turn tail.

MENATO. I'm not saying he wouldn't, but it seems to me that

when you went off to war you were talking about all the big things you were going to do—capturing and plundering. What about all that?

RUZZANTE. Phooey! I just had arse-hard luck, that's all! But, at least, I did get to see a bit of the world.

MENATO. Well, you did travel. How far did you get?

RUZZANTE. Don't ask me how far I traveled. I got as far as Ghieradadda. You know, where the big battle took place where we lost so many? Oh, man, all you could see was piles and piles of bones, and the sky above them.

MENATO. Pox on it all, I'll say you traveled far! What sort of language do they speak there? Can you understand them? Are they men of flesh and blood there? Like you and me? Are they? Are they like us?

RUZZANTE. Oh, sure, they're flesh and blood, just like us. And the language is almost the same. But they don't pronounce it so good, like those louts who sell seeds in the villages. But they get christened in church, and they make bread the same way we do. Why, they even get married! But, to tell the truth, though, what with war and soldiers, there isn't much love going on anywhere. They've sent love packing, like a kick in the arse.

MENATO. What kind of land is it? Good farming land?

RUZZANTE. Like what it is here. You get willows, poplars, vineyards, fruit trees . . .

MENATO. Can you buy land cheap there? I mean, people like us, who might go and live there, you know . . .

RUZZANTE. Don't say another word, friend. I know what you're driving at. No, you wouldn't be any better off there than you are here. Stick to Padua, and pay no attention to those fine tales you may of heard about other places. They're all alike. But there's something I've been meaning to ask, only you kept me talking about everything else. Hold on, I'm going to ask it right now. Have you got any news of my wife?

MENATO. Oh, Ruzzante, has she put on airs! Why, the bitch won't even lower herself to pass the time of day with her old friends. As soon as you left Padua, she began hanging around with those low-down, riffraff types in the Cardinal's stables. Then when they left she moved over here to Venice. Now she's living with God knows who—as big a bunch of pimps, brutes, and back-alley braggarts as you could hope to meet anywhere. Do you want me to go on, Ruzzante? I used to, er, *visit* her myself, you know. God, she's turned into an insolent and snotty bitch. She won't pay any attention to you now, especially since you're wearing those rags!

RUZZANTE. That's where you're wrong, my friend. Why, as soon as she sets eyes on me, she'll throw herself into my arms! You'll see.

MENATO. Don't be too sure!

RUZZANTE. Do you know where she lives? Come on. Let's go find her!

MENATO. Now, wait a minute, Ruzzante. We've got to take it easy. That's a rough bunch she's hanging around with.

RUZZANTE. Pooh! So what! Tell me, do you know anyone tougher than I am? What if they are a bunch of bruisers? So am I. I can't wait to get my hands on them. And her! Just let me swing this pike around a bit. You'll soon see that I've been in the army, all right. Here's how we do it. A couple of jabs with the point, like this, and then a good bash or two. What do you think of that, Menato? Am I a tough character or not? Once I get going, it's to hell with friendship, to hell with family! I get so boiled up I don't care who I'm fighting. You know what? I may have a soft spot in my heart for you, but if it came to a fight, I'd let you have it the same way I'd give it to them! I'd be so blind! See?

MENATO. I'll say, Ruzzante. It wouldn't be safe to hang round you in a fight.

RUZZANTE. You're damn right it wouldn't. It's better to keep clear. So let's get going. And don't be scared!

MENATO. But I'm telling you, Ruzzante. It's a tough situation. After all, one little blow and you're dead!

RUZZANTE. Nonsense. Suppose you'd been in my place that time when there were three thousand of them coming at me at once? Why be scared? Besides, don't you see, I've got this pike.

MENATO. Hey, look. There she is, Ruzzante. Coming this way. Over there. It's her, all right, no doubt about it.

RUZZANTE. That's her, all right. Now, just you watch her fall into my arms. Hey! Yes, you! Who do you think I'm talking to? Come on, you hot piece of tail, don't you recognize me? It's me! Back at last!

GNUA. Ruzzante? Is it really you? Huh! So you're still alive? Ugh! Aren't you a sight! Scruffy, filthy, and you've got that nasty hanging look! I suppose you've managed not to get a thing out of all this?

RUZZANTE. Isn't it enough I've brought my carcass home to you?

GNUA. Your lousy carcass! That'll make me fat! I should think you'd at least bring me back a dress or something.

RUZZANTE. My God! Isn't it enough that I've come back in one piece? With all my arms and legs in their proper places?

GNUA. You can take your arms, and your legs, and stick them up your arse! You'd have done better to bring me something useful. Well, anyway, it's time I was going. There's someone waiting for me.

RUZZANTE. You're certainly in a hurry to get away. Anyone would think you had a cannon at your backside. Wait a minute.

GNUA. What for? Why should I hang around here when you've got nothing to offer me? Let me go!

RUZZANTE. So, it's to hell with all the love I've given you, is it? You want to go off and hide somewhere? And here I am, come back from the wars to see you.

GNUA. All right, you've seen me, haven't you? If you want to know the truth, I don't want you messing up my life now that I've got someone who takes care of me and treats me decently. You don't meet such good luck every day.

RUZZANTE. So he treats you decently, huh? Well, so did I. You know very well I never treated you badly. Besides, he couldn't love you the way I do.

GNUA. Ruzzante, do you know who loves me the best? The one who shows it the most.

RUZZANTE. Exactly! And haven't I?

GNUA. What's the good of something you've given me in the past? I need things *now, now!* Don't you understand that I have to eat every day? If I could keep alive on one meal a year, you'd do fine for me. But I have to eat every day, so you'd better show me how much you love me *now*, because *now* is when I need it.

RUZZANTE. So what! What you really ought to think of is the difference between one man and another. Now I, as you know, am a *good* man, and a very able one.

GNUA. That may be, but there's also a difference between being well off and badly off. Listen, Ruzzante, if I thought you could keep me in style, I'd take you back quick enough. Oh, I'd love you then, you'd see. It's not that I wish you any trouble, it's just that I can't stand the miserable condition you're in. If you were rich, I'd like you plenty. We'd both be in clover.

RUZZANTE. Well, if I'm poor, I'm at least faithful.

GNUA. What good does your being faithful do me if you can't give me any practical proof of it? What have you got to give me? A few lice, I suppose.

RUZZANTE. But you know that if I did have anything I'd give it to you, just as I always have. Do you want me to go thieving and get myself hung? Is that what you want?

GNUA. And do you want me to live on air? And keep hoping for you to fish up something until I drop from hunger? A fine husband you are, if that's what you want!

RUZZANTE. Hell and damnation! Well, there's still one way to get you. I'm going to faint! Haven't you any pity for me?

GNUA. Sure, but what about me? I've got a wholesome fear of dying of starvation. You never think of that. Haven't you got any conscience at all? I want something more out of life than selling leeks and radishes. How, in Heaven's name, do you expect me to live?

RUZZANTE. But if you leave me, I'll die of love for you! I *am* dying! I tell you, I'm passing out!

GNUA. And I'm telling you that because of what you've done, love has run out my backside. To think that you haven't brought me back a thing! What about what you *should* have brought?

RUZZANTE. God damn! Huh! You're worried about what you haven't got. Well, I'm all right. I got all that's needed.

GNUA. Yes, a big heart, and you're shaky on your pins. Oh no, I don't see anything there I want.

RUZZANTE. But I just got here!

GNUA. But it's four months since you left.

RUZZANTE. But it's also four months since I last—*troubled* you.

GNUA. And you're certainly giving me enough trouble now, when I see you looking like a beggar. Anyhow, I've been nicely *troubled* all the time you were away, because I had an idea this is the way you'd turn up.

RUZZANTE. But it's just that I had bad luck.

GNUA. Then take your punishment! You don't expect me to take it for you, do you? Or do you think that would be the decent housewifely thing to do, eh? Eh, sweetheart? Huh! I don't happen to think so.

RUZZANTE. But it's not my fault!

GNUA. Oh no! It's all mine, of course. Ruzzante, the man who's afraid to take a few risks will never get fat. I don't even believe you tried to get anything. Otherwise you'd have something to show for it. So help me God, I bet you never even set eyes on a battlefield. You probably spent all your time loafing in some hospital. Can't you see what a wretched, villainous, hanging look you've got?

MENATO. There you are, Ruzzante! Just what I said. You should have got your face all messed up, slashed to ribbons. That'd be much better. Then maybe she'd think you were a real soldier.

GNUA. That's the truth, good neighbor Menato! I'd rather have him lose an arm or a leg, or get one of his eyes gouged out, or his nose sliced off, so that people would think he was a brave fellow and that he got wounded going after plunder, or that his love had spurred him on! See? I'm not interested in the plunder, if you get what I mean, good neighbor Menato. Because I don't really need anything. It's just that it'll look as if he doesn't give a damn about me. And people

will think he behaved like a lily-livered coward. Look! He
swore to me he'd come back loaded with plunder or die in
the attempt. And now he comes back like this. It's not that
I really wish he'd gotten hurt, Menato, it's just that he
ought to look like he's been in a battle.

MENATO. I know what you mean, good neighbor Gnua, and,
by God, you couldn't be righter, and I told him, too! I said
what you'd like is for him to have some sort of mark that'd
show he's been in the fighting, so it'd look like he's been up
front and in the thick of things. A scratch, at least!

GNUA. Yes. So that when he showed it to me he could say, "I
got this for your sake!"

RUZZANTE. To hell with plunder and the man who first
thought of it!

GNUA. And to hell with all lazy good-for-nothings and turn-
tails. And to hell with whoever it was that made them! What
did you promise me?

RUZZANTE. I tell you, I was just unlucky.

GNUA. You never said a truer word. And as for me, well, now
that I'm well taken care of, I'm *not* unlucky. And I'm going
to stay like that. And not get mixed up in your troubles.
You mind your business, and I'll mind mine. Damn! There's
my man now. Let me go!

RUZZANTE. Shit on your man! I'm the only man for you!

GNUA. Let me go, you miserable, low-down, good-for-nothing
dog! You thieving, vagabonding, lousy . . .

RUZZANTE. *You come with me!* I tell you, you bitch, you won't
get rid of me! Watch out I don't lose my temper. You don't
know what I'm like now. You're not going to lead me by
the nose any more, the way you used to.

MENATO. You better get going before he kills you!

GNUA. Huh! Let him go kill lice! That's more in his line, the
thieving rat!

SCENE 2

The bullying lout who is GNUA's *protector arrives at this moment. He gives* RUZZANTE *a thorough beating. (It is clear,
from the phrasing of the original stage directions, that*
RUZZANTE's *pike is turned to effective and painful use against
him.) When he has finally gone* RUZZANTE *gets up.*

RUZZANTE. Hey, Menato! Have they gone yet? Any of them
still hanging around? Take a good look.

MENATO. No, Ruzzante, he's gone, and she's gone with him.
There's no one here.

RUZZANTE. But what about the others? Are they gone too?

MENATO. What others? I only saw one.

RUZZANTE. You ought to have your eyes examined. There
must have been a hundred of them, all beating me up.

MENATO. Sure as hell there wasn't, Ruzzante.

RUZZANTE. Sure as hell there was, Menato! Do you think you'd
know better than me? That'd be a great joke! So you think
I'm piling it on a little, huh? *A hundred against one,* that's
what it was! See? The least you could have done was to
pitch in, Menato, or helped me out somehow.

MENATO. Not on your life! Why should I get mixed up in it
when you just told me you were a real hotheaded fighter
and that once you got going I better keep clear, because
you might let me have it too? Because you get so worked
up you can't even recognize your friends and relations!

RUZZANTE. All right, that's what I said, but just the same,
when you saw me holding off a bunch like that single-
handed, you should have helped me! Who do you think I
am, Roland?

MENATO. But honestly, Ruzzante, there was only one of them!
Honest there was! And I thought you were letting him have
a good go at you to wear him down, and that when he got

good and tired, you'd jump on him and make up for it. See what I mean, Ruzzante? I figured that when you'd really worn him down and beat him up, he wouldn't be in any condition to go off with Gnua. Or I thought maybe you had some other plan. You should have told me.

RUZZANTE. No, Menato, I didn't think of that! I didn't budge an inch because I was playing dead. Just like I did on the battlefield. So they'd go away. See? It's the only thing to do when you're up against so many of them.

MENATO. But honest, Ruzzante, honest, *there was only one of them!* Why didn't you use your pike?

RUZZANTE. You can say what you want, but I know what I'm talking about, *and I happen to know what happened! I'm* used to it, let me tell you! *It was a hundred of them against one!* And if you think I'm exaggerating, you're talking through your backside!

MENATO. But, Ruzzante, he was all by himself. I swear he was! On my word of honor.

RUZZANTE. Well, if he was all by himself, there's trickery in it somewhere! Some witchcraft, or God knows what! She did it! That's it! She's a witch! What do you know? And she bewitched me into thinking she was the most beautiful woman in the world, when I know all the time she isn't and that there are plenty better than her. There you are! And then she goes and makes me see a hundred men instead of one. God help me if I didn't see a whole forest of weapons whirling around ready to hit me. There was one moment when I saw so many sharp ends coming at me I thought I was going to be sliced into thin air. And didn't I say my prayers then! Oh, didn't I! Pheeew! Pox gripe her guts! I'd like to burn her alive, that's what I'd like to do. Damn it, Menato, why didn't you tell me there was only one of them? Bloody hell, you should've told me.

MENATO. Bloody hell, yourself! I thought you saw him! He was close enough to you.

RUZZANTE. But I tell you I saw more than a hundred of them! Oh well! Say, what do you think of me, Menato? Me, who took a beating like that and didn't bat an eyelid? Am I, or am I not, one brave, tough guy?

MENATO. Did you say *beating*, Ruzzante? Hell, it could've killed a horse. I couldn't see a bit of you. All I saw was a patch of sky and wallop-wallop-wallop-wallop-wallop! Doesn't it hurt, Ruzzante? I don't know why you're alive to tell the tale, honest I don't.

RUZZANTE. Oh, I'm used to it, good neighbor! I've grown myself a thick skin. I don't feel a thing now. But what does hurt me is knowing what you just told me—that there was only one of him. If I'd known that, well, I'd have thought up the best trick I ever cooked up in my life. I'd have tied him and her together and then, with the two of them stuck together like that, I'd have tossed them in the canal. Christ Almighty, wouldn't that have been funny? Hell, man, you should have told me! By God, what a laugh we'd have had. Mind you, I'm not saying I'd have gone so far as to give him a walloping. Out of love for her, I wouldn't do that. After all, I don't want to cause her any pain, because I still sort of love her, if you see what I mean. But it sure would have been damned funny! Ho! Ho! Ho! Ho!

MENATO. I'll be damned! The way you're splitting your sides laughing, anyone would think there was a big joke somewhere! Or else that you'd just come from seeing a funny play. Or else that you'd gotten drunk at a wedding!

RUZZANTE. What the hell, Menato? What does it matter? What do I care? It really would have been a riot, though, if I'd tied the two of them together! But then, I suppose you'd have told me not to put on any more comedies.*

* The ending is probably by way of *envoy*. It sounds like a cue for applause and shouts of "More."

THE
THREE CUCKOLDS

An anonymous scenario of the commedia dell' arte
converted into a play by Leon Katz

CHARACTERS

(In order of their appearance)

ARLECCHINO

COVIELLO

FLAMINIA

PANTALONE

ZANNI

FRANCESCHINA

DEVIL

LEANDRO

CINTIA

MUSICIAN

SCENE: *A street before three houses*

ACT I

SCENE 1

ARLECCHINO *comes in calling to someone, it seems, off stage.*

ARLECCHINO. Arlecchino! Arlecchino! Look what we've found! Move, you scrawny little centipede! Oh, look at him move —like a couple of worms wrapping themselves around a stick! Hurry up, run, we've stumbled on the door of salvation! Oh you snail, can't you shove along any faster? We're only four steps, three hugs, two kisses and a how-are-you from a mountain of food and drink!

Then, as though he has just come in, bedraggled, exhausted, he answers himself.

Food and drink? Where? Zno food and drink. Just doors, houses. Kicks, bruises. No sleep, no meat, no wine, no——

He interrupts himself impatiently.

Doors and houses! Yes, but whose?

Not interested.

Whose?

Shouting at himself impatiently.

Cintia's! We've stumbled on Cintia's door!

His weariness disappearing.

Cintia, the kitchen queen?

Going to her door.

Oh, sweet promise, sweetest Cintia, remember when last we met? Remember the knock at the door? And remember how soon we parted? And what did you whisper to me when that husband, that snooper, that rheumy Coviello was burrowing through your cupboards and nosing through your pails? "A lover? A lover? A lover?" he shrieked. And, injured as you were, what was it you whispered to your poor Arlecchino hanging by a nail from your window? "Come back," you sighed, "come back and we'll be quits with the old fool for what he has made us bear."

He pretends to open wide an enormous pocket in his clothing.

Pocket, remember? Do you have it still? I begged you to hold tight to Cintia's promise.

He so-to-speak lifts it from his pocket and holds it up tenderly.

Sweet promise, dear sweet promise! How long we've waited to embrace our Cintia's dinners, breakfasts, suppers, and in-between-times meals! And to devour with passion her leeks, her vegetables, her tender meats, her white wines and her red wines, her stews, her pastries and her dear sweet love!

He turns to the audience and points to where he was.

Everybody, look! Look at poor Arlecchino! Drawn, wasted, starved for food, starved for the love of the kitchen queen, starved, too, for a good joke on somebody. He hasn't tricked anyone for weeks. His mind is wasting. He's thought of nothing but a few little pranks—making the old doctor pull out all his fingernails to save himself forever from the plague, making the old merchant eat a bowl of mud from the bottom of the river to get back his youthful appetites —little things, hardly worth mentioning. Arlecchino will surely die of waste, wasting away for the want of a meal, wasting away for the want of a prank, wasting away for the want of that foul, beautiful, exquisite, dirty, queenly, wretched, tender, powerful, tasteful, tasty, toothsome, loath-some, lovesome, likesome, wantsome, needsome Cintia! Everybody, weep!

A great voice from CINTIA's *door shouts, "Out, out!" and a pot is flung through the door as* COVIELLO *is hurtled onto the stage floor.*

SCENE 2

COVIELLO. Oh, you there—man! Help me. You are a friend?
ARLECCHINO. I am, I am that if nothing else.

COVIELLO. You are a fellow man?

ARLECCHINO. A fellow man.

COVIELLO. Fellow man, do you know what I am?

ARLECCHINO. You are a bird.

COVIELLO. I am a husband! Coviello, the husband!

ARLECCHINO. Friend, tell me—what sort of a bird is a husband?

COVIELLO. What indeed? What is he but the chattel of a wife, who is given beatings for his charity and mercy——

ARLECCHINO. And maggoty meat for his dinner.

COVIELLO. Whose love and faithfulness is rewarded with slander, suspicion, lying and being found out——

ARLECCHINO. And who gets no dinner because of it.

COVIELLO. Who feels in one day all the tortures of all the martyrs in the Pope's book——

ARLECCHINO. And who gets nothing to eat at the end of it.

COVIELLO. Whose body is full of bruises, his head full of shouts and commands, his heart full of grief and despair——

ARLECCHINO. And only his belly is empty.

COVIELLO. Who is accused of living like a bishop, loving like an abbé, singing and laughing all day like a monk, and does he? No——

ARLECCHINO. No! He fasts and starves like an anchorite!

COVIELLO. Then will you, my friend, help me in my vow of abstinence? Witness that, from this time forth, Coviello will abstain from wives, from all wives—all but one.

ARLECCHINO. Ah, of course—Cintia.

COVIELLO. Flaminia!

ARLECCHINO. Who?

COVIELLO. Flaminia, of course, Flaminia!

ARLECCHINO. But—but you have abstained from all wives.

COVIELLO. All wives, all! All but one—Pantalone's. Ah, Pantalone's wife is not a wife.

ARLECCHINO. Not your wife.

COVIELLO. She is not a wife, she is an elegant repast, a savor of fine living, a dinner cooked for the celebration of the archduke's only daughter's betrothal to the cardinal's favorite mistress's son. Flaminia is the vapor of the white wine, the aroma of the salads, the sauce of the meats, the nectar of the fruits—no, they are all too gross for Flaminia! She is the distillation of the vapor, the swoon of the aroma, the sauciness of the sauce, the aphrodisiac of the nectar!

ARLECCHINO. Come—I will help you eat her.

COVIELLO. Not so fast, my friend. First we must dispose of the old goat Pantalone.

ARLECCHINO. Ah, leave the disposal of the husbands to me.

COVIELLO. Oh, that is my friend! If you do that for me, I make you a great promise.

COVIELLO *becomes solemn.*

If we get Flaminia alone with me, we will share in my harvest.

ARLECCHINO, *incredulous.* Share?

COVIELLO. Yes, dearest friend. Pantalone is a rich man, a very rich man. And Flaminia keeps his keys. I promise you that once I have spent the night with Flaminia, you, my dear friend, will be rewarded well with anything that Pantalone owns.

ARLECCHINO. Anything?

COVIELLO. From the bottom of my heart.

ARLECCHINO. A promise!

COVIELLO. A promise!

COVIELLO *knocks at* FLAMINIA'S *door.*

ARLECCHINO. There goes the old goat Coviello doing in the old goat Pantalone. Oh these old bearded geldings with all their manhood dangling from their spittle and their chins!

COVIELLO. Holla! Flaminia!

ARLECCHINO. Holla! Flaminia! His voice cracking like a boy's of thirteen, hawking wares he hasn't got, crying promises he can't pay.

COVIELLO. Holla, Flaminia!

ARLECCHINO. Holla, Flaminia! He'll spend the night! Up until midnight. And then he wraps the winding sheet on again and goes back to Hell. Eh, Coviello! Ghost! Gelding!

COVIELLO. She doesn't answer, comrade!

ARLECCHINO. Knock again, love!

Continuing to himself.

Knock, and when we get Flaminia alone with you, we get
Cintia alone with me, eh, palsy? I swear if I didn't love your
kitchen slop so that I have no mind for any woman but her,
I could love Pantalone's banquet just to spite you, you
lame unicorn, twice in a single night.

Suddenly ARLECCHINO *jumps to one side of himself, and begins to sneer at the figure he cuts.*

Look at you, Arlecchino, bragging of loving two in a single
night! Which of them would have you? Would any? You
lying, stinking, starving, cheating, whining, shrinking little
exclamation point! I saw you at the fair, remember, when
you made love to the farmer's wife, and the old sow she was
selling fell on her back in her litter and laughed herself to
death.

Proudly, concealing his chagrin, he answers himself.

I? I? You mistake me, whoever you are, for some lovesick
Arlecchino. Look again, sir, look, and may you die of awe
and wonder, may you be racked in Hell with the special
torments they have there for the jealousy of Arlecchino, look
at me once, strike yourself dumb and blind, stumble into
the nearest ditch, die and join the damned writhing with the
jealousy of me. And remember Arlecchino, the lover of a
thousand conquests, for all his fat belly.

*He whips around and, squinting, looks hard for the man he
described.*

Where? Where? I make out only a thin wavy line. What is
it? A wisp of smoke? A visible breath of foul air? Or the
dangling string of a hurried sneeze?

He rises to his full towering self and directs the seeker.

Shut your eyes, shut your eyes and turn around this way.
And when you open them, may you be struck dumb at once
by the radiance of my visible passion, my easily read ardor,
and my audibly heroic manly mold!

*He shuts his eyes, gropes his way until he faces about,
braces himself, and looks. He controls himself for a moment,*

then pointing at the figure he cuts, he looses a hideous yawp of a laugh, and cries:

That!

Wheeling about, he slaps himself hard in the face and says, deeply wounded:

Beast!

COVIELLO. Come, come quickly. She is opening the door.

FLAMINIA *appears from her house.* ARLECCHINO, *overcome by her beauty, gasps and drops into* COVIELLO'S *arms.*

SCENE 3

FLAMINIA. Ardent, ardent Coviello!

COVIELLO, *with* ARLECCHINO *resting in his arms.* Angel Flaminia!

FLAMINIA. Ah! What is that frightful bundle you are holding? Ah-h! Is it a dead beast?

COVIELLO. No, no, my angel, don't be frightened. You see, it is only a man. It is my friend, who has come from heaven to help us, angel. He did not mean to frighten you. Did you mean to frighten my angel, my friend?

ARLECCHINO, *still dangling.* I did not mean to frighten his angel, my angel. Did I mean to frighten my angel, his friend? No, no, his friend did not mean to frighten his angel, his angel.

FLAMINIA. Is he out of his mind, Coviello?

COVIELLO. No, my dear, he is here to help us. Will you forgive him?

FLAMINIA. Anything, anything but another night with Pantalone. As my sweet Coviello knows, I abide by custom, decorum, and so on, but always—Flaminia confesses her fault—she has been a slave to fashion. As the world knows, the fashion has not yet been born that has escaped me, none has left me more than two days behind, or just time enough to get at my husband's chest when he was asleep and into the shops when he was away. I confess it, yes, it was my sin. Now, now it has become my penance. In what mad turn of fashion did it become fashionable for young girls to marry old men? And why had the fashion come to me just when I turned the fashionable age to marry? It has undone me, twice over it has undone me. For now that the fashion for two whole weeks has dictated that wives be virtuous, I have made a solemn vow to break with it. Coviello, help me be brave and true to my oath.

COVIELLO. Oh, my frail innocence, trust in me. I will help you be true to your vow. And here is the ideal friend who has promised to help me help you keep your vow to break your vow.

FLAMINIA. And I can trust him?

COVIELLO. My honesty, as you can trust in me.

FLAMINIA. Walk off a moment, dear Coviello, let me speak to him.

COVIELLO *walks off.* FLAMINIA *beckons to* ARLECCHINO.

Dear friend. Come close to me.

ARLECCHINO *approaches her shufflingly, stands before her, hangdog with embarrassment.*

What is your name?

ARLECCHINO. Arlecchino.

FLAMINIA. Dear Arlecchino, would you—could you—help me?

ARLECCHINO *falls to his knees with a moan and almost grabs the hem of her gown to kiss it.*

FLAMINIA, *in the tone of a woman who has mastered the art of saying, "Don't!"* Ardent, ardent Arlecchino!

ARLECCHINO. Gracious banquet, ask anything, anything of me.

FLAMINIA. Then you will help me undo my husband?

ARLECCHINO. Fair aroma, he and any other.

FLAMINIA. And you will get Coviello into my house tonight?

ARLECCHINO. This night or any other, tender meat, this or any other.

FLAMINIA, *more surprised than outraged.* Tender meat!

ARLECCHINO. Forgive me, I was dreaming of a feast.

FLAMINIA. So!

ARLECCHINO. But I can content myself with its fragrance. If I am promised that, I will help another man to dine his fill.

FLAMINIA. Ah, you dear, clever tradesman! If you can but think of a way to get Coviello into the house, you shall have meat of me as well as fragrance.

ARLECCHINO. Meat of you!

FLAMINIA. A banquet, everything that lies in my power to spread before you.

ARLECCHINO. Then I will help the young pheasant to an old onion, and win for myself, if I understand aright, at least a bit of the dessert?

FLAMINIA, *graciously extending her hand*. A promise.

ARLECCHINO, *gallantly taking it*. A promise! Coviello, here is our plan!

COVIELLO, *joyfully*. Everything is arranged?

ARLECCHINO. Everything is arranged.

COVIELLO. Loyal friend!

ARLECCHINO. Both of you are to pretend that Arlecchino is mute, and that he is a country cousin of Coviello's. When we meet Pantalone, be aghast at the foul odor of his breath and urge him to see a dentist.

COVIELLO. But how am I to get into Pantalone's house tonight?

ARLECCHINO. Ah, an old man is a natural fool. Nothing is easier. For instance, let Flaminia make it known to him that his son and heir is on the way.

FLAMINIA. What? Then the old fool will never leave my side, dote on me night and day, give me things to suck, pillows to lie on, and wait on me with the devotion of a profligate son standing with pen and parchment over his father's deathbed.

ARLECCHINO. That I should live to teach a woman womanly wisdom! Little pheasant, until the heir is apparent—which, Heaven bless old Pantalone however it will, can never be for him—the cold stone of an ancient husband is as a pebble in the hands of a young wife. Want this and that. Need things here and there. Command night and morning. Bring him near, send him far. He comes into the presence, dismiss him. Dismissed, recall him. His friends, the merchants, are at your door? You need solitude. Your friends, the comedians, are in the square? You need bustle, excitement, noise, distraction. From morning to night you cry after him: Pantalone, for my salvation and your own delight, lie with me tonight. From night to morning, you whisper hoarsely as though the convulsion is overtaking you: Pantalone, Pantalone, if you love your wife and your own posterity, sleep on the carpet in the other room. Begin with lemons.

FLAMINIA. Lemons?

ARLECCHINO. You need lemons, you dote on them. You have the taste for lemons, and would he be so niggardly a father that he would deny you harmless little lemons? Father, says Pantalone, FATHER! Honest Flaminia, can you find it in your virtue to fool the old fool from there?

FLAMINIA. Honest Arlecchino, you are a masterpiece!

COVIELLO. My friend, my friend!

The morning coughing and wheezing of old PANTALONE *is heard within.* ARLECCHINO *jumps from the house in surprise.*

ARLECCHINO. Do you keep horses in the very house of so wealthy a merchant as Pantalone?

FLAMINIA. Horses? What horses?

The wheezing is heard again.

ARLECCHINO. Ah no. It is the cook tossing the swill into the canal from the other side of the house.

FLAMINIA. It is swill, and it is going into the canal, but it is not the cook who is tossing it in.

ARLECCHINO. Who, then?

FLAMINIA, *at the door, with tragic dignity.* My husband, when he rises in the morning, goes to the window overlooking the canal——

She shudders.

to clear his throat.

She goes into the house.

SCENE 4

COVIELLO, *almost in tears.* Save her, my friend, save her from
that old man.

ARLECCHINO. You remember your promise?

COVIELLO. Yes, yes, what shall I do now?

ARLECCHINO. Stand away from the door, and as Pantalone
comes out, I will meet him.

COVIELLO. But he does not know you.

ARLECCHINO, *laughing.* He will know me soon enough.

SCENE 5

The door opens and PANTALONE *comes out.* ARLECCHINO
*has assumed the attitude of a beggar standing at his door
for alms. He says nothing, pretending to be mute, but approaches* PANTALONE *and signifies his dire poverty and the
old merchant's opportunity to store up good deeds for
salvation.*

PANTALONE, *glowers at him and barks into his face.* What are
you doing here? Is this a house of God that you should beg
before my door?

ARLECCHINO, *getting a whiff of* PANTALONE'S *breath in this
outburst, sails back across the stage, and falls into* COVIELLO'S
arms like an asphyxiated bird.

Coviello, what is the matter with the beggar?

COVIELLO. Beggar! My good friend Pantalone, this is my good
friend Arlecchino, my country cousin who has come to visit.

PANTALONE. Have I offended him then?

COVIELLO. Arlecchino! Arlecchino! Stand up and greet our
good friend Pantalone.

ARLECCHINO *points to* PANTALONE *and pretends to cry.*

Pantalone wants to know if he has offended you.

ARLECCHINO *moans.*

Stop bawling, Arlecchino, and you will have his apology from his own mouth.

ARLECCHINO *moans even louder and tries to run away.*

With his own breath——

ARLECCHINO *breaks loose and runs behind* COVIELLO *to hide.*

Forgive him, Pantalone. Cousin Arlecchino is beloved by his country neighbors, he has a good heart, and he's the merriest of the village idiots.

ARLECCHINO *takes a moment to digest this injury.*

PANTALONE. Merriest? Ah, a little joke. Ha, ha! You see, Pantalone can laugh at an idiot as well as any man. Ha, ha, ha!

And he laughs directly into COVIELLO's *face. Stiff as a board,* COVIELLO *falls face forward against* PANTALONE's *chest.*

What is the matter with you? Coviello, were you merry in the village too?

COVIELLO. That breath—— Oh, that breath——

ARLECCHINO *runs up to him and pulls his sleeve. He motions vigorously toward his own mouth and shakes his head wildly.*

Cousin Arlecchino says that is not breath!

ARLECCHINO *mimes swallowing a savory morsel, falls dead, sits up, studies* PANTALONE, *and then as though coming to a decision, shakes his head slowly.* PANTALONE *looks to* COVIELLO *for translation of this.*

Cousin Arlecchino says that dead men stuffed with garlic wouldn't smell like that.

PANTALONE, *lurches toward them, outraged.* Stuffed with garlic!

ARLECCHINO *motions toward them to attend his next charade, extends a hand toward* PANTALONE, *as if to say, "Tell me, Pantalone," jumps into a handspring, and eases himself down on his head.*

COVIELLO, *shouting to* PANTALONE *and getting ready for flight with* ARLECCHINO. Cousin Arlecchino wants to know, when you were talking to him were you standing on your head?

ARLECCHINO, *reinforcing* COVIELLO's *translation with attentive nods, is patting his backside.*

Because Cousin Arlecchino thinks——

PANTALONE, *starting after them, raging.* Idiots! What does the idiot cousin think?

COVIELLO, *while he and* ARLECCHINO *are running.* Cousin Arlecchino thinks——

FLAMINIA *appears at the door.*

SCENE 6

FLAMINIA, *with mock horror, since her husband has stopped dead two inches from her.* Ardent, ardent Pantalone!

PANTALONE, *turning aside, to himself.* Oh, my plague!

FLAMINIA, *indignantly, to* PANTALONE. Have you taken to beating your friends in the streets? Why? Have they offended you?

Then, indignantly to the other two.

Have you offended my dear husband Pantalone?

PANTALONE. Yes, yes, they have abused the dignity of my middle age!

FLAMINIA. How? In what way? Tell me, and we will make a public scandal of them.

PANTALONE. No, no, it is a private matter. Hardly anything—— *Aside.*

Public scandal indeed! One in our household is enough!

To FLAMINIA.

It was nothing, nothing at all——

FLAMINIA, *fanning herself.* I am faint—— Ugh—— Help me, I am falling.

PANTALONE, *runs to her, and* FLAMINIA *screams and retreats from him. Furious, he blurts out*: What is the matter with me? Tell me, Flaminia, before I walk through the streets this morning.

FLAMINIA. No, no, it is nothing, nothing at all.

PANTALONE. Nothing at all! I have cut down three people in three minutes just by opening my mouth and you say it is nothing at all. What is the matter with me? Am I the plague? Am I the Last Messenger?

FLAMINIA. Stand away, Pantalone—over there. Open your mouth—— Wide—wider——

The three of them rise on their toes and peer into PANTA-LONE's *mouth from across the stage. They groan and shake their heads.* FLAMINIA *begins to weep as though widowed.*

PANTALONE, *anxiously.* What is it?

To ARLECCHINO.

What do you see?

ARLECCHINO *points to his mouth.*

COVIELLO. Cousin Arlecchino says: teeth!

PANTALONE. Teeth! Teeth! Of course he saw teeth! Did he expect to see scythes and hourglasses?

ARLECCHINO *mimes taking out his teeth one by one.*

COVIELLO. Cousin Arlecchino says when your teeth come out, then the smell will go too.

PANTALONE. Must they come out?

ARLECCHINO, *arms crossed, stamps his foot.*

COVIELLO. They must.

PANTALONE. How many must I lose?

ARLECCHINO *mimes grasping all his teeth in his fist and pitching them on the floor.*

COVIELLO. All.

PANTALONE, *elaborately tragic.* Suddenly I have become old.

The other three register surprise at this intelligence.

FLAMINIA, *running to him.* Ah, my Paolo, my Hercules, my Pan—old? Hercules old? A bacchant old? No, no, no, no, no! *Waggling one finger under* PANTALONE's *nose, with her other hand she is motioning* COVIELLO *into the house.* ARLECCHINO, *who has caught the signal, is prodding*

COVIELLO *on. When they get to the door,* ARLECCHINO *opens it with the unhurried aplomb of a rich man's porter and bows* COVIELLO *in.*

Can a few teeth change a man's passion? Can a husband's virtues be undone in the mouth? Pantalone, Pantalone, what curious discerning woman was ever put off by a mumble? For me my Apollo will shine with or without his teeth. I will find a dentist for you, Achilles!

PANTALONE. How can I thank you enough, my Iphigenia?

ARLECCHINO, *aside to* FLAMINIA. Get to the lemons, Clytemnestra.

FLAMINIA, *as* PANTALONE *has begun to walk off.* Pantalone! Come here to me!

PANTALONE. A command! Are you commanding me, Helen?

FLAMINIA. When you return today, you will bring me some lemons.

PANTALONE. I? I will bring you lemons? I, Agamemnon? I, Achilles?

FLAMINIA, *imperiously.* I, Diana, will have lemons! I have a craving for them, I dote on them, I NEED lemons, and will you be so niggardly a father that you will deny me harmless little lemons?

PANTALONE. Anchises bearing lemons home from battle! A father bringing the gift of lemons—FATHER!

He gapes at FLAMINIA *for a moment, then throws out his arms to her.*

HECUBA!

FLAMINIA. My dear——

PANTALONE, *beside himself.* You shall have lemons! An armful of lemons, a bushel! No, a chest, a chest! All the lemons in the stalls will be yours. Pantalone—father Pantalone—will drag the chest through the streets himself! Tonight, Flaminia, lemons will be at your feet!

FLAMINIA. And they will be ripe, Pantalone?

PANTALONE. Ripe! Ripe! A father will bring ripe lemons!

FLAMINIA. And in a chest? A large chest?

PANTALONE. In a chest! Ripe! Ripe! A father!

FLAMINIA. And you will lock the lemons in a chest?

PANTALONE. A father will lock them in a chest!—Ripe! Ripe!
—Tonight—lemons—a ripe father—locked in a chest!
He runs out.

SCENE 7

ARLECCHINO. You have your lemons tonight, Flaminia?

FLAMINIA. Dear Arlecchino!

ARLECCHINO. And I my meat?

FLAMINIA. A promise!

ARLECCHINO. A promise!
*She extends her hand to him regally, he takes it royally,
and they go in.*

SCENE 8

PANTALONE, *returning in haste.*

Flaminia, there is something I have forgotten to tell you!
Where are you?—Oh, what news, what news to celebrate!
—Ah, she is gone! Flaminia, dearest mother! Dearest, dearest
Flami—— Plague on her, let her go! Her news put me off
entirely. And I had meant to tell her before I left that I
would not be home at all tonight, for my business is calling
me elsewhere. Well, she will have her lemons, I'll bring the
chest. And then, to business! Oh, that business is a comfort
to a man's heart when he is plagued with the coquetry of a
young wife who has eyes for everyone but her husband. An
honest wife is what a fair husband needs. And Pantalone,
you have found her!—if that plague my coquette whom I
took for a wife doesn't find me out. I'll call her, my
Franceschina, that good woman with the honest tongue,
and if she can get rid of her husband tonight, Pantalone
will celebrate his new fatherhood with an enviable try for

another son. Ah, Zanni, what a lucky man you are to have such a woman as Franceschina to bear you sons, and such a man as Pantalone to provide them for you.

He goes to FRANCESCHINA's *house.*

Franceschina, Franceschina, your fond merchant Pantalone is here with his wares. Franceschina, come out and have a look at your purchase. Come out, good Franceschina, and together we will drive a hard bargain.

SCENE 9

FRANCESCHINA *comes out of her house. She bawls at the top of her voice with great joy at seeing him.*

FRANCESCHINA. Pantalone, my sweet lover and my impotent husband's cuckolder, how are you?

PANTALONE. Not so loud, good Franceschina——

FRANCESCHINA, *still shouting.* When can we be in bed again together? Can you be rid of your harlot wife tonight and taste the joys of an honest woman's love, or is your painted slut so malicious that she will tie you like a dog to the foot of her bed to keep you virtuous and in sight while she romps all night with lewd actors and mountebanks before your very eyes?

PANTALONE. Good Franceschina, I know how evil evil appears in your eyes.

FRANCESCHINA. Bawdry is my abomination.

PANTALONE. But a little deceit now and then is the salt of love.

FRANCESCHINA. Deceit! Let a deceiver near me and I will crush his bones. Ah, my protector Pantalone, never speak to me of deceivers!

PANTALONE. Sh! Franceschina, we had better whisper than shout, eh! Zanni may hear us.

FRANCESCHINA. Don't trouble about Zanni! Zanni is too deaf to hear even his wife, too blind to see even a lover, and too old to be even a husband. I am proud I need conceal nothing from him.

PANTALONE. Then tonight I will be with you, good woman, and there will be nothing to hinder us. Before I come, we will send a sign, a message that we are free.

FRANCESCHINA. Make it plain and honest, Pantalone. No deceitful lover's notes. I hate a deceitful message.

PANTALONE. Till tonight, virtue!

FRANCESCHINA. Till tonight, centaur!

PANTALONE *goes out, and* FRANCESCHINA *goes into her house.*

SCENE 10

ARLECCHINO *comes out of* FLAMINIA's *house in a fury.*

ARLECCHINO. Curse her innocence! Curse her virtuous beauty! And curse that decaying lecher Coviello! She gave me meat! Meat! Am I starving or am I a starving man? Ah, your promise, says Coviello. First your promise to our good friend Arlecchino. No, no, says Arlecchino, let that go now for a while. Arlecchino can wait. Wait, says Coviello, my friend wait? My own Flaminia, have you Pantalone's keys? I have. Can you get at his stores at once? I can. Have you dined, Flaminia, my purity? I have. Has the household dined? The household, says Arlecchino, have we made promises to the household? The cook, says Coviello, the footmen, the servants, the seamstress, the gardener, the porter, the messenger, the coachman, the scullery maids, the kitchen boys and the stableboys? They have, says Flaminia, dined their fill. And the monkey, says Coviello, the monkey in your blessed boudoir. Has he been nourished? Is he content? He is, says Flaminia. Content, full, yawning, and ready to sleep. Then bring a platter, says Coviello, bring a platter for our devoted friend. All, all the rest, says he, is yours. Take, partake, eat, sup, repast.

ARLECCHINO *mimes the great platter being brought before*

him by FLAMINIA. *He mimes searching the great surface of the platter, setting it on the ground, putting his nose closer and closer to its immaculate surface, and at last finding a minute particle on it which might be edible. He lifts it in his hands with great care lest it drop and disappear, and says to them, as though overwhelmed by their bounty:*

For me? A promise, says Flaminia. Good-by, says Coviello, *And* ARLECCHINO *imitates his weeping.*

never shall we forget. Never, never. Good-by, dear friend. Good-by.

And he mimes COVIELLO's *shutting the door firmly on the last good-by.*

Arlecchino, you clever, clever, clever lover! Arlecchino the rogue! Arlecchino the trickster! Everybody, look! Look at Arlecchino! Only Arlecchino is clever enough to be cuckolded without even having a wife!

Suddenly he turns on himself and begins to address himself again.

Come, Arlecchino, can you sing with the lovers? No! Then growl with the husbands. Join with the cuckolds and you will have your revenge.

Shouting at the top of his voice.

Pantalone! Thieves are in your house! Come. Come quickly! Pantalone, Pantalone, they are stealing your treasures. Come, Pantalone, save your meat! If you don't hurry, we'll be calling you by other names! Do you want other names? Other names, Pantalone!

SCENE 11

ZANNI *comes out of his house. In a small plaintive voice, he asks with innocent curiosity.*

ZANNI. Are you calling my neighbor Pantalone?

ARLECCHINO. Hello! Who is this bag of wrinkles?

To ZANNI.

Venerable old gentleman, do you know where I can find
Pantalone?

ZANNI. Venerable? Do you call me venerable? A man with his
blood raging for his posterity? Pantalone is venerable, call
him an old gentleman, not a man with a quick step and a
clear eye!

ARLECCHINO, *aside*. Oho! A sprightly cadaver! What does this
rosy babe want with his posterity? Oh, Arlecchino, a perfect customer! To business!

To ZANNI.

Young man, look at me. Do you see me?

ZANNI, *who is facing the other way*. Why should I not? Of
course I see you! Ask Pantalone the mole if he is blind, not
Zanni the eagle!

ARLECCHINO. But what do you see? Only Arlecchino! My
child, under Arlecchino's vanities and frills

In a whisper to ZANNI.

there lies concealed a practitioner!

ZANNI. A man of the science?

ARLECCHINO. Of *the* science, friend, *the* science. Only now I
was calling Pantalone on a medical matter.

ZANNI. Poor man, he is dropping into the grave, I know.

With commiseration.

Is he dying?

ARLECCHINO. No, no, it was not his death but his birth I was
to tell him about. Pantalone has just been delivered of a
son.

ZANNI. He-he! That ancient monument? Impossible!

ARLECCHINO. I have delivered a son to Pantalone that is a
solemn tribute to the father!

ZANNI. That fallow unicorn? That worn-through shoe? How
could it be?

ARLECCHINO. A son that will be his heir, his posterity, his
future!

ZANNI. Oh, that discarded calendar, that yesterday's gossip,
that dry dug! How could he beget a child?

ARLECCHINO. Through the magic of Dr. Arlecchino's science!

ZANNI. That alone?

ARLECCHINO. And the help of Pantalone's wife, of course. As a medical confidence, young man, let me tell you that Flaminia is a great aid in begetting a son.

ZANNI. That is all very well for Flaminia, but my wife is too lazy to do anything, and in fact—in strictest confidence of course to the esteemed doctor—it is not my fault at all that we have no child, but Franceschina's.

ARLECCHINO. Well, well, perhaps, but the malady senectatis has been known since Galen's time to be the worst betrayer of a man's productivity.

ZANNI. Yes, you would think so, and never would I contradict the learned doctor—and all appearances would point to it too: I, wise, matured, and—let me admit it quite frankly—a little past the first bloom—and Franceschina, young, lusty, the darling of the world, a sweet pouting apple if ever one lived. But it is she, she, not Zanni, the most willing and able of husbands, who keeps children from us. Never was there so lazy a creature as Franceschina. Would you believe it, good doctor—a confidence, you understand, since no one lives who suspects—sometimes you would think she had reason not to lust for my manhood.

ARLECCHINO, *astonished*. For *your* manhood? She does not lust for you? What reason, Zanni?

ZANNI, *shaking his head with the old perplexity*. Who can say what is in a woman's mind?

ARLECCHINO. Zanni, I have the cure! Pantalone's cure! Dr. Arlecchino will dig a son out of the very earth! Is it agreed that I can use your wife?

ZANNI, *joyfully*. Use her, use her, good doctor!

ARLECCHINO. Perfect husband! Then quickly, Zanni, bring a spade——

ZANNI. A spade——

ARLECCHINO. A rope——

ZANNI. A rope——

ARLECCHINO. And a great basket to carry the child into the house.

ZANNI, *amazed*. Will she beget it here?

ARLECCHINO. Here and nowhere else.

ZANNI, *rejoicing*. Today I will be a father too!

ARLECCHINO. Call your wife, bring the basket, and we will begin.

ZANNI, *running to his door*. Franceschina! Franceschina! Come out! This good doctor is going to give you a child!

SCENE 12

FRANCESCHINA *comes out bellowing*.

FRANCESCHINA. Why are you calling me, you decayed cheese, you sunken vessel? What stupidity is exciting you now?

ZANNI. Worthless! Worthless lazy plum of a young, tantalizing, unrewarding female! You will thank your husband yet, who is good enough to bless you with a child with the help of this good doctor who is standing before you now.

FRANCESCHINA. That!

She starts to leave.

ZANNI. Come back! Come back, unnatural woman, and listen to the doctor, do you hear!

ARLECCHINO. Listen to the doctor, good Franceschina, after your husband has gone for the basket.

FRANCESCHINA, *catching the note in his voice, stands and looks at him fixedly*.

Dr. Arlecchino, good wife, humble practitioner and master minister to a woman's needs, will explain to you what a blessing in disguise has come to you this day.

ZANNI. Listen to the doctor, follow his instructions to the letter, and though you do not deserve it, he will get you a child.

ZANNI *goes into the house for the basket*.

SCENE 13

FRANCESCHINA, *bawls out directly to* ARLECCHINO *without a moment's hesitation*. A blessing in disguise is a lover. There is no other for a woman, and if you—who are no more a doctor than my husband—are an honest lover who is lying his way into my house, say so at once, take off your disguise, give me a chance to vouch for your blessing, and I will get you into my bed before my idiot husband is out of the house. If you are, then say the one word yes. If not, I will beat you down the street, have you hung for an impostor, a charlatan, an obscene betrayer of honest wives looking for plain lovers, and a cheater of woman's hopes. What is your answer?

ARLECCHINO, *overwhelmed*. Bountiful wife——

FRANCESCHINA, *ready to strike*. What is your answer?

ARLECCHINO, *quickly*. Yes, yes, yes!

FRANCESCHINA. Then hide in the basket that you tell the old fool will hold the child. He will carry it into the house, deposit it beside my bed, and after I have abused him for a clumsy idiot and locked him out, you will come out of the basket and give me your entire blessing. And remember, none of your tricks!

ARLECCHINO. A promise!

FRANCESCHINA. A promise!

SCENE 14

ZANNI *comes out of the house with the basket*.

ZANNI. Here is everything you called for, worthy doctor. Is there anything else I need to dig for the child?

ARLECCHINO. It is not you who digs, Zanni, but your wife.

ZANNI. And what should Zanni do while she digs?

ARLECCHINO. Spin.

ZANNI. A miracle! A miracle is coming to pass! That men should be taken out of earth, out of dust! Oh, the wonders of Medicine!

ARLECCHINO. And Latin too, Zanni, Medicine and Latin together. Do you have no faith in Latin?

ZANNI. Do you take me for Pantalone? Latin too, of course. Every wise man knows that, together, Latin and Medicine can make all things come to pass. Why, they have made men out of beasts——

ARLECCHINO. And beasts out of men——

ZANNI. Wise men out of fools——

ARLECCHINO. And fools out of wise men——

ZANNI. Truth out of error——

ARLECCHINO. And error out of truth——

ZANNI. Children out of dust——

ARLECCHINO. And dust out of children.

ZANNI. Dig, dig, Franceschina!

ARLECCHINO. And the Devil bless our enterprise!

FRANCESCHINA *begins to dig in the ground.*

Repeat after me, Franceschina: *Ignei, aerii, aquatani*——

FRANCESCHINA. *Ignari, alii, aquitinale*——

ZANNI. *Aquatani!*

FRANCESCHINA. *Aquitinale*——

ARLECCHINO. *Spiritus, salvete!*

FRANCESCHINA. *Spinatyphus, salvete!*

ARLECCHINO. *Spiritus, spiritus!* The Devil would blush at your Latin! *Spiritus*, Franceschina!

FRANCESCHINA, *thundering. Spinatyphus, salvete!*

ARLECCHINO. *Inferni ardentis monarcha*——

FRANCESCHINA. *Inferi adamas, monarcha*——

ZANNI. *Inferni ardentis!* Or your child will be stone! Say *inferni ardentis*, before the fires go out!

ARLECCHINO. *Propitiamus vos*——

FRANCESCHINA. *Propitiamus vos——*

ARLECCHINO. *Ut surgat Mephistophilis.*

FRANCESCHINA. *Ut surgat ma spinatyphus.*

From the hole that FRANCESCHINA *is digging, there is suddenly heard a cry of OUCH! after a particularly sharp lunge.*

ZANNI, *jumping to the hole and digging furiously.* We are blessed!

From the hole he has dug, some small stones come flying out onto the stage floor.

Look, look, Doctor. Franceschina, the little imp is playing already!

Shouting into the hole.

Wait, wait, my son, a few more blows and you're out!

He begins to dig like a madman. ARLECCHINO *grabs the rope from the basket and cries out to him.*

ARLECCHINO. The rope, the rope!

ZANNI *grabs the rope and shouts into the hole.*

ZANNI. Grab the rope, take hold of the rope, you little darling!

There is a growl from below like the roar of thunder.

Don't cry, little darling! Daddy is holding on!

Suddenly ZANNI *yells with fright and lunges into the hole head first, still hanging onto the rope.* FRANCESCHINA *and* ARLECCHINO *grab and pull,* ARLECCHINO *on* ZANNI'S *legs,* FRANCESCHINA *on* ARLECCHINO'S. *The tug of war goes back and forth, with* ZANNI *sometimes disappearing down to the ankles, sometimes emerging so that his face is visible for an instant before he goes down again. Finally, with a terrific yank on* FRANCESCHINA'S *part, they get* ZANNI *out of the hole, and the three of them lie sprawled on the stage floor. In the hole, his chin just clearing the ground, a blood-red* DEVIL *is looking out at them angrily. He folds his arms under his chin and rests them on the edge of the hole.*

DEVIL, *in a deep baritone.* Which of you had the strength to pull the Devil out of Hell?

ZANNI, *beside himself with joy, shouts.* A boy! It's a boy!

DEVIL. That old toad couldn't do it. And that wisp of straw

over there couldn't lift his eyes. Then it must have been the woman!

The DEVIL *gets very excited about this.*

What news this will be for Hell! What an event!

FRANCESCHINA. What news?

DEVIL. That a woman should stop the Devil in his work!

ZANNI. Child, give me your hand so that I can pull you out. Franceschina, bring the boy some swaddling clothes. Do you want him to freeze?

DEVIL. Pull me out? Come here and try, you old corpse.

ZANNI. What spirit! What a voice! Give me your hand, little angel!

ZANNI grasps the DEVIL's *hand, and with his back to the hole, tugs it along the ground. The* DEVIL *remains calmly in the hole, watching as his hand detaches itself, and* ZANNI *puffs and pants with the weight of his burden. As he drags the arm.*

Oh, what a child! The little darling weighs more than his father! Are you all right, angel?

DEVIL. My toe is caught.

ZANNI. Don't worry, sweetheart. I'll have you out. Hang on!

The DEVIL *groans as though with the effort of being dragged.*

A little more, angel, just hold on a little longer.

DEVIL. There we are.

ZANNI. Ah, there we are. All out, sweetheart? All safe and sound?

He turns around, sees the detached arm in his grasp. With a shriek, he drops it.

Where's the rest of the child?

DEVIL. Here I am.

ZANNI. There you are, so you are. But I've pulled off his dear arm! How will he manage with one arm?

DEVIL. Oh, I'll manage.

ZANNI. My little angel has only one arm!

DEVIL, *bellowing.* I'll manage! Stop your wawling!

And he throws another arm at ZANNI *to make him stop.*

ZANNI, *almost knocked over by the arm, shrieks.* He's without arms! My angel has no arms!

DEVIL. Lots of arms, lots of arms——

And he throws arms out at ZANNI.

And legs, lots of legs——

And he throws three or four legs at ZANNI *for good measure.*

ZANNI, *at a loss as to how to manage this.* Franceschina, don't stand there gaping. Help me deliver our son before he throws away *all* his precious parts!

FRANCESCHINA. You're mad, you old fossil! Lunatic! Lunatic old Zanni!

ZANNI, *running to the* DEVIL, *grabs him about the head.* Monster mother! Look at your monster mother, darling, who won't even help your father bear his child! Both together now, darling! Heave ho!

DEVIL. Heave ho!

And the DEVIL's *neck distends a couple of inches.*

ZANNI, *preparing for the second tug.* Heave ho!

DEVIL. Heave ho!

And the DEVIL's *neck emerges a foot out of the hole.*

ZANNI. Once more and you're ours, child! Heave ho!

DEVIL. Heave ho!

And this time the DEVIL's *head emerges five feet out of the hole and emits smoke through his mouth and ears.* ZANNI, *taking in the sight, faints dead away. The* DEVIL's *head, in a flash, shoots down into the hole and disappears.*

FRANCESCHINA, *inspects* ZANNI, *and then, with a kick at his prostrate form.* Ach! Wake up the old fool and tell him the child is safe in the basket.

ARLECCHINO. And you remember your promise, madonna?

FRANCESCHINA. Agreed.

ARLECCHINO, *shaking* ZANNI *awake.* Zanni, Zanni, you can wake up now! The child has risen! Wake up, Zanni, wake up and sing the praises of the doctor!

ZANNI *wakes, crawls on all fours to the hole, and looks in.*

Quem quaeritis in caverno, O pater Zanni?

ZANNI. *Bambinum Franceschinum, O magicola.*

ARLECCHINO. *Non est hic; surrexit, sicut praedixero.*

ZANNI. Hallelujah! My child has risen!

He looks toward FRANCESCHINA *with gentle piety and asks:*

Franceschina, what is that sweet thing on thy knee?

FRANCESCHINA *makes ready to smite him, but* ARLECCHINO *interrupts.*

ARLECCHINO. Not there, Zanni! Our child is safe in the basket.

ZANNI. *Arlecchinum laudamus!* Let me see him! Let me see!

ARLECCHINO. No, no, the little darling is fast asleep.

ZANNI. Tell me, Doctor——

ARLECCHINO. Does something trouble you, father?

ZANNI. Did he seem a bit red in the face?

ARLECCHINO. No, he had, I thought, a kind of pallor.

ZANNI. And tall? Advise me, Doctor, can a child be born taller than his father?

ARLECCHINO. Would you give birth to a snail? The child born to Pantalone was a head taller than the old man.

ZANNI. A head taller! Then my child is a mite—a sickly little flea—and Pantalone will always laugh at me!

ARLECCHINO. Take my word for it, consecrated father, your child, with the help of Lucifer, is bigger than Pantalone's.

ZANNI. Ah, so—bigger than Pantalone's—he-he-he!—Franceschina, you good-for-nothing wife, I bore a child bigger than Pantalone's.

And, he-heing to himself, bursting with vanity, he announces to the world as he goes into the house:

Bigger than Pantalone's!

SCENE 15

ARLECCHINO. Ha! My darling Franceschina, did I play the doctor well?

FRANCESCHINA. If you can stop your lies and deceits for a moment, climb into the basket and that dolt, that imbecile will carry you into the house if Franceschina has to break his back to do it.

ARLECCHINO, *getting into the basket, happily.* And the promise, gentle wife, the promise. You will give as you promised to your honest lover?

FRANCESCHINA. Villain! Thief! Player with words! Didn't Franceschina say once she had something for her honest lover? Is there anyone still living who doubts Franceschina's word?

ARLECCHINO. Madonna! Does Arlecchino have the valor to doubt?

ARLECCHINO *closes the lid over his head.* ZANNI *comes scampering out with bags of money and jewels in his arms.*

SCENE 16

ZANNI. Where is the blessed doctor? A boon, a boon for the good man! Where has he gone, Franceschina?

FRANCESCHINA. The doctor played his last joke on the fiend of hell in delivering your child. A great devil came by and stuffed him into a basket, and another devil was pressed into shouldering the burden and carrying him to his last torment.

ZANNI. The good doctor spirited away? Ah, but he will fool them. Take my word for it, good-for-nothing, that devil will be sorry he carried that basket an inch from where it rested.

He turns to the basket to lift it.

Come, my little curer of old age. Into the house with you. Franceschina, for your own good if not for mine, help me lift our blessed little intruder.

FRANCESCHINA. Be careful of your bones, dray horse, be careful you don't crumble into powder as you lift him, and make him bump his precious bottom.

ZANNI, *lifting the basket on his back and walking to the door of his house.* He-he-he! Old Zanni delivered him once; he can deliver him again. Heave ho!

ARLECCHINO, *inside the basket, imitating the* DEVIL. Heave ho!

ZANNI. He-he-he! Oh, the weight, the precious weight of him!

FRANCESCHINA *follows him and holds up the back of the basket.* ARLECCHINO *opens the lid, throws his arms wide, and embraces* FRANCESCHINA *with abandoned sweeps of his arms while the two are bearing him into the house.*

Feel the weight of him, Franceschina!

FRANCESCHINA. I will, you dolt, I will!

ZANNI. And, good-for-nothing, he wants a mother's love. Fondle him, Franceschina, promise you will fondle him.

FRANCESCHINA. Go on, you fool, I have promised.

ZANNI. And he'll want strength. Suckle him, suckle him tenderly, Franceschina.

FRANCESCHINA. Long and tenderly, old ruin, long and tenderly.

ZANNI. And that envious old merchant will never laugh at me again, do you hear. Oh no, my precious burden is bigger than Pantalone's.

ARLECCHINO, *making the sign of horns over him and speaking in the* DEVIL's *voice.* Much bigger, much bigger.

ZANNI. He-he-he! Oh, what spirit. What a child.

They go into ZANNI's *house.*

SCENE 17

COVIELLO *comes out of* FLAMINIA's *house.*

COVIELLO. Zanni carrying a heavy basket! Is it possible? Never did I think he could still lift a crutch! Ah, Coviello! Zanni will be your friend. Why should not Zanni carry the chest into Pantalone's house? Surely the old fool will want to help me make a fool of the old fool Pantalone.

SCENE 18

ZANNI *comes merrily out of his house.*

ZANNI. Coviello, I am a happy man!

COVIELLO. My good friend Zanni, what has come over you?

ZANNI. My wife has just driven me from the house, thrown a box, a mirror and a shoe at me, and forbid me ever to return to her sight until I have cast off forty of my years, and I am the happiest man in the world.

COVIELLO. What husband would not be happy, Zanni, with such a loving forbid. Ah, where is such another wife who forbids as Zanni's wife forbids? Lucky Zanni, my good friend. Oh, that I could share your good fortune. I weep for your joy, Zanni, joy to you and to all husbands.

ZANNI, *affected, begins to weep too.* Joy to us all, eh, Coviello, joy to all husbands!

Both weeping, they embrace and give comfort to each other.

COVIELLO. Joy to all husbands in single blessedness.

ZANNI, *detaching himself.* No, no, no. It's not that. There is a secret joy which I cannot tell. It is a secret from Pantalone.

COVIELLO. Zanni, we are friends indeed. I have a secret from Pantalone I am bursting to share with you.

ZANNI, *incredulous.* You have?

COVIELLO. Yes, and you must help me. You must carry a chest for me as I just saw you carry one into your own house.

ZANNI. Is there a chest to be carried into your house too? Has that accursed doctor spawned a whole generation of children from hell?

COVIELLO. No, no, Zanni, not my house. Into Pantalone's house.

ZANNI. Then Pantalone could not carry his own burden into his house? And my burden was bigger than Pantalone's! Tell me, Coviello, is it true that Pantalone could not lift his own child?

COVIELLO, *aside*. Curse him, he's gone mad!

To ZANNI.

No, no, Zanni, not a child, a chest of lemons, lemons! Listen, Zanni, tonight Pantalone will bring a chest of lemons to his door which his wife entreated of him.

ZANNI. A chest of lemons! What would his wife want with a chest of lemons?

COVIELLO. That's it, Zanni, that's it! Flaminia has led the old mange to believe that he is going to have a son. And Pantalone is mad to satisfy her every craving. Her first demand was for lemons, which Pantalone, to give her her full measure of delight, is sending in a chest.

ZANNI, *dully*. But what delight will there be for Flaminia in the lemons?

COVIELLO. No, no, you old—dear friend, there will be no lemons in the chest.

ZANNI. But you just said——

COVIELLO, *shouting at him in a frenzy of impatience*. Coviello, Coviello will be in the chest! It is I Pantalone will furnish for his wife's delight!

ZANNI, *as comprehension finally seizes him*. In a chest! He-he-he!

Pointing at COVIELLO *and shouting at him through his paroxysms of joy*.

Lemons!—Lemons!—Coviello in Pantalone's chest!—He-he-he!

COVIELLO. And I have come to ask you if you will carry the chest into Pantalone's house.

ZANNI. For his wife's delight! He-he! Yes, yes—Zanni will carry the chest.

COVIELLO. And it pleases you, Zanni? My good friend!

He is on the verge of tears again.

ZANNI. Zanni has carried a chest before. And he will carry it again. He-he-he! For his wife's delight!

They go off together.

SCENE 19

LEANDRO *comes in. He puts one hand to his mouth and calls in a low voice to* CINTIA's *door.*

LEANDRO. Coo-ee-ee! Coo-ee-ee! Cintia! It is Leandro! Surely she hasn't forgotten my love. I must remind her.

Again to CINTIA's *house.*

Cintia! It is Leandro of the meadow calling. Cintia! Leandro, behind the bridge, when the tide came in and woke us? Leandro, Cintia! Leandro who jumped from your window with nothing concealed but his modesty! Leandro, who offered you his heart—which you almost took from him with a kitchen knife! Leandro, Leandro, Venus and Mars, with whom and for how long will you be in there consoling yourself for my loss?

ARLECCHINO, *storming out of* FRANCESCHINA's *house.* Oh, what form of a pest is this? Wait until he's gone, Leandro!

SCENE 20

ARLECCHINO. Something for a lover! Yes, which lover? Mercury Arlecchino, the messenger, the lackey! Arlecchino the puppy who runs with billet-doux between his teeth from lover to lover. From lover to lover! Here, says she, is something for my lover. Out of the basket, you lying doctor, you fraud, out of the basket and run with this to Pantalone. Why are you standing in the basket? What are you waiting for? A-A-H-H, she screams, did you come to tamper with my virtue? Out, out, you cheat, you filthy, lewd, designing man! You charlatan, you fraudulent alchemist, you devil's mate! Sorcerer, cheater, lecher, liar, out of the house of an honest woman! Run with this note to Pantalone, and never let me hear that you broke a promise again! Straight to Pantalone, do you hear, deliverer! Franceschina does not forget your promises!

Again he opens wide the imaginary pocket in his clothing.

Pocket, here! A letter for you!

Suddenly astonished by what he sees in the pocket.

Pocket, is there room? Look at you, stuffed, bulging with promises! Was there ever a man who carried such a bundle of promises!

Pretends to lift them out one at a time as he studies them.

Why, look at this dinner from Flaminia, days and days of dainties, all she has in her power to spread before me. Poor promise!

He puts it back tenderly and takes another.

And here is one for robes and furred gowns, pearls and lapis lazuli, all the wealth of the rich merchant Pantalone, signed my "dearest friend Coviello." Ah, here is a lusty, bawdy, plain-spoken promise, to be had just for jumping into a basket, paid on delivery!

Looks at the promise with impatience and pitches it back.

What a bruised little promise you are! What's this one at the bottom?

As he looks at it, he begins to jump and tremble with delight.

Oh, look at this sweet little promise!

Slapping his head.

Arlecchino, you simple seeker for salvation, here is a darling little whisper of a promise that says, "Come back and we'll be quits with the old fool for what he has made us bear." Cintia, queen of the kitchen! Arlecchino will be a respectable, well-fed lover of an old man's wife yet! Cintia will be my salvation!

He runs with anticipatory delight to CINTIA's *door, and knocks loudly on it.*

Oh, Cintia! Open the door for my salvation! Come out, Cintia, your little conspirator is here! Vengeance, Cintia, sweet vengeance is calling you! Come out, you great enchanter of the stomach! Arlecchino is here, sly Arlecchino, to help you be quits with that husband!

SCENE 21

CINTIA, *through the door, her voice brays at* ARLECCHINO. Who is bawling like a vulgar fishwife for Cintia? Doesn't he know that I must have silence in my kitchen?

ARLECCHINO. We are plighted to conspiracy, dearest mustard-seed. Come out and see who it is.

A pot flies across the stage, missing ARLECCHINO.

CINTIA. Silence!

ARLECCHINO. Vinegar has puckered her temper. Try again, Arlecchino.

He moves to one side of the door.

But we had better get out of harm's way. Remember, pod? "Come back and together we'll be quits with the old fool?" Put down your ladle and open the door.

CINTIA, *coming out and recognizing* ARLECCHINO. *With no great joy, she says:* Ah, it's you. You've come back.

ARLECCHINO. And that's all? No more?

CINTIA. Welcome.

ARLECCHINO. We have a great plot, Cintia. Do you remember our plot?

CINTIA, *as* LEANDRO *appears and throws her a kiss, she cries with ardor.* Ah, you've come back. Welcome, my heaven, my joy, a thousand welcomes!

LEANDRO, *behind* ARLECCHINO, *puts his fingers to his lips.*

ARLECCHINO. My ecstasy! Now you remember!

CINTIA, *as* ARLECCHINO *attempts to embrace her.* Don't touch me, poltroon!

ARLECCHINO. Now what in the Devil's name has gotten into this stockpot? Have you forgotten our plan? Have you forgotten what we have suffered together? Cintia, have you forgotten your promise?

LEANDRO, *in unison with* ARLECCHINO, *is urging all his words on* CINTIA *in silence.*

CINTIA, *responding to* LEANDRO. Never! How can you accuse me? Have I ever loved as I have loved you? Have I known such tenderness with my winter, my husband? What do I spice when I spice my mutton but the dear remembrance of your saucy advances? What do I wring when I strangle chickens but my husband's neck? The wine of your laughter, the milk of your ardor, the oil of your tongue, are mixed with my memories and stir my blood, and the reek, the stench, the filth of my husband's glance, his word, his motion, his—ugh—I throw every day into the canal. Everything I beat, scatter, mash, poison and throw away is my husband's; and everything I store, treasure, fondle and keep in my heart is——

ARLECCHINO. Arlecchino! Blessed and happy man! You are beatified, sanctified, transmuted! No more tears, my poor Cintia, you have persuaded me! No more entreaty, I am won!

CINTIA. Are you in truth? Can I trust my heart?

ARLECCHINO. Forever and ever, my love!

CINTIA. And if I wait, if I tell you now when to come to me, you will come?

ARLECCHINO. Though twenty men were at your door when I came, my faithful Cintia, I and I alone will be at your side.

CINTIA. And if some stupid clown of a pretending lover bars your way, you will not be put off, you will not let him deceive you, my own?

ARLECCHINO. No stupid clown will bar love's way, my true and loving Cintia! Love, not clowning, passion, not tricks, will win you.

CINTIA. And if I ask some small, some little indignity of you that you may come and go as you please, so that we will not be detected or interrupted, so that you may come to my door at any time and even be admitted by my husband, so that never again need you ask assurance or wonder how to gain admittance, so that never again need a stupid conspiracy stand between us and the ecstasy of our pleasure, will you suffer this tiny indignity for our love?

ARLECCHINO. My heart is too full, dear Cintia, to mouth more promises. All, all, I promise to give to you eternally. What indignity would I not suffer for you now? You have given me the gift of perfect love.

CINTIA. Then tonight and forever after, as you please and without let or hindrance, disguise yourself as a dull clod of a girl and come to visit me with some little parcel, some small gift, and even my husband will know you well and trust you as my sweet, beguiling country cousin!

ARLECCHINO. Ah, love, not even Arlecchino could dream up a ruse at once so simple, so sure, and so eternally rewarding.

CINTIA. Then go now, my promised lover! No kiss, no touch, no word between us—until tonight!

LEANDRO *throws a kiss to her, he departs and* CINTIA *goes into her house.*

SCENE 22

ARLECCHINO. It was a dream, and never will I believe that such words were spoken to ragamuffin Arlecchino. But what a dream! After tonight, my heart, my soul, my stomach, and my pride will all be filled. Pocket, here! Take this tenderly. Hug Cintia's promise close to your sides. Don't tear, pocket. It's a very great and heavy promise, but hold it just until tonight. Because after tonight, pocket, after tonight— our cup runneth over!

He runs out with a bound.

ACT II

SCENE 1

ARLECCHINO *enters dressed as a woman.*

ARLECCHINO, *very feminine.* Oh, la, what a dish! Arlecchino, you're just a darling irresistible! And if you aren't the country cousin to end all country cousins.

He hoists his bodice so that he protrudes indecently and walks liquidly about the stage.

Kind gentleman, a kind word for a kind lady? La, la, la, that's a harsh word. You'd better just give me a kind look. Oh, la, that's a scowl. Settle a smile on your face, dear man, and give me a taste of a little kiss?

ARLECCHINO *puckers his mouth and closes his eyes in anticipation, then lurches back with a wee cry.*

Oh! A man can be such a beast! Now you see, Arlecchino, the secret of woman's virtue. Give her scorn for her love, and she is outraged to the point of virtue. Walk the paths of a furious virtue, Signora Arlecchino.

ARLECCHINO *yanks the bodice flat, and takes on the look of a too-old duenna.*

Don't touch me, you deliciously indecent man. If you come near me, you devilish temptation, you tasty morsel of sin, I'll scream, you impetuous fool, you non-stop daredevil, I'll call my lame husband, you hotheaded libertine, and he'll tell you to go away. Don't turn your back when I talk to you, don't run off when I'm repulsing you, you outrageous potency, you sinister sweetheart!

SIGNORA ARLECCHINO *looks older and wiser.*

There you see, Arlecchino, what a vice virtue is. How can a virtuous woman tempt without temptations? How does she do it, Arlecchino? Study the ways of woman.

He studies them.

Oh! Arlecchino, you're blushing. Don't blush, Arlecchino. What happier thing can a forced virtue become than a practiced bawd? Listen to me, Signora Arlecchino, when you so rust that lovers run from your modest indignation, the time has come to fetch lovers for the lovers. A happy bawd! Fetch and carry lusty maids and lusty men, trip to your grave with love's gold in one hand, love's letters in the other, love's memories in your head and love's trinkets in your pockets, and lie down at last in a paralyzed decorum!

He is seized by the pleasure of his role.

Oh, what a thing it is to be incognito! Everybody, look! Look at the incognito! Who is inside this little darling? Whose memories lie behind these pretty eyes? Whose bosom is swelling behind this swelled bosom? Whose wisdom is behind this folly? Magical Arlecchino, how thoroughly you are tucked away! Nothing can find you out but Cintia and your own salvation. There it is, Arlecchino. Knock, and it will open. Lift your skirts and walk right in! And nothing that has eyes to see can have the wit to stop you. No husbands, no lovers, no old men, no young men——

SCENE 2

FLAMINIA *comes out of her house, and, seeing* ARLECCHINO's *back, says at once.*

FLAMINIA. Arlecchino, have you forgotten about me?

ARLECCHINO. Woman! I have forgotten about you!

FLAMINIA. Cruel Arlecchino, why are you dressed like that? Is this what comes of your promise? Is this how you remember about my husband's teeth?

ARLECCHINO. Your husband's teeth! Little promiser, since I left you, I have been gnashing my own. Arlecchino had neither wine nor meat nor dessert nor what he intended from you, and he has tossed your business from his pocket and is in a hurry pursuing a business of his own.

FLAMINIA. How wrongfully you abuse me, Arlecchino. Could

you not see in my impatience how I longed to be rid of
that old crow Coviello and give you that banquet I promised you so fully? Only this favor, only play this one trick
on my husband, and see how Flaminia can answer for a
promise.

ARLECCHINO. Wise lady, do you think that Arlecchino lives by
foolish impulse? Who knows better than Arlecchino the folly
of learning the same lesson twice? I will tell you a secret,
Flaminia. Once when Arlecchino was rich enough to own a
very long sheet of paper, he catalogued on one side all the
virtues of wisdom, all the lessons of caution, all the maxims
of restraint, and—would you believe it?—they added up to
the blessed truth. On the other side, he catalogued all the
follies of the world, all sweet promises, all tantalizing hopes,
all yearnings and lovely cravings, all the hungers of the
body, the soul and the mind, and—do you know?—they
added up to heartbreak, anguish, disenchantment and despair. Little promiser, how was a man to choose?

FLAMINIA. Very well, you chose wisdom and so will have
nothing to do with me. Then good-by.

ARLECCHINO. No, no, I left wisdom to the wise men, and
hugged all the sweet follies to my heart. Wonderful
Flaminia, only make your promises tantalizing enough, and
you can ask anything of me. Promise me bliss, and tell me
what you want me to do.

FLAMINIA. Arlecchino! You dear, clever madman! Hurry into
my house and be ready for Pantalone. I have sent for my
husband and told him I have found a dentist for him to
cure his breath. Hurry into the house, disguise yourself as a
dentist, and return. Disappear, Arlecchino, he is coming!

ARLECCHINO. I fly!

FLAMINIA. And remember, not a word of this to Coviello, that
awful, jealous man.

ARLECCHINO. Not a word!

He runs into FLAMINIA's *house.*

SCENE 3

PANTALONE *comes in dragging the chest of lemons.* COVIELLO *and* ZANNI *are superintending his labor and urging him on*

COVIELLO. This way, Pantalone, shove it this way and pull a little harder! Don't fall, oh, the poor man is falling! His strength——

ZANNI. His strength, keep up his strength, Coviello! He-he-he! Don't fall, Pantalone! Oh, if he falls, the poor man will never get up!

PANTALONE, *aside.* I'll get up, curse you, as you'll never again get up.

COVIELLO. Don't tip the basket, Pantalone!

He screams.

Ah, he's crushing his foot!

ZANNI, *in terror.* His poor old foot! He'll never walk again!

PANTALONE, *aside.* Right through your door, you old eunuch, and walk into your bedroom, and into your bed.

ZANNI. Save his foot!

PANTALONE, *aside.* And keep on walking!

COVIELLO. Thank heaven he didn't stuff it too full of lemons so that he could still drag it along. You didn't stuff it too full of lemons, did you, Pantalone?

PANTALONE, *as he finally brings the chest to rest.* No, no, there's room enough for a body in it!

ZANNI. Room enough for a body! He-he-he!

COVIELLO. Thank heaven, for your sake, Pantalone. What a burden for a man to drag!

Testing it.

And it's a firm chest, Pantalone? It won't come apart?

PANTALONE. No, no, it could hold a man's weight and not come apart.

ZANNI, *delighted.* A man's weight, oh, a man's weight! He-he-he!

COVIELLO. I'm pleased for your sake, Pantalone. A firm chest and it will not come apart. Aren't you pleased, Zanni, for Pantalone's sake?

ZANNI, *quite obviously.* Delighted, delighted for Pantalone!

COVIELLO, *with ceremony.* Flaminia, my kind neighbor, here is the chest of lemons Pantalone carried for you with the help of his good friend Zanni and myself.

FLAMINIA. A thousand thanks, dear neighbor, and depend upon it, Pantalone will find a way to reward you.

COVIELLO. Generous neighbor! Coviello wants no other reward than the joy of seeing Pantalone foster the delight and comfort of his wife, a good woman, happy to bear her husband many sons, yea, many sons.

PANTALONE. Where is this dentist, Flaminia? Pantalone is ready, girded for his sacrifice.

ZANNI. Girded and trussed! Stuffed, tied, and feathered!

FLAMINIA. Then you are ready, dear husband, for whatever befalls?

ZANNI. Ready? He's ripe and spoiling! Did you ever see a man so ripe for what befalls?

COVIELLO. So be it, honest Flaminia! Let him come.

FLAMINIA, *going to her door and opening it.* Come out, good dentist! My husband is asking for whatever befalls!

SCENE 4

ARLECCHINO *comes out with the air of a high priest emerging from the tabernacle. He wears an immense cloak, a huge hat, and carries a great satchel with instruments.*

ARLECCHINO. *In nomine patris.* Where is the hapless man?

FLAMINIA. Worthy practitioner! Did you find all your comforts while waiting in my house?

ARLECCHINO. *Sanctum sanctorum.* Lead me to my object.

FLAMINIA. Praise heaven and your craft, good man. Here is the willing patient.

ARLECCHINO, *surveying him, raising his hand in blessing. Simplex simplicimus!* Shall we begin?

PANTALONE. Begin.

ARLECCHINO, *drops his satchel to the ground. It falls as though it were laden with bricks.* Bring him a chair!

COVIELLO, *running into* FLAMINIA's *house for it.* A chair, a chair for Pantalone!

ARLECCHINO. A rope!

ZANNI. A rope? He-he, I have just the rope for Pantalone. *And he runs into his house to get it.* COVIELLO *deposits the chair in the middle of the stage.*

PANTALONE. A rope? Why do you need a rope?

ARLECCHINO. Be seated, Pantalone.

PANTALONE, *not sitting.* Somebody tell me why he needs a rope.

FLAMINIA. Put your faith in the dentist, Pantalone.

ARLECCHINO *kneels down, pulls open the top of the satchel, and begins the elaborate business of extracting the implements. First, an object resembling a two-foot-long corkscrew. Then, a something that looks like a sledge hammer. He removes an instrument that looks like monstrous calipers. And last, a set of immense pliers, which he holds aloft.*

PANTALONE, *getting ready to run off.* Pantalone, this is your Day of Judgment!

FLAMINIA, *as she,* COVIELLO *and* ZANNI *run to stop him.* Running away? Husband, where is your great courage?

COVIELLO. Stop, Pantalone. What is there to be afraid of?

ZANNI. Is there anyone afraid? Who is afraid? He-he! Not Pantalone!

COVIELLO, *leading* PANTALONE *to the chair, with the help of the others.* No, not Pantalone. Not with his wife beside him. Not with his friends here to give him courage.

PANTALONE, *as he is gently but forcibly seated in the chair.* Tell me why he needs a rope.

ARLECCHINO. Tie him!

PANTALONE *moves to spring out of his chair.*

FLAMINIA, *holding him.* Don't move, Pantalone. For your own sake, dear man, hold your seat!

ZANNI, *dancing and skipping completely around the chair as he winds the rope round and round* PANTALONE *until the patient is completely immobilized.* For your own sake, for your very own sake, dear sweet Pantalone. For your sake, for you, he-he, for nobody else but you!

ARLECCHINO. *In manus tuas!*

Humming, he moves toward PANTALONE'S *mouth, while the others stand absolutely silent and breathless with interest. He moves the pliers toward* PANTALONE'S *mouth, almost sticks his nose into it, then, hurling himself back across the stage away from* PANTALONE'S *offending breath, he shouts at him, waving the pliers to emphasize his wrath.*

Rubrificationibus! Excrementabilis! Fungi! Fungi!

He lunges back into his satchel and produces two long handles which he attaches to the pliers, and, thus keeping his distance, examines the open maw of PANTALONE *from about six feet away. He m'hms and ahas for a while, and pokes about in* PANTALONE'S *mouth with the functional end of the pliers. Suddenly he barks:*

All!

and waves the pliers with a broad gesture, almost knocking PANTALONE'S *teeth out of his mouth at a stroke.* PANTALONE *groans.*

PANTALONE. Learned sir, hunt about for a while and see if there are any you can save.

ARLECCHINO. We shall see. OPEN!

PANTALONE *throws his mouth open, and* ARLECCHINO *again puts the pliers into it.*

Gently, gently——

And when he presumes he has them where he wants them, with a shout he leaps at PANTALONE, *and, standing on the patient's lap, he works them up and down like a man possessed.* PANTALONE *shrieks and groans in agony, tilts his chair backward, and the spectators of his torment, in various*

*conditions of helpfulness and excitement, support the chair,
lend a hand to* ARLECCHINO *in working the pliers and shout
instructions to* PANTALONE *as follows:*

FLAMINIA. Hold on a little longer, Pantalone!

ZANNI. You're doing well, Pantalone, very well!

COVIELLO. Let it happen, Pantalone! Don't fight it!

At last ARLECCHINO *dismounts with a great white object,
dripping blood from its ragged end, trapped in the teeth
of the pliers.*

PANTALONE, *hanging limp with exhaustion, lifts his head like
a dying man.* Flaminia! Where is he? Has he flown away?

ARLECCHINO, *holding up the pliers like a sword, announces:*
ONE! !

PANTALONE, *galvanized into life by this announcement, yells:*
No more, no more!

ZANNI. No more?

FLAMINIA. Husband! The good dentist has only just begun!

ARLECCHINO. Open! Open again!

PANTALONE. Not for the Devil himself! Devil! Not for salvation!

ARLECCHINO. *Deus avertat!* Open his mouth!

He bangs the sledge hammer on the ground.

PANTALONE. Never! Never will that fiend see the inside of my
mouth again!

FLAMINIA. See it! He will smell it! In the North of England
they will smell it! Do you want me to die of the stink of
your breath?

PANTALONE, *in a spasm of fury, throws the chair at* ARLEC-
CHINO, *who runs out amid screaming.* If I kill the world with
this breath, let that hellhound be the first to go! Let it stink!
Let it breathe fire! But it will stay as it is! Stay as it is!

He has been tossing ARLECCHINO's *instruments and satchel
after the fleeing* ARLECCHINO, *who runs out to the left, and
after* ZANNI *and* COVIELLO, *who run out to the right.*
FLAMINIA *takes refuge in her house.*

As they run:

ZANNI. He's mad! Mad!

COVIELLO. Pantalone's gone mad!

FLAMINIA. Help! My husband is possessed!
And they are gone.

SCENE 5

PANTALONE. POSSESSED!! Of what am I possessed? Of a devil wife who brings devils to tear teeth out of my jaws! Of a breath that fells men, would shrink flowers, and make even the canal hold its nose! Oh, my life, what a toothache you've become! Where is that consolation? Find her out, Pantalone, find her and have her! Time or no time, tooth or no tooth, hug your consolation to you now! Franceschina! Franceschina! A beggar is at your door! Your fond Pantalone has come begging!

SCENE 6

FRANCESCHINA *has come out of her house.*

FRANCESCHINA. Sweet Pantalone! What thievish lout has been knocking the teeth out of your mouth?

PANTALONE. No, my own wife charged me to submit to a dentist, a devilish executioner, who has cost me the remains of my beauty.

FRANCESCHINA. Beauty lies deeper in a man than his teeth. What curious discerning woman was ever put off from a man by the loss of a few teeth?

PANTALONE. Iphigenia! Oh, I pray God your understanding doesn't lead to such another remedy.

FRANCESCHINA. Franceschina has a simple remedy for a man's sorrows. Come with Franceschina, and the whole loss will be made up to you!

PANTALONE, *holding back*. First tell me, good woman—what is my breath?

FRANCESCHINA. What is it? It is breath!

PANTALONE. It doesn't offend you?

FRANCESCHINA. No more than my own!

PANTALONE. Oh, my consolation!

FRANCESCHINA. How, Pantalone?

PANTALONE. We are the same odor!

They go into FRANCESCHINA's *house.*

SCENE 7

LEANDRO *comes in disguised as a woman. His disguise is identical with* ARLECCHINO's.

LEANDRO. A clear night, a clear road, a clear disguise—a clear pleasure! Oh, what a man will do to keep a husband smiling! Waste no time on monologues, Leandro. Get into Cintia's house before that other country maiden comes to call.

He knocks at her door.

Cintia! Oh Lord, will she put me to the test of ardor before I get into the house?

CINTIA, *from inside the house.* Who is there? Can it be my little country cousin?

LEANDRO. She will! Well, Leandro, it's a battle of metaphors tonight, right up to the door of the bedroom.

CINTIA, *coming out.* Ah, Leandro! So humbled as to mock his manhood! Cruel Cintia, to humble her lover with a foolish disguise! Oh my darling, be sure, be sure that from this debasement, Cintia will have you rise. She will see to it!

LEANDRO. My tender minister, how could I doubt? Don't I remember how, out of baseness, you have made me rise before?

CINTIA. Memories, Leandro, precious memories. How many memories we have hoarded up, Leandro!

LEANDRO. Of meetings and partings, of fallings and risings——

CINTIA. In the brightness of the moon, remember?

LEANDRO. In the downpour at noon, can I forget?

CINTIA. At Matins, at Lauds, at each of the canonical hours!

LEANDRO. Oh, my breviary, my canon, my office! Oh, my divine service!

CINTIA. My sanctity!

LEANDRO. My holiness, come—let us pray!

He rushes her into the house.

SCENE 8

COVIELLO *and* ZANNI *come in cautiously.*

COVIELLO. Is he gone?

ZANNI. He is gone. Oh, Pantalone! Now you're a mad dog as well as a fool!

COVIELLO. Do you have the keys to the chest?

ZANNI. Yes, from Pantalone's pocket.

COVIELLO, *stops and puzzles over this.* When did you get them?

ZANNI. When the fool was tied in the chair, and howling about losing a tooth.

COVIELLO. But you were not near his pocket!

ZANNI, *opening the chest.* I have them just the same.

COVIELLO. But, Zanni, if you weren't near his pocket, the action isn't probable. It isn't even possible!

ZANNI, *irate.* Is this Aristotle or *commedia*? Get into the chest.

COVIELLO. Curses on these lemons. Can you carry me and all the lemons too?

ZANNI. Yes, yes, get in. Zanni can bear the burden for Pantalone. Have no fear, Coviello. Get in.

COVIELLO *gets into the chest.* ZANNI *locks the chest and sits on it.*

Oh, let me sit down and enjoy this moment! Oh, Pantalone, you no-father! Here is your offspring in this chest, and here is your deliverer sitting on it. In a moment, in less than a moment, Zanni will undo you, you no-husband!

COVIELLO, *from inside the chest*. What are you waiting for, Zanni? Pick up the chest and carry me into the house.

ZANNI. He-he-he! If you could see me now, Pantalone! Wherever you are, what a pity you can't see me now, you fool, you trusting folly, you no-father and no-husband!

COVIELLO. Hurry and get me inside and go back to your own house before you are missed there. Don't you want to hurry home?

ZANNI. Yes, yes, there is entertainment for me at home too, but this moment is so blessed, I can't bear to give it up for what is waiting for me in my own house. He-he-he! Oh, Pantalone, you old, blind, deaf, mad, trusting fool! Older than the wisest man, and he knows nothing!

COVIELLO. Zanni, what's the matter? Is the chest too heavy for you?

ZANNI. Too heavy for me? He-he! Zanni can bear anything for Pantalone! If only it is for Pantalone, Zanni can bear it. Come, into the house!

He lifts the chest with one hand, and holding it as though it were paper, he trots to FLAMINIA's *door*. Flaminia, here are your lemons!

FLAMINIA, *opening the door and calling with rapture*. Welcome, welcome, Zanni!

ZANNI *runs into the house with the chest*.

SCENE 9

ARLECCHINO *comes in dressed as a woman again*.

ARLECCHINO. At last, a clear road to Cintia's door! A clear night, a clear disguise—a clear pleasure! Oh, what a man will do to keep a husband smiling! What a lovely conceit, Arlecchino! Where is the lover who, on the brink of his salvation, can conceit you such a conceit? It's a wise head you carry, Arlecchino!

Going to CINTIA's *door.*

Oh, Cintia! Wisdom is here for salvation! Your little cousin is here from the country, just arrived, Cintia, to learn all about the town's good ways.

CINTIA, *from inside the house.* My little country cousin is already in my house! What devil is out there wanting to make a fool of Cintia?

ARLECCHINO. No, Cintia, I am not in your house, I am out here waiting to get in. Open the door and you will see me just as you expected to.

CINTIA, *inside.* Go away and stop your lying. You're not out there, but sitting beside me now, and—oh!

She laughs.

You're tickling me!

ARLECCHINO. Tickling you? I'm not even near you. Open the door and I'll be glad to tickle you.

CINTIA. Stop tickling me!

ARLECCHINO. Not until you let me in. Let me in and I'll stop tickling you gladly, Cintia.

CINTIA, *inside.* Oh, that's better, darling little cousin. Darling, darling little cousin, that's very nice.

ARLECCHINO. What's very nice? Open the door, Cintia, so that I can see what I am doing! Come out here and you'll see me where I say I am. Won't you believe your senses? Won't you believe your eyes?

CINTIA, *poking her head out the door.* My senses much more than my eyes. What a dreadful liar you are! You tell me I can see you there when all the time I can feel you here.

ARLECCHINO. But you *see* me! I am here, Cintia, see? You can't feel me there if you see me here.

CINTIA. Dull man! To feel only what he sees! Well then see what Cintia feels and feel as you please about what you see!

She ushers LEANDRO *into* ARLECCHINO's *sight.*

SCENE 10

ARLECCHINO. Arlecchino! What am I doing there?

He turns around and speaks to the space behind him.

Arlecchino, Arlecchino—are you with me? If you are with me here, then what are you doing there?

He walks closer to LEANDRO *and says to him:*

You, Arlecchino—tell me—which of me are you?

LEANDRO, *in echo.* You, Arlecchino—tell me—which of me are you?

ARLECCHINO, *turning to the invisible* ARLECCHINO. You, Arlecchino—— Where are you?—Oh—tell me——

Whispering to the invisible one.

Did you know about this abbreviated Arlecchino?

Turning to LEANDRO *prayerfully.*

Oh, little ghost of Arlecchino, go away from the door and let me be alone with Cintia!

LEANDRO, *echoing again.* Oh, little ghost of Arlecchino, go away from the door and let me be alone with Cintia!

ARLECCHINO, *pinching himself to demonstrate.* But look at me, ghost, I am not a ghost! I am flesh, flesh, and need no help from you, spirit, to win my salvation! Go away!

LEANDRO, *pinching himself also, and echoing* ARLECCHINO *again.* But look at me, ghost, I am not a ghost! I am flesh, flesh, and need no help from you, spirit, to win my salvation! Go away!

He goes back into the house, after CINTIA.

SCENE 11

ARLECCHINO, *crying after the departed* LEANDRO. Arlecchino! Don't go back alone! Oh my soul, what good is your salva-

tion without my flesh to share in it? Spirit Arlecchino! *Me*
Arlecchino! Take this devilish flesh with you!

Turning away from the house in despair.

Oh, Arlecchino, this is the worst trick of all! To have your
soul saved without your body! What man can endure such
a cheat and disappointment!

*He stops suddenly, and says to himself, as though he didn't
want to be overheard:*

Hey, Arlecchino! Come here! Can you live like a clever liar?
No! Then die like an honest man! Throw off your disguises
and be yourself!

*He begins to tear off his disguise and throws the pieces of
it into the audience.*

Pick your lying spirit clean, cast out your fraudulent soul,
throw away your art, that phantom, toss off that cheat, your
laughter. Let your immortal flesh die as naked as the truth.

He is divested of his disguise, and left plain ARLECCHINO.

There you are, Arlecchino—— All right—kill yourself.

He clutches his throat and begins to choke himself.

SCENE 12

ZANNI *comes out of* FLAMINIA'S *house.*

ZANNI, *seeing* ARLECCHINO. Doctor! Miraculous doctor! How
did you save yourself from Hell?

ARLECCHINO. I was interrupted.

ZANNI. Were you there, great man? Did the Devil carry you
all the way to Hell?

ARLECCHINO. To its very door.

ZANNI. What did you see there? Tell me, whom did you meet?

ARLECCHINO. I'll tell you. When I got to the very gate, when
I knocked to get in—on the strength of a promise, mind you
—the door opened, someone came out to meet me—— And
who do you think it was?

ZANNI. Who? Who? A devil?

ARLECCHINO. Worse, much worse!

ZANNI. A monster? A three-headed thing?

ARLECCHINO. Worse than that!

ZANNI. What? What? What horror met you?

ARLECCHINO. Myself! Myself came to the door, told me to go away, and went back in without me!

ZANNI. A miracle. A miracle in Hell. Come, Franceschina must hear about this. Franceschina! Franceschina!

ARLECCHINO. Another time, Zanni. The doctor must get back to some business he was attending to.

ZANNI. No, no. Franceschina must see the good doctor again, and have a magician to tend her child. Come out, Franceschina, the magical doctor is back!

SCENE 13

FRANCESCHINA *comes out with the laundry basket, this time filled with laundry.*

FRANCESCHINA. Why are you interrupting me in the midst of nursing your child?

ZANNI. Forgive me, Franceschina, were you in the midst of nursing him?

FRANCESCHINA. Right in the midst of it, you idiot, when you shouted.

ZANNI. Are you fondling him, Franceschina, are you showing him great love and tenderness?

FRANCESCHINA. More than you could imagine, you fool, greater than you could dream of.

ZANNI. Let me come in and play a bit with the little dear. Do you think, Doctor, he will be happy to see his father?

FRANCESCHINA. Play with him? You mad old folly, what are you thinking of? He will scratch out your eyes.

ZANNI. What? He would scratch out the eyes of his loving father?

FRANCESCHINA. Run to the market stalls and bring him a toy. Come to see him with a toy in your hands, and then you can play with him.

ZANNI. A toy? Where am I to get a toy in the middle of the night?

FRANCESCHINA. Run, you old palsy, and don't come back until you find him a toy.

ZANNI. If I do, will he be happy to see me then?

FRANCESCHINA. He will kiss you and bless you, kiss you and bless you forever.

ZANNI. I'll find him a toy, Franceschina. Keep him happy, good mother, until I return.

FRANCESCHINA, *as* ZANNI *is running out.* He'll be happy until you return, I promise you.

ZANNI *runs out.*

SCENE 14

FRANCESCHINA, *turns furiously on* ARLECCHINO *as soon as* ZANNI *has gone.* Liar. Cheat. You fraud of a doctor. Are you standing there accusing me of breaking my word?

ARLECCHINO. Good woman, I haven't opened my mouth.

FRANCESCHINA. Deceit! Deceit! I swear, Franceschina will be quits with you for this abuse. What are you supposing, you lecherous fraud? That Franceschina promised you her virtue, that she swore she would lie with you?

ARLECCHINO. I am supposing nothing, modest lady, except that I want to be off and that you want me to go.

FRANCESCHINA. Lie with you, you foul beast? Give you Franceschina's virtues, you scheming hypocrite? That's what you supposed I promised?

ARLECCHINO. I supposed you supposed——

FRANCESCHINA. You supposed! You supposed! You supposed I promised and then, you cheat, you supposed I would never redeem my promise. Franceschina, to whom honesty is more than all the other virtues. Very well then, you outrage, if you supposed I would bed you, I will bed you for days and days without number, I'll redeem that promise a hundred times, a thousand times over, that you will know that Franceschina knows how to keep her word, and then she will be quits with your lying deceit forever.

ARLECCHINO, *outraged.* Oh, you woman, you think Arlecchino doesn't remember what promises are made to him. Then listen to Arlecchino, for Arlecchino is going to swear by his sacred flesh and blessed hungers. I will hold you to every letter of your oath, woman. Put me through any trial on my memory or my understanding you can think of, and not one iota of it will I forget, not a word, not a sigh, not a wink, not a movement of your limbs will I remember or repeat of what you did without the most perfectly accurate recollection.

FRANCESCHINA. Then you dare Franceschina! Then listen to Franceschina, man, for she will confess what she has never confessed. My lover Pantalone is with me now, and when the will of heaven wears down his own, he will leave my house and you can come in. Wait in this basket——

ARLECCHINO. Oh, that basket!

FRANCESCHINA. In that basket, until he is gone, and then we will see which of us can manage a powerful promise.

ARLECCHINO. Then you dare Arlecchino! I, who can manage a million promises, promises without number. Very well, we shall see!

He climbs into the basket in a fury while saying this.

FRANCESCHINA. Yes, we shall see. Are you ready?

ARLECCHINO. Ready.

And she stuffs the clothing over him in the basket, and ARLECCHINO *sits inside it at the door of her house, invisible.*

FRANCESCHINA. And none of your shouting and yawping, do you hear? It is night, and my neighbors are tucked away in their beds, snoring and dreaming of modesty and heavenly rewards. Don't wake them, do you hear? Don't let them suppose that Franceschina's house is less virtuous than any of theirs. Whisper to me, do you understand?

ARLECCHINO, *whispering from inside the basket.* I understand.

FRANCESCHINA. Then when Pantalone finds it in his weakness to leave, you will enter. Sh! If you value my virtue, not a sound!

She goes in.

SCENE 15

A musician crosses the empty stage, playing and singing. The song to follow Act IV of The Mandrake *might be used.*

SCENE 16

When he is gone PANTALONE *comes out of* FRANCESCHINA'S *house. He yawns and stretches.* LEANDRO *comes out of* CINTIA'S *house and does the same thing. They see each other and start.*

LEANDRO. Pantalone! I thought I was meeting Coviello.

PANTALONE. Leandro! Coming from Coviello's house at this hour!

LEANDRO. And from whose house is Pantalone coming at this hour? Surely not Zanni's, eh, Pantalone?

PANTALONE. We lovers can abide each other's confidence. It was Zanni's house, to be sure. Zanni is such a blind fool, Leandro. What a comfort it is to have such a friend as Zanni!

LEANDRO. As comfortable as having such a friend as Coviello. Quickly, come down the street with me and help me get rid of my masquerade.

PANTALONE. Yes, yes. Then we can come back and masquerade as innocent friends.

LEANDRO. Leandro and Pantalone. Away all night on important business.

PANTALONE. Spoken like a lover.

They go off together.

SCENE 17

ARLECCHINO *sticks his head out of the basket, with the linen draped around him.*

ARLECCHINO. What a fool that vinegar husband is to mix with that oily lover. And what a fool that lover is to let a husband look over his shoulder. Arlecchino, you are wise to stay in the basket in the morning when all the husbands are popping about. Get down, Arlecchino, here come two more wise men.

SCENE 18

COVIELLO *comes out of* PANTALONE's *house as* ZANNI *comes in with toys.*

COVIELLO. Zanni, what are you carrying?

ZANNI. Ah, Coviello, advise me. Will the little darling like to play with these? Franceschina forbade me to come back without them, and all night long Zanni has run about getting them. Will they make him happy, Coviello? Will they please him?

COVIELLO. How did you come by a child, Zanni? Has someone left one at your door?

ZANNI. That is my secret. Mine and the crafty doctor's who is tending him. And Pantalone will never laugh at me again.

COVIELLO. But we will laugh at him, eh, Zanni? We have both outwitted him. Think, Zanni, that a man lives who is such a fool!

ZANNI. Ah, the world is not wise, Coviello, the world is not wise.

SCENE 19

PANTALONE *and* LEANDRO *come in.*

PANTALONE. Zanni! You have just returned?

LEANDRO. Coviello! How fortunate to meet you now.

COVIELLO. My good friend Leandro!

ZANNI. Pantalone, my dear.

PANTALONE. What are you carrying there, Zanni?

ZANNI. Toys. For my newly arrived child, Pantalone.

PANTALONE. A child! Where is it, Zanni?

ZANNI. With his mother, who has been watching over him this past night.

PANTALONE. Oh, blessed child!

ZANNI. Are you to be blessed too, Pantalone?

PANTALONE. Not so blessed as you, Zanni. Could I be honest, and hope to be blessed in my child as you are in yours?

ZANNI. True, Pantalone, very true.

PANTALONE. Very true, very true.

COVIELLO, *to* PANTALONE. And you have had a good night too, Pantalone?

PANTALONE. Oh, very good, Coviello.

COVIELLO. Untroubled, content?

PANTALONE. As untroubled as Zanni's, good friend.

LEANDRO. But Zanni has been busy all night chasing another's pleasure.

PANTALONE. Pantalone too, my friend.

LEANDRO. Zanni has found pleasure in his charity, and the toys he has there for his loved one.

PANTALONE. Pantalone too, my friend, Pantalone too, as you know better than any man.

ZANNI. And have you found pleasure in charity too, Leandro?

LEANDRO. Oh, great charity. And from a kind of toy, too. And Coviello, the good man, he has shown charity too tonight, don't you think so, Pantalone?

COVIELLO. Charity with toys, Leandro. My whole night has been nothing but charity and toys.

PANTALONE. Charity indeed, Coviello. Great charity.

ZANNI. Well, it was a blessed night indeed, of which all of us have nothing to remember but charity and mercy, and nothing to reap in the morning but gratitude and contentment.

COVIELLO. Yes, a blessed morning.

PANTALONE. A blessed morning, a good morning.

SCENE 20

FLAMINIA *comes out of her house.*

FLAMINIA. Pantalone! Husband! At last you are with me again.

PANTALONE. My own wife, did you miss me?

FLAMINIA. Not once did I shut my eyes for remembering you were gone.

PANTALONE. Dear Flaminia.

CINTIA *comes out of her house.*

CINTIA. Husband! Coviello! Thank God you are back this morning.

COVIELLO. My own Cintia, were you anxious about my being gone?

CINTIA. All night I lay awake wondering when you would return.

COVIELLO. My own Cintia.

FRANCESCHINA *comes out of her house.*

FRANCESCHINA. Zanni, my husband! At last you are back from your errand.

ZANNI. Safe and sound, good Franceschina. Are you happy I did not despair and come back without the toys?

FRANCESCHINA. If you had given up and come back without them, your Franceschina would have been lost.

ZANNI. Excellent mother!

FLAMINIA. A celebration! Dear neighbors, this is a morning for rejoicing. Pantalone and Flaminia ask you all to dine and we will celebrate these happy reunions of true wives and contented husbands.

SEVERALLY. A banquet. Come. Oh, blessed morning—a banquet.

FRANCESCHINA. Zanni, dear husband, bring my laundry basket into the house before we settle to this banquet.

ZANNI. Yes, dear mother, yes, yes.

PANTALONE. Let us help you, Zanni. Coviello, let us help Zanni carry his burden.

ZANNI. Ah, Zanni needs no help with baskets, Pantalone. Zanni can carry baskets.

COVIELLO. For your sake, Zanni.

PANTALONE. For Zanni's sake. All together——

COVIELLO. All together——

ZANNI. All together, friends—heave ho!

Since they have all grasped the basket at the same end, it overturns as they lift it and ARLECCHINO *falls out onto the ground. Consternation.*

COVIELLO. My friend!

PANTALONE. The beggar!

ZANNI. The doctor!

FLAMINIA. My little helper!

CINTIA. My conspirator!

FRANCESCHINA. My promise!

ZANNI. Doctor! What are you doing in my basket?

PANTALONE. Is this the bundle to be carried into your house? What a kindness we were doing for your wife!

ZANNI. Kindness for my wife? Then it was a kindness returned, because only last night I carried a chest into your house, with just such a burden inside it.

COVIELLO. Zanni, don't let the world know that our good friend has a lover coming to his house.

PANTALONE. No, and Pantalone will keep it secret that only this morning did he meet a lover coming out of Coviello's house, who is, as all the world knows, a cuckold!

COVIELLO. Ha! Then tell it he is a lover too, and of Pantalone's wife, whom Pantalone could not please!

PANTALONE. Not please? I, who am a lover and a father too, not please! This from an old jealous cuckold and an impotent old fool!

ZANNI. I impotent! Pantalone calls me impotent! I, who produced a child bigger than Pantalone's! No, no, he did not even produce a child. He produced a chest of lemons. Nothing but a chest of lemons! Ask this devilish doctor what a child I produced yesterday.

PANTALONE. Doctor! That is Coviello's mad country cousin, who cannot utter a syllable out of his mouth.

ZANNI. Latin! Latin comes out of his mouth. And children out of the ground! That is how mad he is.

Running to ARLECCHINO.

Shout Latin at him, shout it and sing it, that he will know you are a man of the science. Tell him in Latin how Zanni gave birth to a child!

PANTALONE. Save your Latin and I will tell you in your mother tongue. If Zanni has a child it is Pantalone's, for Pantalone has lain with his wife and shown her how children are begotten, and how he begot them on the sworn oath of his own wife. Not as old dead fools and cuckolds beget them in their sick fancies!

COVIELLO. Listen to this sick fancy then, and tell Coviello how better to beget a child for Pantalone than by bringing me into his house in a chest of lemons so that I might do what the both of you have lost the memory of, to please a wife and beget a child!

ZANNI. The both of us! A cuckold talks about the both of us! A cuckold tells us how to please a wife!

PANTALONE. Tell us, tell us how to call Leandro to our beds and please our wives. Cuckold!

COVIELLO. I a cuckold!

Pointing to the both of them.

There are cuckolds! Cuckolds! Cuckolds!

PANTALONE *and* ZANNI *also point to both the other old men and all three, jumping about in a circle and pointing at the other two, shout in a blue fury at the others.*

PANTALONE, ZANNI, COVIELLO. Cuckolds! Cuckolds! Cuckolds!

FRANCESCHINA *screams with rage and stops the dance of the cuckolds dead.*

FRANCESCHINA, *when there is silence.* Who are these men to besmirch our virtues? Pantalone! What have you confessed?

FLAMINIA. Coviello! Has your wife deserved this indignity?

CINTIA. Leandro! What has the world learned of our love?

LEANDRO, *coming to the middle of the stage and addressing them all.* What it would have learned without my word, or your reassurance. What it would learn of all these husbands and wives, for now the cat is out of the bag. And what have you lost now that it has learned all? Honest wives, be honest, and just husbands, be fair, do any of you find yourselves this morning bereft of what you had last night? The lovers did not steal and the wives did not lose their virtue in a single night. Virtue sets off meekly in the eye, in the leg, in the beckoning finger, in the slip of the tongue long before she gallops away in the bed. And the eye, the leg, the finger and the tongue are not born bawdy, but learn to wander after the example of the husband or the lesson of the wife. Pantalone, teach your wife modesty, and she will teach you the seemliness of love. Coviello, teach your wife contentment, and she will show you the abandon of love. Zanni— Zanni. Give your wife patience and pray for a heavenly reward. With all this done, you will have wisdom for your folly, and remember this night always as a blessing in disguise.

ARLECCHINO, *approaches* LEANDRO *and pulls his sleeve.* Wise man, can you teach me how I too can find a blessing in this night's disguise? What am I to do to lose my folly and be content with my lot?

LEANDRO, *pointing to the audience.* Do as these good people here are doing. Find wisdom and contentment in a folly greater than your own. Go to the *commedia,* and laugh at Arlecchino.

ARLECCHINO. Wise man, I am Arlecchino, and I have laughed at him until I have cried. Now I am lost, doubly damned, and triply desperate. Thank you for your counsel, wise man. Do you take a fee?

FLAMINIA, *addressing everybody.* Friends, good neighbors, with the help of the basket and the wise Leandro, this morning has been blessed twice over. Come. Into our house, and we can celebrate a contentment that no husbands and wives before us, and on my honor none that will follow us, can ever know on earth. Look at us. Leandro, come, look at your work. Three husbands and three wives, all smiling, and not a single one with a deceit inside him he can call his own. Miraculous lover who makes husbands happy as well as wives, come in and sit beside me, and tell me the secret of turning plain honesty to so much profit. Good neighbors, come.

LEANDRO goes into PANTALONE's house. FLAMINIA offers her hand to PANTALONE.

Husband!

PANTALONE. Dear wife!

They go in hand in hand.

CINTIA. Coviello!

COVIELLO. Dearest Cintia!

They go in hand in hand.

FRANCESCHINA. Zanni!

ZANNI. Ah, well!

They go hand in hand. ARLECCHINO stands before the door alone for a moment. FLAMINIA comes out as he begins to depart.

SCENE 21

FLAMINIA. Arlecchino, have we forgotten you? Come in, dear fool, and share in our banquet.

ARLECCHINO. Thank you, kind lady, but not for Arlecchino.

FLAMINIA. But, dear Arlecchino, here is a promise without tricks, without buts, without anything that can come of it but a true harvest.

ARLECCHINO. Dearest of all promises, Arlecchino can share no food and drink with you. What would become of Arlecchino with so much meat and wine inside him? Arlecchino has many follies, dear lady, but he is not so foolish as to digest his injuries and drown his wit.

FLAMINIA. But what better thing can you do, fool, than fill your empty stomach and put your folly to sleep?

ARLECCHINO. I can leave them alone, Flaminia. From my empty stomach I get my whole wisdom, and from my folly, my whole prosperity. Besides, dear lady, Arlecchino is in a great hurry to be off to Bergamo.

FLAMINIA. What is in Bergamo?

ARLECCHINO. Oh, there is a certain Isabella, who has a rich husband and a full larder, and—do you know?—Isabella keeps his keys. If I get there before nightfall, she will open the door for me, and Arlecchino will win her and his salvation and everything with his love.

FLAMINIA. Then Flaminia is not so unkind that she will spoil your happiness with meat and wine. Good-by, fool.

ARLECCHINO. Wise and beautiful lady, good-by.

FLAMINIA *goes in.*

SCENE 22

ARLECCHINO. Move, Arlecchino! Oh, you scrawny little centipede, look at him move! Hurry up, Arlecchino. Bergamo by
nightfall! Run, run, to Bergamo and your own salvation!
He leaps out.

THE SERVANT OF
TWO MASTERS

Carlo Goldoni

English Version by Edward J. Dent

CHARACTERS

PANTALONE DEI BISOGNOSI, *a Venetian merchant*

CLARICE, *his daughter*

DR. LOMBARDI

SILVIO, *his son*

BEATRICE RASPONI, *a lady of Turin, disguised as her brother*
FEDERIGO RASPONI

FLORINDO ARETUSI, *of Turin, lover of* BEATRICE

BRIGHELLA, *an innkeeper*

SMERALDINA, *maidservant to* CLARICE

TRUFFALDINO, *servant first to* BEATRICE, *and afterward to*
FLORINDO

FIRST WAITER

SECOND WAITER

FIRST PORTER

SECOND PORTER

The scene is laid in Venice.
The action takes place within a single day.

ACT I

SCENE 1

A Room in the House of PANTALONE

PANTALONE, THE DOCTOR, CLARICE, SILVIO,
BRIGHELLA, SMERALDINA

SILVIO, *offering his hand to* CLARICE. Here is my hand, and with it I give you my whole heart.

PANTALONE, *to* CLARICE. Come, come, not so shy, give him your hand too. Then you will be betrothed, and very soon you will be married.

CLARICE. Dear Silvio, here is my hand. I promise to be your wife.

SILVIO. And I promise to be your husband.

They take hands.

DR. LOMBARDI. Well done. Now that is settled, and there's no going back on it.

SMERALDINA, *aside.* There's luck for you! And me just bursting to get married!

PANTALONE, *to* BRIGHELLA *and* SMERALDINA. You two shall be witnesses of this betrothal of my daughter Clarice to Signor Silvio, the worthy son of our good Dr. Lombardi!

BRIGHELLA, *to* PANTALONE. We will, sir, and I thank you for the honor.

PANTALONE. Look you, I was witness at your wedding, and now you are a witness to my daughter's. I have asked no great company of friends and relations, for the doctor too is a man of my sort. We will have dinner together; we will enjoy ourselves and nobody shall disturb us.

To CLARICE *and* SILVIO.

What say you, children, does that suit you?

SILVIO. I desire nothing better than to be near my beloved bride.

SMERALDINA, *aside*. Yes, that's the best of all foods.

DR. LOMBARDI. My son is no lover of vanities. He is an honest lad; he loves your daughter and thinks of nothing else.

PANTALONE. Truly we may say that this marriage was made in Heaven, for had it not been for the death of Federigo Rasponi, my correspondent at Turin, you know, I had promised my daughter to him.

To SILVIO.

I could not then have given her to my dear son-in-law.

SILVIO. I can call myself fortunate indeed, sir; I know not if Signora Clarice will say the same.

CLARICE. You wrong me, dear Silvio. You should know if I love you. I should have married Signor Rasponi in obedience to my father; but my heart has always been yours.

DR. LOMBARDI. 'Tis true indeed, the will of Heaven is wrought in unexpected ways.

To PANTALONE.

Pray, sir, how did Federigo Rasponi come to die?

PANTALONE. Poor wretch, I hardly know. He was killed one night on account of some affair about his sister. Someone ran a sword through him and that was the end of him.

BRIGHELLA. Did that happen at Turin, sir?

PANTALONE. At Turin.

BRIGHELLA. Alas, poor gentleman! I am indeed sorry to hear it.

PANTALONE, *to* BRIGHELLA. Did you know Signor Federigo Rasponi?

BRIGHELLA. Indeed and I did, sir. I was three years at Turin. I knew his sister too—a fine high-spirited young woman— dressed like a man and rode a-horseback; and he loved her more than anyone in the world. Lord! Who'd ha' thought it?

PANTALONE. Well, misfortune waits for all of us. But come, let us talk no more of sad things. Do you know what I have in mind, good master Brighella? I know you love to show your skill in the kitchen. Now, I would have you make us a few dishes of your best.

BRIGHELLA. 'Tis a pleasure to serve you, sir. Though I say it that shouldn't, customers are always well contented at my house. They say there's no place where they eat as they do there. You shall taste something fine, sir.

PANTALONE. Good, good. Let's have something with plenty of gravy that we can sop the bread in.

A knock at the door.

Oh! Someone is knocking. Smeraldina, see who it is.

SMERALDINA. Yes, sir.

Goes to door.

CLARICE, *wishing to retire.* Sir, may I beg your leave?

PANTALONE. Wait; we are all coming. Let us hear who is there.

SMERALDINA, *coming back.* Sir, there is a gentleman's servant below who desires to give you a message. He would tell me nothing. He says he would speak to the master.

PANTALONE. Tell him to come up. We'll hear what he has to say.

SMERALDINA. I'll fetch him, sir.

Exit.

CLARICE. May I not go, sir?

PANTALONE. Whither then, madam?

CLARICE. I know not—to my own room——

PANTALONE. No, madam, no; you stay here.

Aside to DR. LOMBARDI.

These lovebirds can't be left alone just yet for a while.

DR. LOMBARDI, *aside to* PANTALONE. Prudence above all things!

SMERALDINA *brings in* TRUFFALDINO.

TRUFFALDINO. My most humble duty to the ladies and gentlemen. And a very fine company too, to be sure! Ve-ry fine, indeed!

PANTALONE. Who are you, my good friend? And what is your business?

TRUFFALDINO, *to* PANTALONE, *pointing to* CLARICE. Who is this fair gentlewoman?

PANTALONE. That is my daughter.

TRUFFALDINO. Delighted to hear it.

SMERALDINO, *to* TRUFFALDINO. What's more, she is going to be married.

TRUFFALDINO. I'm sorry to hear it. And who are you?

SMERALDINA. I am her maid, sir.

TRUFFALDINO. I congratulate her.

PANTALONE. Come, sir, have done with ceremony. What do you want with me? Who are you? Who sends you hither?

TRUFFALDINO. Patience, patience, my good sir, take it easy. Three questions at once is too much for a poor man.

PANTALONE, *aside to* DR. LOMBARDI. I think the man's a fool.

DR. LOMBARDI, *aside to* PANTALONE. I think he's playing the fool.

TRUFFALDINO, *to* SMERALDINA. Is it you that are going to be married?

SMERALDINA, *sighs*. No, sir.

PANTALONE. Will you tell me who you are, or will you go about your business?

TRUFFALDINO. If you only want to know who I am, I'll tell you in two words. I am the servant of my master.

Turns to SMERALDINA.

To go back to what I was saying——

PANTALONE. But who is your master?

TRUFFALDINO, *to* PANTALONE. He is a gentleman who desires the honor of paying his respects to you.

To SMERALDINA.

We must have a talk about this marriage.

PANTALONE. Who is this gentleman, I say? What is his name?

TRUFFALDINO. Oh, that's a long story. Si'or Federigo Rasponi of Turin, that's my master, and he sends his compliments, and he has come to see you, and he's down below, and he sends me to say that he would like to come up and he's waiting for an answer. Anything else, or will that do?

All look surprised.

To SMERALDINA, *as before.*

Let's begin again.

PANTALONE. Come here and talk to me. What the devil do you mean?

TRUFFALDINO. And if you want to know who I am, I am Truffaldin' Battocchio from Bergamo.

PANTALONE. I don't care who *you* are. Tell me again, who is this master of yours? I fear I did not understand you rightly.

TRUFFALDINO. Poor old gentleman! He must be hard of hearing. My master is Si'or Federigo Rasponi of Turin.

PANTALONE. Away! You must be mad. Signor Federigo Rasponi of Turin is dead.

TRUFFALDINO. Dead?

PANTALONE. To be sure he's dead, worse luck for him.

TRUFFALDINO, *aside*. The devil! My master dead? Why, I left him alive downstairs!

To PANTALONE.

You really mean he is dead?

PANTALONE. I tell you for an absolute certainty, he is dead.

DR. LOMBARDI. 'Tis the honest truth; he is dead; we can have no doubt about it.

TRUFFALDINO, *aside*. Alas, my poor master! He must have met with an accident.

To PANTALONE *as if retiring*.

Your very humble servant, sir.

PANTALONE. Can I do nothing more for you?

TRUFFALDINO. If he's dead, there's nothing more to do.

Aside.

But I'm going to see if it's true or not.

Exit.

PANTALONE. What are we to make of this fellow? Is he knave or fool?

DR. LOMBARDI. I really don't know. Probably a little of both.

BRIGHELLA. I should say he was just a zany. He comes from Bergamo; I can't think he is a knave.

SMERALDINA. He's not such a fool, neither.

Aside.

I like that little dark fellow.

PANTALONE. But what is this nightmare about Signor Federigo?

CLARICE. If 'tis true indeed that he is here, it would be the worst of news for me.

PANTALONE. What nonsense! Did not you see the letters yourself?

SILVIO. If he *is* alive and here after all, he has come too late.

Re-enter TRUFFALDINO.

TRUFFALDINO. Gentlemen, I am surprised at you. Is that the way to treat a poor man? Is that the way you deceive strangers? Is that the behavior of a gentleman? I shall insist upon satisfaction.

PANTALONE, *to* DR. LOMBARDI. We must be careful, the man's mad.

To TRUFFALDINO.

What's the matter? What have they done to you?

TRUFFALDINO. To go and tell me that Si'or Federigo Rasponi was dead!

PANTALONE. Well, what then?

TRUFFALDINO. What then? Well, he's here, safe and sound, in good health and spirits, and he desires to pay his respects to you, with your kind permission.

PANTALONE. Signor Federigo?

TRUFFALDINO. Si'or Federigo.

PANTALONE. Rasponi?

TRUFFALDINO. Rasponi.

PANTALONE. Of Turin?

TRUFFALDINO. Of Turin.

PANTALONE. Be off to Bedlam, my lad; that's the place for you.

TRUFFALDINO. The Devil take *you* there, sir! You'll make me swear like a Turk. I tell you he's here, in the house, in the next room, bad luck to you.

PANTALONE. If you say any more I'll break your head.

DR. LOMBARDI. No, no, Signor Pantalone; I tell you what to

do. Tell him to bring in this person whom he thinks to be Federigo Rasponi.

PANTALONE. Well, bring in this man that is risen from the dead.

TRUFFALDINO. He may have been dead and risen from the dead, for all I know. That's no affair of mine. But he's alive now, sure enough, and you shall see him with your own eyes. I'll go and tell him to come.

Angrily to PANTALONE.

And 'tis time you learned how to behave properly to strangers, to gentlemen of my position, to honorable citizens of Bergamo.

To SMERALDINA.

Young woman, we will have some talk together when you will.

Exit.

CLARICE. Silvio, I am all of a tremble.

SILVIO. Have no fear; whatever happens, you shall be mine.

DR. LOMBARDI. Now we shall discover the truth.

PANTALONE. Some rogue, I dare say, come to tell me a string of lies.

BRIGHELLA. Sir, as I told you just now, I knew Signor Federigo; we shall see if it be he.

SMERALDINA, *aside*. That little dark fellow doesn't look like a liar. I wonder, now, if——

Curtsy to PANTALONE.

By your good leave, sir.

Exit.

Enter BEATRICE, *dressed as a man.*

BEATRICE. Signor Pantalone, that courtesy which I have so much admired in your correspondence is but ill matched in the treatment which I have received from you in person. I send my servant to pay you my respects, and you keep me standing in the street for half an hour before you condescend to allow me to enter.

PANTALONE, *nervously*. I ask your pardon. But, sir, who are you?

BEATRICE. Your obedient servant, sir, Federigo Rasponi of Turin.

All look bewildered.

PANTALONE. Extraordinary!

BRIGHELLA, *aside.* What does this mean? This is not Federigo, this is his sister Beatrice.

PANTALONE. I rejoice to see you, sir, alive and in health, after the bad news which we had received.

Aside to DR. LOMBARDI.

I tell you, I am not convinced yet.

BEATRICE. I know; 'twas reported that I was killed in a duel. Heaven be praised, I was but wounded; and no sooner was I restored to health than I set out for Venice, according to our previous arrangement.

PANTALONE. I don't know what to say. You have the appearance of an honest man, sir, but I have sure and certain evidence that Signor Federigo is dead, and you will understand that if you cannot give us proof of the contrary——

BEATRICE. Your doubt is most natural; I recognize that I must give you proof of my identity. Here are four letters from correspondents of yours whom you know personally; one of them is from the manager of our bank. You will recognize the signatures and you will satisfy yourself as to who I am.

Gives four letters to PANTALONE, *who reads them to himself.*

CLARICE. Ah, Silvio, we are lost.

SILVIO. I will lose my life before I lose you.

BEATRICE, *noticing* BRIGHELLA, *aside.* Heavens! Brighella! How the devil does he come to be here? If he betrays me——

Aloud to BRIGHELLA.

Friend, I think I know you.

BRIGHELLA. Indeed yes, sir; do you not remember Brighella Cavicchio at Turin?

BEATRICE. Ah yes, now I recognize you.

Goes up to him.

And what are you doing in Venice, my good fellow?

Aside to BRIGHELLA.

For the love of heaven do not betray me.

BRIGHELLA, *aside to* BEATRICE. Trust me.

Aloud.

I keep an inn, sir, at your service.

BEATRICE. The very thing for me; as I have the pleasure of your acquaintance, I shall come to lodge at your inn.

BRIGHELLA. You do me honor, sir.

Aside.

Running contraband, I'll be bound.

PANTALONE. I have read the letters. Certainly they present Signor Federigo Rasponi to me, and if you present them, I am bound to believe that you are—the person named therein.

BEATRICE. If you are still in doubt, here is Master Brighella; he knows me, he can assure you as to who I am.

BRIGHELLA. Of course, sir, I am happy to assure you.

PANTALONE. Well, if that be so, and my good friend Brighella confirms the testimony of the letters, then, dear Signor Federigo, I am delighted to see you and I ask your pardon for having doubted your word.

CLARICE. Then, sir, this gentleman is indeed Signor Federigo Rasponi?

PANTALONE. But of course he is.

CLARICE, *aside to* SILVIO. Oh misery, what will happen to us?

SILVIO, *aside to* CLARICE. Don't be frightened; you are mine and I will protect you.

PANTALONE, *aside to* DR. LOMBARDI. What do you say to it, Doctor? He has come just in the nick of time.

DR. LOMBARDI. *Accidit in puncto, quod non contingit in anno.*

BEATRICE, *pointing to* CLARICE. Signor Pantalone, who is that young lady?

PANTALONE. That is my daughter Clarice.

BEATRICE. The one who was promised in marriage to me?

PANTALONE. Precisely, sir; that is she.

Aside.

Now I am in a pretty mess.

BEATRICE, *to* CLARICE. Madam, permit me to have the honor.

CLARICE, *stiffly*. Your most humble servant, sir.

BEATRICE, *to* PANTALONE. She receives me somewhat coldly.

PANTALONE. You must forgive her, she is shy by nature.

BEATRICE, *to* PANTALONE, *pointing at* SILVIO. And this gentleman is a relative of yours?

PANTALONE. Yes, sir; he is a nephew of mine.

SILVIO, *to* BEATRICE. No, sir, I am not his nephew at all; I am the promised husband of Signora Clarice.

DR. LOMBARDI, *aside to* SILVIO. Well said, my boy! Don't lose your chance! Stand up for your rights, but do nothing rash.

BEATRICE. What? You the promised husband of Signora Clarice? Was she not promised to me?

PANTALONE. There, there, I'll explain the whole matter. My dear Signor Federigo, I fully believed that the story of your accident was true, that you were dead, in fact, and so I had promised my daughter to Signor Silvio; but there is not the least harm done. You have arrived at last, just in time. Clarice is yours, if you will have her, and I am here to keep my word. Signor Silvio, I don't know what to say; you can see the position yourself. You remember what I said to you; and you will have no cause to bear me ill-will.

SILVIO. But Signor Federigo will never consent to take a bride who has given her hand to another.

BEATRICE. Oh, I am not so fastidious. I will take her in spite of that.

Aside.

I mean to have some fun out of this.

DR. LOMBARDI, *sarcastically*. There's a fine fashionable husband! I like him.

BEATRICE. I hope Signora Clarice will not refuse me her hand.

SILVIO. Sir, you have arrived too late. Signora Clarice is to be *my* wife, and you need have no hope that I will yield her to you. If Signor Pantalone does me wrong, I will be avenged upon him; and whoever presumes to desire Clarice will have to fight for her against this sword.

DR. LOMBARDI, *aside*. That's a fine boy, by the Lord!

BEATRICE, *aside*. Thank you, but I don't mean to die just yet.

DR. LOMBARDI. Sir, I must beg to inform you that you are too late. Signora Clarice is to marry my son. The law, the law, sir, is clear on the point. *Prior in tempore, potior in jure.*

Exeunt DR. LOMBARDI *and* SILVIO.

BEATRICE, *to* CLARICE. And you, madam bride, do you say nothing?

CLARICE. I say—I say—I'd sooner marry the hangman.

Exit.

PANTALONE. What, you minx! What did you say?

Starts to run after her.

BEATRICE. Stay, Signor Pantalone; I am sorry for her. It is not the moment for severity. In course of time I hope I may deserve her favor. Meanwhile let us go into our accounts together, for, as you know, that is one of the two reasons that have brought me to Venice.

PANTALONE. Everything is in order for your inspection. You shall see the books; your money is ready for you, and we will make up the account whenever you like.

BEATRICE. I will call on you at some more convenient time. Now, if you will allow me, I will go with Brighella to settle some little business which I have to do.

PANTALONE. You shall do as you please, and if you have need of anything, I am at your service.

BEATRICE. Well, if you could give me a little money, I should be greatly obliged; I did not bring any with me, for fear of being robbed on the way.

PANTALONE. I am delighted to serve you; but the cashier is not here just now. The moment he comes I will send the money to your lodgings. Are you not staying at my friend Brighella's?

BEATRICE. Yes, I lie there. But I will send my servant; he is entirely honest. You can trust him with anything.

PANTALONE. Very well. I will carry out your wishes, and if you may be pleased to take pot luck with me, I am yours to command.

BEATRICE. For today I thank you. Another day I shall be happy to wait upon you.

PANTALONE. Then I shall expect you.

Enter SMERALDINA.

SMERALDINA, *to* PANTALONE. Sir, you are asked for.

PANTALONE. Who is it?

SMERALDINA. I couldn't say, sir.

PANTALONE. I will come directly. Sir, I beg you to excuse me. Brighella, you are at home here; be good enough to attend Signor Federigo.

BEATRICE. Pray do not put yourself about for me, sir.

PANTALONE. I must go. Farewell, sir.

Aside.

I don't want to have trouble in my house.

Exit with SMERALDINA.

BRIGHELLA. May I ask, Signora Beatrice——?

BEATRICE. Hush, for the love of Heaven, don't betray me. My poor brother is dead. 'Twas thought Florindo Aretusi killed him in a duel. You remember, Florindo loved me, and my brother would not have it. They fought, Federigo fell, and Florindo fled from justice. I heard he was making for Venice, so I put on my brother's clothes and followed him. Thanks to the letters of credit, which are my brother's, and thanks still more to you, Signor Pantalone takes me for Federigo. We are to make up our accounts; I shall draw the money, and then I shall be able to help Florindo too, if he has need of it. Be my friend, dear Brighella, help me, please! You shall be generously rewarded.

BRIGHELLA. That's all very well, but I don't want to be responsible for Signor Pantalone paying you out money in good faith and then finding himself made a fool of.

BEATRICE. Made a fool of? If my brother is dead, am I not his heir?

BRIGHELLA. Very true. Then why not say so?

BEATRICE. If I do that, I can do nothing. Pantalone will begin by treating me as if he were my guardian; then they will all worry me and say my conduct is unbecoming and all that sort of thing. I want my liberty. Help me to it. 'Twill not last long.

BRIGHELLA. Well, well, you were always one for having your own way. Trust me, and I'll do my best for you.

BEATRICE. Thank you. And now let us go to your inn.

BRIGHELLA. Where is your servant?

BEATRICE. I told him to wait for me in the street.

BRIGHELLA. Wherever did you get hold of that idiot? He cannot even speak plain.

BEATRICE. I picked him up on the journey. He seems a fool at times; but he isn't really a fool and I can rely on his loyalty.

BRIGHELLA. Yes, loyalty's a fine thing. Well, I am at your service. To think what love will make people do!

BEATRICE. Oh, this is nothing. Love makes people do far worse things than this.

BRIGHELLA. Well, here's a good beginning. If you go on that way, Lord knows what may come of it!

Exeunt BEATRICE *and* BRIGHELLA.

SCENE 2

A *Street with* BRIGHELLA'S *Inn*

TRUFFALDINO *solus*

TRUFFALDINO. I'm sick of waiting; I can hold out no longer. With this master of mine there's not enough to eat, and the less there is the more I want it. The town clock struck twelve half an hour ago, and my belly struck two hours ago at least. If I only knew where we were going to lodge! With my other masters the first thing they did, as soon as they came to a town, was to go to a tavern. This gentleman—Lord no! He leaves his trunks in the boat at the landing stage, goes off to pay visits, and forgets all about his poor servant. When they say we ought to serve our masters with love, they ought to tell the masters to have a little charity toward their servants.

Here's an inn. I've half a mind to go in and see if I could find something to tickle my teeth; but what if my master comes to look for me? His own fault; he ought to know better. I'll go in—but now I come to think of it, there's another little difficulty that I hadn't remembered; I haven't a penny. Oh poor Truffaldin'! Rather than be a servant, devil take me, I'd—what indeed? By the grace of Heaven there's nothing I *can* do.

Enter FLORINDO *in traveling dress with a* PORTER *carrying a trunk on his shoulder.*

PORTER. I tell you, sir, I can go no farther; the weight's enough to kill me.

FLORINDO. Here is the sign of an inn. Can't you carry it these few steps?

PORTER. Help! The trunk is falling.

FLORINDO. I told you you could not carry it; you're too weak; you have no strength at all.

FLORINDO *rearranges the trunk on the* PORTER'S *shoulder.*

TRUFFALDINO. Here's a chance for sixpence.

To FLORINDO.

Sir, can I do anything for you?

FLORINDO. My good man, be so good as to carry this trunk into the inn there.

TRUFFALDINO. Yes, sir, let me take it, sir. See how I do it.

To the PORTER.

You be off!

TRUFFALDINO *puts his shoulder under the trunk and takes it by himself, knocking the* PORTER *down at the same time.*

FLORINDO. Well done!

TRUFFALDINO. It weighs nothing. A mere trifle.

Goes into the inn with the trunk.

FLORINDO, *to* PORTER. There! You see how it's done.

PORTER. I can do no more. I work as a porter for my misfortune, but I am the son of a respectable person.

FLORINDO. What did your father do?

PORTER. My father? He skinned lambs in the town.

FLORINDO. The fellow's mad.

To PORTER.

That will do.

Going towards the inn.

PORTER. Please your honor——

FLORINDO. What do you want?

PORTER. The money for the porterage.

FLORINDO. How much am I to give you for ten yards? There's the landing stage!

Pointing off.

PORTER. I didn't count them. I want my pay.

Holds out his hand.

FLORINDO. There's twopence.

Gives money.

PORTER. I want my pay.

Still holding out his hand.

FLORINDO. Lord, what obstinacy! Here's twopence more.

Gives money.

PORTER. I want my pay.

FLORINDO, *kicks him.* Go and be hanged!

PORTER. Thank you, sir, that's enough.

Exit.

FLORINDO. There's a humorous fellow! He was positively waiting for me to kick him. Well, let us go and see what the inn is like——

Re-enter TRUFFALDINO.

TRUFFALDINO. Sir, everything is ready for you.

FLORINDO. What lodging is there here?

TRUFFALDINO. 'Tis a very good place, sir. Good beds, fine looking glasses, and a grand kitchen with a smell to it that is very comforting. I have talked with the waiter. You will be served like a king.

FLORINDO. What's *your* trade?

TRUFFALDINO. Servant.

FLORINDO. Are you a Venetian?

TRUFFALDINO. Not from Venice, but of the State. I'm from Bergamo, at your service.

FLORINDO. Have you a master now?

TRUFFALDINO. At the moment—to tell the truth, I have not.

FLORINDO. You are without a master?

TRUFFALDINO. You see me, sir. I am without a master.

Aside.

My master is not here, so I tell no lies.

FLORINDO. Will you come and be *my* servant?

TRUFFALDINO. Why not?

Aside.

If his terms are better.

FLORINDO. At any rate, for as long as I stay in Venice.

TRUFFALDINO. Very good, sir. How much will you give me?

FLORINDO. How much do you want?

TRUFFALDINO. I'll tell you: another master I had, who is here no more, he gave me a shilling a day and all found.

FLORINDO. Good, I will give you as much.

TRUFFALDINO. You must give me a little more than that.

FLORINDO. How much more do you want?

TRUFFALDINO. A halfpenny a day for snuff.

FLORINDO. Oh, I'll give you that and welcome.

TRUFFALDINO. If that's so, I'm your man, sir.

FLORINDO. But I should like to know a little more about you.

TRUFFALDINO. If you want to know all about me, you go to Bergamo; anyone there will tell you who I am.

FLORINDO. Have you nobody in Venice who knows you?

TRUFFALDINO. I only arrived this morning, sir.

FLORINDO. Well, well, I take you for an honest man. I will give you a trial.

TRUFFALDINO. You give me a trial and you shall see.

FLORINDO. First of all, I am anxious to know if there are letters at the Post for me. Here is half a crown; go to the Turin Post and ask if there are letters for Florindo Aretusi; if there are, take them and bring them at once. I shall wait for you.

TRUFFALDINO. Meanwhile you will order dinner, sir?

FLORINDO. Yes, well said! I will order it.

Aside.

He is a wag, I like him. I'll give him a trial.

FLORINDO *goes into the inn.*

TRUFFALDINO. A halfpenny more a day, that's fifteen pence a
month. 'Tis not true that the other gentleman gave me a
shilling; he gives me six pennies. Maybe six pennies make
a shilling, but I'm not quite sure. And this gentleman from
Turin is nowhere to be seen. He's mad. He's a young fellow
without a beard and without any sense neither. He may go
about his business; I shall go to the Post for my new
gentleman.

As he is going, BEATRICE *enters with* BRIGHELLA *and meets
him.*

BEATRICE. That's a nice way to behave! Is that the way you
wait for me?

TRUFFALDINO. Here I am, sir. I am still waiting for you.

BEATRICE. And how do you come to be waiting for me here,
and not in the street where I told you? 'Tis a mere accident
that I have found you.

TRUFFALDINO. I went for a bit of a walk to take away my
appetite.

BEATRICE. Well, go at once to the landing stage; fetch my
trunk and take it to the inn of Master Brighella.

BRIGHELLA. There's my inn, you cannot mistake it.

BEATRICE. Very well, then, make haste, and I will wait for you.

TRUFFALDINO. The devil! In *that* inn?

BEATRICE. Here, you will go at the same time to the Turin
Post and ask if there are any letters for me. You may ask if
there are letters for Federigo Rasponi and also for Beatrice
Rasponi. That's my sister. Some friend of hers might perhaps
write to her; so be sure to see if there are letters either for
her or for me.

TRUFFALDINO, *aside.* What *am* I to do? Here's a pretty kettle
of fish!

BRIGHELLA, *to* BEATRICE. Why do you expect letters in your
real name if you left home secretly?

BEATRICE. I told the steward to write to me; and I don't know which name he may use. I'll tell you more later.

To TRUFFALDINO.

Make haste, be off with you to the Post and the landing stage. Fetch the letters and have the trunk brought to the inn; I shall be there.

Exit BEATRICE *into the inn.*

TRUFFALDINO. Are you the landlord?

BRIGHELLA. Yes, I am. You behave properly and you need have no fear, I will do you well.

Exit BRIGHELLA *into the inn.*

TRUFFALDINO. There's luck! There are many that look in vain for a master, and I have found two. What the devil am I to do? I cannot wait upon them both. No? Why not? Wouldn't it be a fine thing to wait upon both of them, earn two men's wages and eat and drink for two? 'Twould be a fine thing indeed, if neither of them found out. And if they did? What then? No matter! If one sends me away, I stay with the other. I swear I'll try it. If it last but a day, I'll try it. Whatever happens I shall have done a fine thing. Here goes. Let's go to the Post for both of 'em.

Enter SILVIO *and meets* TRUFFALDINO.

SILVIO, *aside.* That is the servant of Federigo Rasponi.

To TRUFFALDINO.

My good man.

TRUFFALDINO. Sir?

SILVIO. Where is your master?

TRUFFALDINO. My master? He's in that inn there.

SILVIO. Go at once and tell your master that I wish to speak to him; if he be a man of honor let him come down; I wait for him.

TRUFFALDINO. My dear sir——

SILVIO, *angrily.* Go at once.

TRUFFALDINO. But I must tell you, my master——

SILVIO. Don't answer me; or, by Heaven, I'll——

TRUFFALDINO. But which do you want?

SILVIO. At once, I say, or I'll beat you.

TRUFFALDINO, *aside*. Well, I don't know—I'll send the first I can find.

Exit TRUFFALDINO *into the inn.*

SILVIO. No, I will never suffer the presence of a rival. Federigo may have got off once with his life, but he shall not always have the same fortune. Either he shall renounce all claims to Clarice, or he shall give me the satisfaction of a gentleman. Here are some more people coming out of the inn. I don't want to be disturbed.

Retires to the opposite side.

Enter TRUFFALDINO *with* FLORINDO.

TRUFFALDINO, *points out* SILVIO *to* FLORINDO. There's the fire-eating gentleman, sir.

FLORINDO. I do not know him. What does he want with me?

TRUFFALDINO. I don't know. I go to fetch the letters, with your good leave, sir.

Aside.

I don't want any more trouble.

Exit.

SILVIO, *aside*. Federigo does not come?

FLORINDO, *aside*. I must find out what the truth is.

To SILVIO.

Sir, are you the gentleman who inquired for me?

SILVIO. I, sir? I have not even the honor of your acquaintance.

FLORINDO. But that servant who has just gone told me that with a loud and threatening voice you made bold to challenge me.

SILVIO. He misunderstood. I said I wished to speak to his master.

FLORINDO. Very well, I am his master.

SILVIO. You his master?

FLORINDO. Certainly. He is in my service.

SILVIO. Then I ask your pardon. Either your servant is exactly like another whom I saw this morning, or he waits on another person.

FLORINDO. You may set your mind at rest; he waits on me.

SILVIO. If that be so, I ask your pardon again.

FLORINDO. No harm done. Mistakes often occur.

SILVIO. Are you a stranger here, sir?

FLORINDO. From Turin, sir, at your service.

SILVIO. The man whom I would have provoked was from Turin.

FLORINDO. Then perhaps I may know him; if he has given you offence, I shall gladly assist you to obtain just satisfaction.

SILVIO. Do you know one Federigo Rasponi?

FLORINDO. Ah! I knew him only too well.

SILVIO. He makes claim, on the strength of her father's word, to the lady who this morning swore to be my wife.

FLORINDO. My good friend, Federigo Rasponi cannot take your wife away from you. He is dead.

SILVIO. Yes, we all believed that he was dead; but this morning to my disgust he arrived in Venice safe and sound.

FLORINDO. Sir, you petrify me.

SILVIO. No wonder! I was petrified myself.

FLORINDO. I assure you Federigo Rasponi is dead.

SILVIO. I assure you that Federigo Rasponi is alive.

FLORINDO. Take care you are not deceived.

SILVIO. Signor Pantalone dei Bisognosi, the young lady's father, has made all possible inquiries to assure himself and is in possession of incontestable proofs that he is here in person.

FLORINDO, *aside*. Then he was not killed in the duel, as everybody believed!

SILVIO. Either he or I must renounce claim to the love of Clarice or to life.

FLORINDO, *aside*. Federigo here?

SILVIO. I am surprised that you have not seen him. He was to lodge at this very inn.

FLORINDO. I have not seen him. They told me that there was no one else at all staying there.

SILVIO. He must have changed his mind. Forgive me, sir, if

I have troubled you. If you see him, tell him that for his own welfare he must abandon the idea of this marriage. Silvio Lombardi is my name; I am your most obedient servant, sir.

FLORINDO. I shall be greatly pleased to have the honor of your friendship.

Aside.

I am confounded.

SILVIO. May I beg to know your name, sir?

FLORINDO, *aside.* I must not discover myself.

To SILVIO.

Your servant, sir, Orazio Ardenti.

SILVIO. Signor Orazio, I am yours to command.

Exit SILVIO.

FLORINDO. I was told he died on the spot. Yet I fled so hurriedly when accused of the crime that I had no chance of finding out the truth. Then, since he is not dead, it will be better for me to go back to Turin and console my beloved Beatrice, who is perhaps in suffering and sorrow for my absence.

Enter TRUFFALDINO, *with another* PORTER *who carries* BEATRICE's *trunk.* TRUFFALDINO *comes forward a few steps, sees* FLORINDO *and, fearing to be seen himself, makes the* PORTER *retire.*

TRUFFALDINO. Come along. This way—— The devil! There's my other master. Go back, friend, and wait for me at that corner.

Exit PORTER.

FLORINDO, *continuing to himself.* Yes, without delay. I will go back to Turin.

TRUFFALDINO. Here I am, sir.

FLORINDO. Truffaldino, will you come to Turin with me?

TRUFFALDINO. When?

FLORINDO. Now; at once.

TRUFFALDINO. Before dinner?

FLORINDO. No, we will have dinner, and then we will go.

TRUFFALDINO. Very good, sir. I'll think it over at dinner.

FLORINDO. Have you been to the Post?

TRUFFALDINO. Yes, sir.

FLORINDO. Have you found my letters?

TRUFFALDINO. I have, sir.

FLORINDO. Where are they?

TRUFFALDINO. I will give you them.

Takes three letters out of his pocket. Aside.

The devil! I have mixed up one master's letters with the other's. How shall I find out which are his? I cannot read.

FLORINDO. Come, give me my letters.

TRUFFALDINO. Directly, sir.

Aside.

Here's a muddle.

To FLORINDO.

I must tell you, sir; these three letters are not all for your honor. I met another servant, who knows me; we were in service together at Bergamo; I told him I was going to the Post, and he asked me to see whether there was anything for *his* master. I think there was one letter, but I don't know which of them it was.

FLORINDO. Let me see; I will take mine and give you the other back.

TRUFFALDINO. There, sir; I only wanted to do my friend a good turn.

FLORINDO, *aside.* What is this? A letter addressed to Beatrice Rasponi? To Beatrice Rasponi at Venice?

TRUFFALDINO. Did you find the one that belongs to my mate?

FLORINDO. Who is this mate of yours who asked you to do this for him?

TRUFFALDINO. He is a servant—his name is Pasqual'——

FLORINDO. Whom does he wait upon?

TRUFFALDINO. I do not know, sir.

FLORINDO. But if he told you to fetch his master's letters, he must have told you his name.

TRUFFALDINO. Of course he did.

Aside.

The muddle's getting thicker.

FLORINDO. Well, what name did he tell you?

TRUFFALDINO. I don't remember.

FLORINDO. What?

TRUFFALDINO. He wrote it down on a bit of paper.

FLORINDO. And where is the paper?

TRUFFALDINO. I left it at the Post.

FLORINDO, *aside*. Confusion! What does this mean?

TRUFFALDINO, *aside*. I am learning my part as I go along.

FLORINDO. Where does this fellow Pasquale live?

TRUFFALDINO. Indeed, sir, I haven't the slightest idea.

FLORINDO. How will you be able to give him the letter?

TRUFFALDINO. He said he would meet me in the Piazza.

FLORINDO, *aside*. I don't know what to make of it.

TRUFFALDINO, *aside*. If I get through this business clean 'twill be a miracle.

To FLORINDO.

Pray give me the letter, sir, and I shall find him somewhere.

FLORINDO. No; I mean to open this letter.

TRUFFALDINO. Oh, sir, do not do that, sir. Besides, you know how wrong it is to open letters.

FLORINDO. I care not; this letter interests me too much. It is addressed to a person on whom I have a certain claim. I can open it without scruple.

Opens letter.

TRUFFALDINO. As you will, sir.

Aside.

He has opened it!

FLORINDO, *reads*. "Madam, your departure from this city has given rise to much talk, and all understand that you have gone to join Signor Florindo. The Court of Justice has discovered that you have fled in man's dress and intends to have you arrested. I have not sent this letter by the courier from Turin to Venice, so as not to reveal the place whither you were bound, but I have sent it to a friend at Genoa to be forwarded to Venice. If I have any more news to tell you, I will not fail to send it by the same means. Your most humble servant, Antonio."

TRUFFALDINO. That's a nice way to behave! Reading other people's letters!

FLORINDO, *aside*. What is all this? Beatrice has left home? In man's dress? To join me? Indeed she loves me. Heaven grant I may find her in Venice.

To TRUFFALDINO.

Here, my good Truffaldino, go and do all you can to find Pasquale; find out from him who his master is, and if he be man or woman. Find out where he lodges, and if you can, bring him here to me, and both he and you shall be handsomely rewarded.

TRUFFALDINO. Give me the letter; I will try to find him.

FLORINDO. There it is. I count upon you. This matter is of infinite importance to me.

TRUFFALDINO. But am I to give him the letter open like this?

FLORINDO. Tell him it was a mistake, an accident. Don't make difficulties.

TRUFFALDINO. And are you going to Turin now?

FLORINDO. No, not for the present. Lose no time. Go and find Pasquale.

Aside.

Beatrice in Venice, Federigo in Venice! If her brother finds her, unhappy woman! I will do all I can to discover her first.

Exit toward the town.

TRUFFALDINO. Upon my word, I hope he is not going away. I want to see how my two jobs will work out. I'm on my mettle. This letter, now, which I have to take to my other master—I don't like to have to give it him opened. I must try to fold it again.

Tries various awkward folds.

And now it must be sealed. If I only knew how to do it! I have seen my grandmother sometimes seal letters with chewed bread. I'll try it.

Takes a piece of bread out of his pocket.

It's a pity to waste this little piece of bread, but still something must be done.

Chews a little bread to seal the letter and accidentally swallows it.

The devil! It has gone down. I must chew another bit.

Same business.

No good, nature rebels. I'll try once more.

Chews again; would like to swallow the bread, but restrains himself and with great difficulty removes the bread from his mouth.

Ah, here it is; I'll seal the letter.

Seals the letter with the bread.

I think that looks quite well. I'm always a great man for doing things cleanly.

     Lord! I had forgotten the porter.

Calls off.

Friend, come hither; take the trunk on your shoulder.

Re-enter PORTER.

PORTER. Here I am; where am I to carry it?

TRUFFALDINO. Take it into that inn; I am coming directly.

     BEATRICE *comes out of the inn.*

BEATRICE. Is this my trunk?

TRUFFALDINO. Yes, sir.

BEATRICE, *to* PORTER. Carry it into my room.

PORTER. Which is your room?

BEATRICE. Ask the waiter.

PORTER. There's one and threepence to pay.

BEATRICE. Go on, I will pay you.

PORTER. Please be quick about it.

BEATRICE. Don't bother me.

PORTER. I've half a mind to throw the trunk down in the middle of the street.

     Goes into the inn.

TRUFFALDINO. Great folk for politeness, these porters!

BEATRICE. Have you been to the Post?

TRUFFALDINO. Yes, sir.

BEATRICE. Any letters for me?

TRUFFALDINO. One for your sister.

BEATRICE. Good; where is it?

TRUFFALDINO. Here.

Gives letter.

BEATRICE. This letter has been opened.

TRUFFALDINO. Opened? No! Impossible!

BEATRICE. Yes, opened, and then sealed with bread.

TRUFFALDINO. I can't think how that can have happened.

BEATRICE. You cannot think, eh? Rascal, who has opened this letter? I must know.

TRUFFALDINO. Sir, I'll tell you, I'll confess the truth. We are all liable to make mistakes. At the Post there was a letter for me; I can't read very much, and by mistake, instead of opening my letter, I opened yours. I ask your pardon——

BEATRICE. If that was all, there's no great harm done.

TRUFFALDINO. 'Tis true, on the word of a poor man.

BEATRICE. Have you read this letter? Do you know what is in it?

TRUFFALDINO. Not a word. I can't read the handwriting.

BEATRICE. Has anyone else seen it?

TRUFFALDINO, *with an air of great indignation.* Oh!

BEATRICE. Take care now——

TRUFFALDINO, *same business.* Sir!

BEATRICE, *aside.* I hope he is not deceiving me.

Reads to herself.

TRUFFALDINO. That's all put straight.

BEATRICE, *aside.* Antonio is a faithful servant and I am obliged to him.

To TRUFFALDINO.

Listen; I have some business to do close by. You go into the inn, open the trunk—here are my keys—and unpack my things. When I come back, we will have dinner.

Aside.

I have seen nothing of Signor Pantalone, and I am anxious to have my money.

Exit.

TRUFFALDINO. Come, that all went well; it couldn't have gone better. I'm a great fellow; I think a deal more of myself than I did before.

Enter PANTALONE.

PANTALONE. Tell me, my good man, is your master in the house?

TRUFFALDINO. No, sir, he is not there.

PANTALONE. Do you know where he may be?

TRUFFALDINO. Not that neither.

PANTALONE. Is he coming home to dinner?

TRUFFALDINO. Yes, I should think so.

PANTALONE. Here, as soon as he comes home give him this purse with these hundred guineas. I cannot stay, I have business. Good day to you.

Exit PANTALONE.

TRUFFALDINO. And a good day to you, sir! He never told me to which of my masters I was to give it.

Enter FLORINDO.

FLORINDO. Well, did you find Pasquale?

TRUFFALDINO. No, sir, I did not find Pasqual', but I found a gentleman who gave me a purse with a hundred guineas in it.

FLORINDO. A hundred guineas? What for?

TRUFFALDINO. Tell me truly, sir, were you expecting money from anyone?

FLORINDO. Yes; I had presented a letter of credit to a merchant.

TRUFFALDINO. Then this money will be for you.

FLORINDO. What did he say when he gave it to you?

TRUFFALDINO. He told me to give it to my master.

FLORINDO. Then of course it is mine. Am I not your master? What doubt could you have?

TRUFFALDINO, *aside.* Yes, but what about t'other one?

FLORINDO. And you do not know who gave you the money?

TRUFFALDINO. No, sir; I think I have seen his face somewhere, but I don't remember exactly.

FLORINDO. It will have been the merchant to whom I had a letter.

TRUFFALDINO. Yes, of course, sir.

FLORINDO. You won't forget Pasquale.

TRUFFALDINO. I'll find him after dinner.

FLORINDO. Then let us go and order our meal.

Goes into the inn.

TRUFFALDINO. We will. Lucky I made no mistake this time. I've given the purse to the right one.

Goes into the inn.

SCENE 3

A Room in the House of PANTALONE

PANTALONE *and* CLARICE

PANTALONE. That's the long and short of it; Signor Federigo is to be your husband. I have given my word and I am not to be cozened.

CLARICE. You have my obedience, sir; but I beseech you, this is tyranny.

PANTALONE. When Signor Federigo first asked for your hand, I told you; you never replied that you did not wish to marry him. You should have spoken then; now it is too late.

CLARICE. My fear of you, sir, and my respect, made me dumb.

PANTALONE. Then your fear and respect should do the same now.

CLARICE. Indeed I cannot marry him, sir.

PANTALONE. No? And why not?

CLARICE. Nothing shall induce me to marry Federigo.

PANTALONE. You dislike him so much?

CLARICE. He is odious in my eyes.

PANTALONE. And supposing I were to show you how you might begin to like him a little?

CLARICE. What do you mean, sir?

PANTALONE. Put Signor Silvio out of your mind, and you will soon like Federigo well enough.

CLARICE. Silvio is too firmly stamped upon my heart; and your own approval, sir, has rooted him there the more securely.

PANTALONE, *aside*. In some ways I am sorry for her.

To CLARICE.

You have got to make a virtue of necessity.

CLARICE. My heart is not capable of so great an effort.

PANTALONE. Come, come; you shall!

Enter SMERALDINA.

SMERALDINA. Sir, Signor Federigo is here and desires to speak with you.

PANTALONE. Tell him to come in; I am at his service.

CLARICE, *weeping*. Alas! What torture!

SMERALDINA. What is it, madam? You are weeping? Truly you do wrong. Have you not noticed how handsome Signor Federigo is? If I had such luck, I would not cry; no, I would laugh with the whole of my mouth.

Exit SMERALDINA.

PANTALONE. There, there, my child; you must not be seen crying.

CLARICE. But if I feel my heart bursting!

Enter BEATRICE *in man's dress.*

BEATRICE. My respects to Signor Pantalone.

PANTALONE. Your servant, sir. Did you receive a purse with a hundred guineas in it?

BEATRICE. No.

PANTALONE. But I gave it to your servant just now. You told me he was a trustworthy man.

BEATRICE. Yes, indeed; there is no danger. I did not see him. He will give me the money when I come home again.

Aside to PANTALONE.

What ails Signora Clarice that she is weeping?

PANTALONE, *aside to* BEATRICE. Dear Signor Federigo, you must have pity on her. The news of your death was the cause of this trouble. I hope it will pass away in time.

BEATRICE, *to* PANTALONE. Do me a kindness, Signor Pantalone, and leave me alone with her a moment, to see if I cannot obtain a kind word from her.

PANTALONE. With pleasure, sir. I will go, and come back again.

To CLARICE.

My child, stay here, I will be back directly. You must entertain your promised husband awhile.

Softly to CLARICE.

Now, be careful.

Exit PANTALONE.

BEATRICE. Signora Clarice, I beg you——

CLARICE. Stand away, and do not dare to importune me.

BEATRICE. So severe with him who is your destined husband?

CLARICE. They may drag me by force to the altar, but you will have only my hand, never my heart.

BEATRICE. You disdain me, but I hope to appease you.

CLARICE. I shall abhor you to all eternity.

BEATRICE. But if you knew me, you would not say so.

CLARICE. I know you well enough as the destroyer of my happiness.

BEATRICE. But I can find a way to comfort you.

CLARICE. You deceive yourself; there is no one who can comfort me but Silvio.

BEATRICE. 'Tis true, I cannot give you the same comfort as your Silvio might, but I can at least contribute to your happiness.

CLARICE. I think it is quite enough, sir, that although I speak to you as harshly as I can, you should continue to torture me.

BEATRICE, *aside*. Poor girl! I can't bear to see her suffer.

CLARICE, *aside.* I'm so angry, I don't care how rude I am.

BEATRICE. Signora Clarice, I have a secret to tell you.

CLARICE. I make no promise to keep it; you had better not tell it me.

BEATRICE. Your severity deprives me of the means to make you happy.

CLARICE. You can never make me anything but miserable.

BEATRICE. You are wrong, and to convince you I will speak plainly. You have no desire for me, I have no use for you. You have promised your hand to another, I to another have already pledged my heart.

CLARICE. Oh! Now you begin to please me.

BEATRICE. Did I not tell you that I knew how to comfort you?

CLARICE. Ah, I feared you would deceive me.

BEATRICE. Nay, madam, I speak in all sincerity; and if you promise me that discretion which you refused me just now, I will confide to you a secret, which will ensure your peace of mind.

CLARICE. I vow I will observe the strictest silence.

BEATRICE. I am not Federigo Rasponi, but his sister Beatrice.

CLARICE. What! I am amazed. You a woman?

BEATRICE. I am indeed. Imagine my feelings when I claimed you as my bride!

CLARICE. And what news have you of your brother?

BEATRICE. He died indeed by the sword. A lover of mine was thought to have killed him, and 'tis he whom I am seeking now in these clothes. I beseech you by all the holy laws of friendship and of love not to betray me.

CLARICE. Won't you let me tell Silvio?

BEATRICE. No; on the contrary I forbid you absolutely.

CLARICE. Well, I will say nothing.

BEATRICE. Remember I count upon you.

CLARICE. You have my promise. I will be silent.

BEATRICE. Now, I hope, you will treat me more kindly.

CLARICE. I will be your friend indeed; and if I can be of service to you, dispose of me.

BEATRICE. I too swear eternal friendship to you. Give me your hand.

CLARICE. I don't quite like to——

BEATRICE. Are you afraid I am not a woman after all? I will give you proof positive.

CLARICE. It all seems just like a dream.

BEATRICE. Yes. 'Tis a strange business.

CLARICE. 'Tis indeed fantastic.

BEATRICE. Come, I must be going. Let us embrace in sign of honest friendship and loyalty.

CLARICE. There! I doubt you no longer.

Enter PANTALONE.

PANTALONE. Well done, well done; I congratulate you.

To CLARICE.

My child, you have been very quick in adapting yourself.

BEATRICE. Did I not tell you, Signor Pantalone, that I should win her round?

PANTALONE. Magnificent! You have done more in four minutes than I should have done in four years.

CLARICE, *aside.* Now I am in a worse tangle than ever.

PANTALONE, *to* CLARICE. Then we will have the wedding at once.

CLARICE. Pray do not be in too much haste, sir.

PANTALONE. What? Holding hands on the sly and kissing, and then in no haste about it? No, no, I don't want you to get yourself into trouble. You shall be married tomorrow.

BEATRICE. Signor Pantalone, 'twill be necessary first of all to arrange the settlement and to go into our accounts.

PANTALONE. We will do all that. These things can be done in a couple of hours.

CLARICE. Sir, I beseech you——

PANTALONE. Madam, I am going straight away to say a word to Signor Silvio.

CLARICE. For the love of Heaven do not anger him.

PANTALONE. What, what? Do you want two husbands?

CLARICE. Not exactly—but——

PANTALONE. Butt me no buts. 'Tis all settled. Your servant, sir.
  Going.

BEATRICE, *to* PANTALONE. Listen, sir——

PANTALONE. You are husband and wife.
  Going.

CLARICE. Had you not better——

PANTALONE. We will talk about it this evening.
  Exit.

CLARICE. Oh, Signora Beatrice, 'tis worse than it was before!

ACT II

SCENE 1

The Courtyard of PANTALONE'S *House*

SILVIO *and the* DOCTOR

SILVIO. Sir, I entreat you to leave me alone.

DR. LOMBARDI. Stay, answer me.

SILVIO. I am beside myself.

DR. LOMBARDI. What are you doing in the courtyard of Signor Pantalone?

SILVIO. I intend either that he should keep his word that he has given me, or that he should render me account for this intolerable insult.

DR. LOMBARDI. But you cannot do this in Pantalone's own house. You are a fool to let yourself be so transported with anger.

SILVIO. A man who behaves so abominably deserves no consideration.

DR. LOMBARDI. True; but that is no reason why you should be so rash. Leave him to me, my dear boy, leave him to me; let me talk to him; maybe I can bring him to reason and make him see where his duty lies. Go away somewhere and wait for me; leave this courtyard; do not let us make a scene. I will wait for Signor Pantalone.

SILVIO. But sir, I——

DR. LOMBARDI. But, sir, I will have you obey me.

SILVIO. I obey you, sir. I will go. Speak to him. I wait for you at the apothecary's. But if Signor Pantalone persists, he will have to settle with me.

Exit SILVIO.

DR. LOMBARDI. Poor dear boy, I feel truly sorry for him. Signor Pantalone ought never to have led him on so far before he was quite certain that man from Turin was dead. I must see him quietly; I must not let my temper get the better of me.

Enter PANTALONE.

PANTALONE, *aside*. What is the doctor doing in my house?

DR. LOMBARDI. Oh, Signor Pantalone, your servant.

PANTALONE. Your servant, Doctor. I was just going to look for you and your son.

DR. LOMBARDI. Indeed? Good! I suppose you were coming to give us your assurance that Signora Clarice is to be Silvio's wife.

PANTALONE, *much embarrassed*. Well, the fact is, I was coming to tell you——

DR. LOMBARDI. No, no; there is no need for explanations. You have my sympathy in a very awkward situation. But we are old friends and we will let bygones be bygones.

PANTALONE, *still hesitating*. Yes, of course, in view of the promise made to Signor Federigo——

DR. LOMBARDI. He took you by surprise, and you had no time for reflection; you did not think of the affront you were giving to our family.

PANTALONE. You can hardly talk of an affront, when a previous contract——

DR. LOMBARDI. I know what you are going to say. It seemed at first sight out of the question that your promise to the Turin gentleman could be repudiated, because it was a formal contract. But that was a contract merely between you and him; whereas ours is confirmed by the girl herself.

PANTALONE. Very true, but——

DR. LOMBARDI. And as you know, in matrimonial cases, *consensus, et non concubitus, facit virum.*

PANTALONE. I am no Latin scholar; but I must tell you——

DR. LOMBARDI. And girls must not be sacrificed.

PANTALONE. Have you anything more to say?

DR. LOMBARDI. I have nothing more to say.

PANTALONE. Have you finished?

DR. LOMBARDI. I have finished.

PANTALONE. May I speak?

DR. LOMBARDI. You may.

PANTALONE. My dear Doctor, with all your learning——

DR. LOMBARDI. As regards the dowry, we can easily arrange matters. A little more or a little less, I will make no difficulties.

PANTALONE. I must begin all over again. Will you allow me to speak?

DR. LOMBARDI. With pleasure.

PANTALONE. I must tell you; I have the greatest respect for your legal learning, but in this case it does not apply.

DR. LOMBARDI. And you mean to tell me that this other marriage is to take place?

PANTALONE. For my part I have given my word and I cannot go back upon it. My daughter is content; what impediment can there be? I was just coming to look for you or Signor Silvio, to tell you this. I am extremely sorry, but I see no help for it.

DR. LOMBARDI. I am not surprised at your daughter's behavior. But I am surprised at yours, sir, at your treating me in this disgraceful way. If you were not perfectly certain about the death of Signor Federigo, you had no business to enter into an engagement with my son; and having entered into an engagement with him, you are bound to maintain that engagement whatever it may cost you. The news of Federigo's death was quite sufficient to justify, even to Federigo, your new intention; he could have no right to reproach you, still less to demand compensation. The marriage which was contracted this morning between Signora Clarice and my son *coram testibus* cannot be dissolved by a mere word given by you to another party. If I were to listen to my son I should insist upon the annulment of the new contract and compel your daughter to marry him; but I should be ashamed to receive into my house so disreputable a daughter-in-law, the daughter of a man who breaks his word as you do. Signor Pantalone, you have done me an injury, you

have done an injury to the house of Lombardi. The time
will come when you will have to pay for it; yes, sir, the
time will come—*omnia tempus habent*.

Exit DOCTOR.

PANTALONE. You may go to the devil for all I care. I don't
care a fig, I'm not afraid of you. The Rasponis are worth a
hundred of the Lombardis. An only son, and as rich as he
is—you won't find that every day. It has got to be.

Enter SILVIO.

SILVIO, *aside*. 'Tis all very fine for my father to talk. Let him
keep his temper who can.

PANTALONE, *seeing* SILVIO, *aside*. Here comes the other.

SILVIO, *rudely*. Your servant, sir.

PANTALONE. Yours to command, sir.

Aside.

He is boiling.

SILVIO. I have just heard something from my father; am I to
believe that it is true?

PANTALONE. If your father said it, it must certainly be true.

SILVIO. Then the marriage is settled between Signora Clarice
and Signor Federigo?

PANTALONE. Yes, sir, settled and concluded.

SILVIO. I am amazed that you should have the face to tell me
so. You are a man of no reputation, you are no gentleman.

PANTALONE. What is all this? Is that the way you speak to a
man of my age?

SILVIO. I don't care how old you are; I have a mind to run
you straight through the body.

PANTALONE. I am not a frog, sir, to be spitted. Do you come
into my own house to make all this turmoil?

SILVIO. Come outside then.

PANTALONE. I am surprised at you, sir.

SILVIO. Come on, if you are a man of honor.

PANTALONE. I am accustomed to be treated with respect.

SILVIO. You are a low fellow, a coward, and a villain.

PANTALONE. You are a most impertinent young puppy.

SILVIO. I swear to Heaven——

Lays his hand to his sword.

PANTALONE. Help! Murder!

Draws a pistol.

Enter BEATRICE *with a drawn sword.*

BEATRICE. I am here to defend you.

To PANTALONE.

PANTALONE. My dear son-in-law, I am much obliged to you.

SILVIO, *to* BEATRICE. You are the very man I want to fight.

BEATRICE, *aside.* I am in for it now.

SILVIO, *to* BEATRICE. Come on, sir.

PANTALONE, *frightened.* My dear son-in-law——

BEATRICE. It is not the first time that I have been in danger.

To SILVIO.

I am not afraid of you.

Presents sword.

PANTALONE. Help! Help!

PANTALONE *runs toward the street.* BEATRICE *and* SILVIO *fight.* SILVIO *falls and drops his sword.* BEATRICE *holds her point to his heart.*

Enter CLARICE.

CLARICE, *to* BEATRICE. Stop, stop!

BEATRICE. Fair Clarice, at your request I grant Silvio his life, and in consideration of my mercy, I beg you to remember your oath.

Exit BEATRICE.

CLARICE. Dear Silvio, are you hurt?

SILVIO. Dear Silvio! Faithless deceiver! Dear Silvio! To a lover disdained, to a betrayed husband!

CLARICE. No, Silvio, I do not deserve your reproaches. I love you, I adore you, I am indeed faithful.

SILVIO. Oh, lying jade! Faithful to me, forsooth! You call that fidelity, to plight your troth to another?

CLARICE. I never did so, nor will I ever. I will die rather than desert you.

SILVIO. I heard just now that you have given your oath.

CLARICE. My oath does not bind me to marry him.

SILVIO. Then what did you swear?

CLARICE. Dear Silvio, have mercy on me; I cannot tell you.

SILVIO. Why not?

CLARICE. Because I am sworn to silence.

SILVIO. That proves your guilt.

CLARICE. No, I am innocent.

SILVIO. Innocent people have no secrets.

CLARICE. Indeed I should be guilty if I spoke.

SILVIO. And to whom have you sworn this silence?

CLARICE. To Federigo.

SILVIO. And you will observe it so jealously?

CLARICE. I will observe it, rather than be a perjuress.

SILVIO. And you tell me you do not love him? He's a fool that believes you. I do not believe you, cruel, deceiver! Begone from my sight!

CLARICE. If I did not love you, I should not have run hither in all haste to save your life.

SILVIO. Then I loathe my life, if I must owe it to one so ungrateful.

CLARICE. I love you with all my heart.

SILVIO. I abhor you with all my soul.

CLARICE. I will die, if you are not to be appeased.

SILVIO. I would sooner see you dead than unfaithful.

CLARICE. Then you shall have that satisfaction.

Picks up his sword.

SILVIO. Yes, that sword should avenge my wrongs.

CLARICE. Are you so cruel to your Clarice?

SILVIO. 'Twas you that taught me cruelty.

CLARICE. Then you desire my death?

SILVIO. I know not what I desire.

CLARICE. I do.

Points the sword at her breast.

Enter SMERALDINA.

SMERALDINA. Stop, stop! What on earth are you doing?

Takes the sword away from CLARICE.

And you, you dog, you would have let her die?

To SILVIO.

Have you the heart of a tiger, of a hyena, of a devil? Look at you, you're a pretty little fellow, that expects ladies to disembowel themselves for you! You are much too kind to him, madam. He doesn't want you any more, I suppose? The man that doesn't want you doesn't deserve you. Let this murderer go to the devil; and you come along with me. There's no shortage of men; I'll promise to find you a dozen before evening.

She throws down the sword, SILVIO *picks it up.*

CLARICE, *weeping.* Ungrateful! Can it be that my death should cost you not a single sigh? But I *shall* die, and die of grief. I shall die, and you will be content. But one day you will know that I am innocent, and then, when it is too late, you will be sorry you did not believe me, you will weep for my misfortune and for your own barbarous cruelty.

Exit CLARICE.

SMERALDINA. Here's something I really don't understand. Here's a girl on the point of killing herself, and you sit there looking on, just as if you were at a play.

SILVIO. Nonsense, woman! Do you suppose she really meant to kill herself?

SMERALDINA. How should I know? I know that if I had not arrived in time, she would have been gone, poor thing.

SILVIO. The point was nowhere near her heart.

SMERALDINA. Did you ever hear such a lie? It was just ready to pierce her.

SILVIO. You women always invent things.

SMERALDINA. We should indeed, if we were like you. It's as the old saw says; we get the kicks and you the halfpence. They say women are unfaithful, but men are committing infidelities all day long. People talk about the women, and they never say a word about the men. We get all the blame, and you are allowed to do as you please. Do you know why? Because 'tis the men who have made the laws. If the women had made them, things would be just the other way.

If I were a queen, I'd make every man who was unfaithful carry a branch of a tree in his hand, and I know all the towns would look like forests.

Exit SMERALDINA.

SILVIO. Clarice faithless! Clarice a traitress! Her pretense at suicide was a trick to deceive me, to move my compassion. But though fate made me fall before my rival, I will never give up the thought of revenge. That wretch shall die, and my ungrateful Clarice shall see her lover wallowing in his own gore.

Exit SILVIO.

SCENE 2

A Room in BRIGHELLA'S *Inn, with a door at each side and two doors at the back, facing the audience.*

TRUFFALDINO *solus*

TRUFFALDINO. Just my luck! Two masters and neither of them comes home to dinner. 'Tis two o'clock, and not one to be seen. Sure enough they will both come at the same time, and I shall be in a mess; I shall not be able to wait on both together, and the whole thing will be found out. Hush, here comes one. All the better.

Enter FLORINDO.

FLORINDO. Well, did you find that fellow Pasquale?

TRUFFALDINO. Didn't we say, sir, that I was to look for him after dinner?

FLORINDO. I am impatient to see him.

TRUFFALDINO. You should have come back to dinner a little sooner.

FLORINDO, *aside*. I can find no way of making certain whether Beatrice is here.

TRUFFALDINO. You told me to go and order dinner, and then you go out. The dinner will have been spoiled.

FLORINDO. I don't want to eat anything.

Aside.

I shall go to the Post; I must go myself; then perhaps I shall find out something.

TRUFFALDINO. You know, sir, at Venice you must eat; if you do not, you will fall sick.

FLORINDO. I must go out; I have important business. If I come back to dinner, well and good; if not, I shall eat in the evening. You can get yourself some food, if you like.

TRUFFALDINO. Very good, sir; just as you please, sir; you're the master.

FLORINDO. This money is heavy; here, put it in my trunk. There is the key.

Gives TRUFFALDINO *the purse and his keys.*

TRUFFALDINO. Certainly, sir; I'll bring the key back at once.

FLORINDO. No, no, you can give it me later. I can't stop. If I do not come back to dinner come to the Piazza; I can't rest till you have found Pasquale.

Exit FLORINDO.

TRUFFALDINO. Well, anyway, he said I could get myself some food; we are agreed about that. If he won't eat his dinner, he can leave it. My complexion was not made for fasting. I'll just put away this purse, and then——

Enter BEATRICE.

BEATRICE. Oh, Truffaldino!

TRUFFALDINO, *aside.* The devil!

BEATRICE. Did Signor Pantalone dei Bisognosi give you a purse of a hundred guineas?

TRUFFALDINO. Yes, indeed he did.

BEATRICE. Then why did you not give it to me?

TRUFFALDINO. Was it meant for your honor?

BEATRICE. Was it meant for me? What did he say when he gave you the purse?

TRUFFALDINO. He told me I was to give it to my master.

BEATRICE. Well, and who is your master?

TRUFFALDINO. Your honor.

BEATRICE. Then why do you ask if the purse is mine?

TRUFFALDINO. Then it will be yours.

BEATRICE. Where is it?

TRUFFALDINO. Here, sir.

Gives BEATRICE *the purse.*

BEATRICE. Is the money all there?

TRUFFALDINO. I never touched it, sir.

BEATRICE, *aside.* I shall count it.

TRUFFALDINO, *aside.* I made a mistake over the purse; but that puts it straight. I wonder what the other gentleman will say? Oh well, if the money wasn't his, he'll say nothing at all.

BEATRICE. Is the landlord in?

TRUFFALDINO. Yes, sir.

BEATRICE. Tell him I shall have a friend to dinner with me, and he must get it ready as soon as ever he can.

TRUFFALDINO. What do you want for dinner, sir? How many dishes?

BEATRICE. Oh, Signor Pantalone dei Bisognosi is not a man who expects a great deal. Tell him to give us five or six dishes; something good.

TRUFFALDINO. You leave it all to me, sir?

BEATRICE. Yes, you order it, do the best you can. I am going to fetch the gentleman, he is not far off; see that all is ready by the time we come back.

Going.

TRUFFALDINO. You shall see how they serve you here.

BEATRICE. Look! Take this paper; put it in my trunk. Be careful with it; 'tis a bill of exchange for four thousand crowns.

TRUFFALDINO. Be sure of it, sir, I'll put it away at once.

BEATRICE. See that everything is ready.

Aside.

Poor old Signor Pantalone—I gave him a terrible fright! I must cheer him up a little.

Exit BEATRICE.

TRUFFALDINO. Now's the time to do myself proud. 'Tis the first time this master of mine has told me to order him a dinner. I'll show him I am a man of good taste. I'll just put away this paper and then—no, I'll put it away afterward, I must not waste time. Ho there! Is nobody at home?

Calling into the inn.

Call Master Brighella, tell him I want to talk to him.

Returning.

Now with a really good dinner 'tis not the having such and such dishes, but the way it is served. A properly laid table is worth more than a mountain of dishes.

Enter BRIGHELLA.

BRIGHELLA. What is it, Si'or Truffaldin'? What can I do for you?

TRUFFALDINO. My master has got a gentleman to dine with him. He wants a good dinner, and that quickly. Have you got enough in the kitchen?

BRIGHELLA. I always have plenty of everything. In half an hour I can put on any sort of dinner you like.

TRUFFALDINO. Very well, then. Tell me what you can give us.

BRIGHELLA. For two persons, we will have two courses of four dishes each; will that do?

TRUFFALDINO. He said five or six dishes—better say six or eight. That will do. What will you give us?

BRIGHELLA. For the first course, I shall give you soup, fried, boiled, and a fricandeau.

TRUFFALDINO. Three of the dishes I know, but I do not know the last.

BRIGHELLA. 'Tis a French dish—a ragout—very tasty indeed.

TRUFFALDINO. Very well, that will do for the first course; now the second.

BRIGHELLA. For the second course the roast, the salad, a meat pie—and a trifle.

TRUFFALDINO, *indignant.* What's that? A trifle? My master and his guest are gentlemen of substance; they won't be satisfied with a mere trifle. A trifle indeed!

BRIGHELLA. You don't understand. I said

Impressively.

a trifle! That's an English dish, a pudding, my very own speciality; there's not another man in Venice knows how to make it!

TRUFFALDINO, *nonchalantly*. Oh well, I dare say it will do. But how are you going to arrange the table?

BRIGHELLA. Oh, that's easy enough. The waiter will see to that.

TRUFFALDINO. No, my good friend, laying the table is a very important matter; that's the first thing about a dinner, to have the table properly laid.

BRIGHELLA. Well, you might put the soup here, the fried there, there the boiled and here the fricandeau.

Makes an imaginary arrangement.

TRUFFALDINO. I don't like that. Don't you put something in the middle?

BRIGHELLA. Then we should want five dishes.

TRUFFALDINO. Good, then let us have five.

BRIGHELLA. We can put the gravy in the middle.

TRUFFALDINO. No, no, friend, you know nothing about laying a table; you can't put the gravy in the middle; soup always goes in the middle.

BRIGHELLA. Then the meat on one side, and the gravy on the other.

TRUFFALDINO. Lord, lord, that won't do at all. You innkeepers may know how to cook, but you have no idea of butlering. Now I'll show you.

Kneels down on one knee and points to the floor.

Suppose this is the table. Now you look how we arrange the five dishes. Like this: here in the middle the soup.

He tears off a piece of the bill of exchange and puts it on the floor to represent a dish.

Now the boiled meat.

Same business.

Here we put the fried opposite,

Same business.

here the gravy and here that—what-d'ye-call-it. There now! Won't that look fine?

BRIGHELLA. H'm, 'twill do; but you have put the gravy too far away from the meat.

TRUFFALDINO. Very well, we must see if we can't put it a little nearer.

Enter BEATRICE *and* PANTALONE.

BEATRICE. What are you doing on your knees?

TRUFFALDINO, *stands up.* I was just planning how to have the table laid.

BEATRICE. What is that paper?

TRUFFALDINO, *aside.* The devil! The letter that he gave me!

BEATRICE. That is my bill of exchange.

TRUFFALDINO. I am very sorry, sir; I will stick it together again.

BEATRICE. You rascal! Is that the way you look after my things? Things of such value too! You deserve a good thrashing. What say you, Signor Pantalone? Did you ever see such a piece of folly?

PANTALONE. To tell the truth, I cannot help laughing. 'Twould be a serious matter if it could not be mended, but I will write you out another and then all will be in order.

BEATRICE. But just think if the bill had been made out not here but in some place a long way off!

To TRUFFALDINO.

You ignorant fool!

TRUFFALDINO. This has all come about because Brighella doesn't know how to lay a table.

BRIGHELLA. He finds fault with everything I do.

TRUFFALDINO. I am a man that knows his business.

BEATRICE, *to* TRUFFALDINO. Go away.

TRUFFALDINO. Things must be done properly.

BEATRICE. Be off, I tell you.

TRUFFALDINO. In the matter of pantry work I won't give way to the first butler in the land.

Exit TRUFFALDINO.

BRIGHELLA. I don't understand that fellow; sometimes he is a knave and sometimes a fool.

BEATRICE. This tomfoolery is all put on. Well, is dinner ready?

BRIGHELLA. If you will have five dishes to each course, 'twill take a little time.

PANTALONE. What's this about courses of five dishes? We'll take pot luck—a risotto, a couple of other dishes, and I shall be most obliged to you. My tastes are simple.

BEATRICE, *to* BRIGHELLA. You hear that? That will do nicely.

BRIGHELLA. Very good, sir; but will you please to tell me if there might be anything you would particularly fancy?

PANTALONE. I should like some rissoles if you have them; my teeth are not very good nowadays.

BEATRICE. You hear? Rissoles.

BRIGHELLA. Very good, sir. If you will sit down here for a moment, gentlemen, dinner will be ready directly.

BEATRICE. Tell Truffaldino to come and wait on us.

BRIGHELLA. I'll tell him, sir.

Exit BRIGHELLA.

BEATRICE. Signor Pantalone, I fear you will indeed have to be content with pot luck.

PANTALONE. My dear sir, I am overcome with all the attention you show me; in fact you are doing for me what I ought to be doing for you. But, you see, I have that girl of mine at home, and until everything is finally settled it would not be proper for you to be together. So I accept your kind hospitality to raise my spirits a little; indeed I still feel quite upset. Had it not been for you, that young scoundrel would have done for me.

BEATRICE. I am glad that I arrived in time.

WAITERS *enter from the kitchen and carry glasses, wine, bread, etc., into the room where* BEATRICE *and* PANTALONE *are to dine.*

PANTALONE. They are very quick about their business here.

BEATRICE. Brighella is a smart fellow. He was servant to a great nobleman at Turin, and still wears his livery.

PANTALONE. There's a very good tavern on the other side of the Grand Canal opposite the Rialto where you can eat very well; I have often been there with various good friends of mine, very sound men, too; I often think of that place. They had some wonderful Burgundy wine there too—'twas a wine for the gods.

BEATRICE. There's nothing one enjoys more than good wine in good company.

PANTALONE. Good company! Ah, if you had known them! That was good company! Good honest fellows, with many a good story to tell. God bless them. Seven or eight of them there were, and there wasn't the like of them in all the world.

The WAITERS *come out of the room and return to the kitchen.*

BEATRICE. You often had a merry time with these gentlemen, eh?

PANTALONE. And I hope I may live to have many more.

Enter TRUFFALDINO *carrying the soup tureen.*

TRUFFALDINO, *to* BEATRICE. Dinner is ready for you in that room, sir.

BEATRICE. Go and put the soup on the table.

TRUFFALDINO, *makes a bow.* After you, sir.

PANTALONE. A queer fellow, that servant of yours.

Goes in.

BEATRICE, *to* TRUFFALDINO. I want less wit and more attention.

Goes in.

TRUFFALDINO. Call that a dinner! One dish at a time! They have money to spend, but they get nothing good for it. I wonder if this soup is worth eating; I'll try it.

Takes a spoon out of his pocket and tastes the soup.

I always carry my weapons about me. Not bad; it might be worse.

Goes into room with soup.

Enter FIRST WAITER *with a dish.*

FIRST WAITER. When is that man coming to take the dishes?

TRUFFALDINO, *re-entering.* Here I am, friend. What have you got for me?

FIRST WAITER. Here's the boiled meat. There's another dish to follow.

Exit FIRST WAITER.

TRUFFALDINO. Mutton? Or veal? Mutton, I think. Let's taste it.

Tastes.

No, 'tis neither mutton nor veal; 'tis lamb, and very good, too.

Goes toward BEATRICE'S *room.*

Enter FLORINDO.

FLORINDO. Where are you going?

TRUFFALDINO, *aside.* Oh dear, oh dear!

FLORINDO. What are you doing with that dish?

TRUFFALDINO. I was just putting it on the table, sir.

FLORINDO. For whom?

TRUFFALDINO. For you, sir.

FLORINDO. Why do you serve dinner before I come in?

TRUFFALDINO. I saw you from the window.

Aside.

I must find some excuse.

FLORINDO. And you begin with boiled meat instead of soup?

TRUFFALDINO. You must know, sir, at Venice soup is always taken last.

FLORINDO. I have other habits. I want my soup. Take that back to the kitchen.

TRUFFALDINO. Yes, sir, as you wish, sir.

FLORINDO. Make haste; afterward I want to have a nap.

TRUFFALDINO. Yes, sir.

Makes as if going to the kitchen.

FLORINDO, *aside.* Shall I never find Beatrice again?

FLORINDO *goes into the other room. As soon as he is in,* TRUFFALDINO *quickly takes the dish in to* BEATRICE. *Enter* FIRST WAITER *with another dish.* FLORINDO *calls from his room.*

FLORINDO. Truffaldino! Truffaldino! Am I always to be kept waiting?

TRUFFALDINO, *coming out of* BEATRICE'S *room.* Coming, sir.

To FIRST WAITER.

Quick, go and lay the table in that other room, the other gentleman has arrived; bring the soup at once.

FIRST WAITER. Directly.

Exit FIRST WAITER.

TRUFFALDINO. What may this dish be? This must be the "fricandeau."

Tastes it.

That's good, upon my word.

Takes it in to BEATRICE.

WAITERS *enter and carry glasses, wine, bread, etc., into* FLORINDO'S *room.*

TRUFFALDINO, *to* WAITERS. Good lads, that's right.

Aside.

They're as lively as kittens. Well, if I can manage to wait at table on two masters at once, 'twill be a great accomplishment indeed.

The WAITERS *come back out of* FLORINDO'S *room and go toward the kitchen.*

TRUFFALDINO. Hurry up, lads, the soup!

FIRST WAITER. You look after your own table; we'll take care of this one.

Exeunt WAITERS.

TRUFFALDINO. I want to look after both, if I can.

Re-enter FIRST WAITER *with* FLORINDO'S *soup.*

TRUFFALDINO. Here, give me that; I'll take it. Go and get the stuff for the other room.

Takes soup from FIRST WAITER *and carries it into* FLORINDO'S *room.*

FIRST WAITER. That's a strange fellow. He wants to wait on everyone. Let him. They will have to give me *my* tip all the same.

TRUFFALDINO *comes out of* FLORINDO'S *room.*

BEATRICE, *calling from her room.* Truffaldino!

FIRST WAITER, *to* TRUFFALDINO. Your master's calling.

TRUFFALDINO. Coming, sir.

Goes into BEATRICE's *room.*

SECOND WAITER *brings the boiled meat for* FLORINDO. TRUF-FALDINO *brings the dirty plates out of* BEATRICE's *room.*

TRUFFALDINO. Here, give it to me.

Exit SECOND WAITER.

FLORINDO, *calls.* Truffaldino!

TRUFFALDINO, *wishes to take the meat from* WAITER. Give it to me.

FIRST WAITER. No, I'm taking this.

TRUFFALDINO. Didn't you hear him call for me?

Takes meat from him and carries it in to FLORINDO.

FIRST WAITER. Well, that's fine! He wants to do everything.

SECOND WAITER *brings in a dish of rissoles, gives it to the* FIRST WAITER *and exit.*

I would take this in myself, but I don't want to have words with that fellow.

Re-enter TRUFFALDINO *from* FLORINDO's *room with dirty plates.*

Here, master Jack-of-all-trades; take these rissoles to your master.

TRUFFALDINO, *takes dish.* Rissoles?

FIRST WAITER. Yes, the rissoles he ordered.

Exit FIRST WAITER.

TRUFFALDINO. Oh, fine! Now which table are these to go to? I wonder which the devil of my two masters can have ordered them? If I go to the kitchen and ask, they'll begin to suspect; if I make a mistake and carry them to the one who didn't order them, then the other will ask for them and I shall be found out. I know what I'll do; I'll divide them on two plates, take half to each, and then I shall see who ordered them.

Takes plates and divides the rissoles.

That's four and that's four. There's one over. Who's to have that? We mustn't cause ill-feeling; I'll eat that one myself.

Eats it.

Now. We'll take the rissoles to this gentleman.

TRUFFALDINO *puts one plate of rissoles on the floor and takes the other in to* BEATRICE. FIRST WAITER *enters with an English pudding (trifle).*

FIRST WAITER. Truffaldino!

TRUFFALDINO, *comes out of* BEATRICE's *room.* Coming!

FIRST WAITER. Take this pudding——

TRUFFALDINO. Wait a moment, I'm coming.

Takes the other dish of rissoles and is going to FLORINDO's *room.*

FIRST WAITER. That's not right, the rissoles belong there.

TRUFFALDINO. I know they do, sir; I have carried them there; and my master sends these four as a courtesy to this gentleman.

Goes into FLORINDO's *room.*

FIRST WAITER. I see, they know each other—friends, you might say? They might as well have dined together.

TRUFFALDINO, *re-entering.* What's this affair?

FIRST WAITER. That's an English pudding.

TRUFFALDINO. Who is it for?

FIRST WAITER. For your master.

Exit FIRST WAITER.

TRUFFALDINO. What the devil is this "pudding"? It smells delicious, and looks like polenta. Oh! If it is polenta, that would be good indeed. I'll taste it.

Brings a fork out of his pocket and tries the pudding.

It's not polenta, but it's very much like it.

Eats.

Much better than polenta.

Goes on eating.

BEATRICE, *calling.* Truffaldino!

TRUFFALDINO, *with mouth full.* Coming, sir.

FLORINDO, *calling.* Truffaldino!

TRUFFALDINO, *with mouth full.* Coming, sir.

To himself.

Oh what wonderful stuff! Just another mouthful and then I'll go.

Goes on eating.

BEATRICE *comes out of her room, sees* TRUFFALDINO *eating, kicks him, and says:*

BEATRICE. You come and wait on me.

She goes back to her room.

Truffaldino!

TRUFFALDINO. Coming!

TRUFFALDINO *puts the pudding on the floor and goes into* BEATRICE'S *room.* FLORINDO *comes out of his.*

FLORINDO, *calling.* Truffaldino! Where the devil is he?

TRUFFALDINO *comes out of* BEATRICE'S *room.*

TRUFFALDINO. Here, sir.

Seeing FLORINDO.

FLORINDO. What are you doing? Where have you been?

TRUFFALDINO. I just went to fetch the next course, sir.

FLORINDO. Is there anything more to eat?

TRUFFALDINO. I'll go and see.

FLORINDO. Make haste, I tell you, because I want to have a nap afterward.

Goes back into his room.

TRUFFALDINO. Very good, sir.

Calling.

Waiter, is there anything more to come?

Aside.

I'll put this pudding aside for myself.

Hides it.

Enter FIRST WAITER *with dish.*

FIRST WAITER. Here's the roast.

TRUFFALDINO, *takes the roast.* Quick, the dessert!

FIRST WAITER. Lord, what a fluster! In a minute.

Exit FIRST WAITER.

TRUFFALDINO. I'll take the roast to this gentleman.

Takes it to FLORINDO.

Re-enter FIRST WAITER.

FIRST WAITER, *with plate of fruit.* Here's the dessert; where are you?

TRUFFALDINO, *re-entering from* FLORINDO's *room.* Here.

FIRST WAITER, *gives him the fruit.* There. Anything more?

TRUFFALDINO. Wait.

Takes the dessert to BEATRICE.

FIRST WAITER. He jumps about here and there like the devil himself.

TRUFFALDINO, *re-entering.* That will do. Nobody wants any more.

FIRST WAITER. I'm glad to hear it.

TRUFFALDINO. And now lay the table for *me.*

FIRST WAITER. In a moment.

Exit FIRST WAITER.

TRUFFALDINO. Now for my pudding! Hurrah! I've got through it all, they are all content, they want nothing more, they've had a very good dinner. I have waited at table on two masters at once, and neither of 'em knew anything about the other. But if I have waited for two, now I am going to eat for four.

SCENE 3

A Street with BRIGHELLA's *Inn*

Enter SMERALDINA.

SMERALDINA. A very proper sort of young lady my mistress is! To send me all alone with a letter to a tavern, a young girl like me! Waiting on a woman in love is a sad business. This young lady of mine does a thousand crazy things, and what I cannot understand is this—if she is so much in love with Signor Silvio as to be ready to disembowel herself for him, why does she send letters to another gentleman? One for summer and one for winter, I suppose! Well, there it is!

I am not going inside that tavern. I'll call; somebody will come out. Hey there! Anyone at home?

FIRST WAITER *comes out of the inn.*

FIRST WAITER. Now, young woman, what do you want?

SMERALDINA, *aside.* I feel thoroughly ashamed.

To WAITER.

Tell me—a certain Signor Federigo Rasponi lodges here, does he not?

FIRST WAITER. Yes, indeed. He has just this moment finished dinner.

SMERALDINA. I have something to say to him.

FIRST WAITER. A message? You can come inside.

SMERALDINA. And what sort of a girl do you take me for? I am the waiting maid of the lady he is to marry.

FIRST WAITER, *more politely.* Well then, pray step this way.

SMERALDINA. Oh, but I don't like to go in there.

FIRST WAITER. Do you expect me to bring him out into the street for you? That would not be at all the right thing; more especially as he has Signor Pantalone dei Bisognosi with him.

SMERALDINA. What, my master? Worse and worse! I'll not come in.

FIRST WAITER. I can send his servant, if you like.

SMERALDINA. The little dark man?

FIRST WAITER. Exactly so.

SMERALDINA. Yes, do send him.

FIRST WAITER, *aside.* I understand. She fancies the little dark man, and is ashamed to come inside. She is not ashamed to be seen with him in the middle of the street.

Goes in.

SMERALDINA. If the master sees me, whatever shall I say? I'll tell him I came to look for *him;* that will do nicely. I'm never short of an answer.

Enter TRUFFALDINO *with a bottle in his hand, a glass and a napkin.*

TRUFFALDINO. Who sent for me?

SMERALDINA. I did, sir. I ask pardon if I have troubled you.

TRUFFALDINO. Not a bit of it. I am here to receive your commands.

SMERALDINA. I fear I must have taken you from your dinner.

TRUFFALDINO. I was having dinner, but I can go back to it.

SMERALDINA. I am truly sorry.

TRUFFALDINO. I am delighted. The fact is, I have had my bellyful, and your bright eyes are just the right thing to make me digest it.

SMERALDINA, *aside.* Very gallant!

TRUFFALDINO. I'll just set down this bottle, and then I'm with you, my dear.

SMERALDINA, *aside.* He called me "my dear"!

To TRUFFALDINO.

My mistress sends this letter to Signor Federigo Rasponi; I do not like to come into the tavern, so I thought I might put you to this trouble, as you are his man.

TRUFFALDINO. I'll take it with pleasure; but first, you must know that I have a message for *you*.

SMERALDINA. From whom?

TRUFFALDINO. From a very honest man. Tell me, are you acquainted with one Truffaldin' Battocchio?

SMERALDINA. I think I have heard him spoken of, but I am not sure.

Aside.

It must be himself.

TRUFFALDINO. He's a good-looking man; short, thickset, with plenty of wit to his talk. Understands butlering too——

SMERALDINA. I don't know him from Adam.

TRUFFALDINO. Yes, you do; and what's more, he's in love with you.

SMERALDINA. Oh! You are making fun of me.

TRUFFALDINO. And if he could only have just a little hope that his affections were returned, he would make himself known.

SMERALDINA. Well, sir, if I were to see him, and he took my

fancy, it might possibly be that I should return his affection.

TRUFFALDINO. Shall I show him to you?

SMERALDINA. I should like to see him.

TRUFFALDINO. Just a moment.

Goes into the inn.

SMERALDINA. Then 'tis not he.

TRUFFALDINO *comes out of the inn, makes low bows to* SMERALDINA, *passes close to her, sighs, and goes back into the inn.*

SMERALDINA. I do not understand this play-acting.

TRUFFALDINO, *re-entering.* Did you see him?

SMERALDINA. See whom?

TRUFFALDINO. The man who is in love with your beauty.

SMERALDINA. I saw no one but you.

TRUFFALDINO, *sighs.* Well!

SMERALDINA. It is you, then, who profess to be in love with me?

TRUFFALDINO. It is.

Sighs.

SMERALDINA. Why did you not say so before?

TRUFFALDINO. Because I am rather shy.

SMERALDINA, *aside.* He would make a stone fall in love with him.

TRUFFALDINO. Well, and what do you say?

SMERALDINA. I say——

TRUFFALDINO. Come, tell me.

SMERALDINA. Oh—I am rather shy too.

TRUFFALDINO. Then if we were joined up, 'twould be a marriage of two people who are rather shy.

SMERALDINA. I must say, you are just my fancy.

TRUFFALDINO. Are you a maid?

SMERALDINA. Need you ask?

TRUFFALDINO. I suppose that means "certainly not."

SMERALDINA. On the contrary, it means "certainly I am."

TRUFFALDINO. I am a bachelor too.

SMERALDINA. I could have been married fifty times, but I never found the man I really fancied.

TRUFFALDINO. Do you think there is any hope for me?

SMERALDINA. Well—to tell the truth—really—I must say— there's a—something about you—— No, I won't say another word.

TRUFFALDINO. If somebody wanted to marry you, what would he have to do?

SMERALDINA. I have neither father nor mother. He would have to speak to my master, or to my mistress.

TRUFFALDINO. And if I speak to them, what will they say?

SMERALDINA. They will say, that if I am content——

TRUFFALDINO. And what will you say?

SMERALDINA. I shall say—that if they are content too——

TRUFFALDINO. That will do. We shall all be content. Give me the letter and when I bring you back the answer, we will have a talk.

SMERALDINA. Here's the letter.

TRUFFALDINO. Do you know what is in it?

SMERALDINA. No—if you only knew how curious I am to know!

TRUFFALDINO. I hope it is not a disdainful letter, or I shall get my face spoiled.

SMERALDINA. Who knows? It can't be a love letter.

TRUFFALDINO. I don't want to get into trouble. If I don't know what is in the letter, I am not going to take it.

SMERALDINA. We could open it—but how are we to seal it again?

TRUFFALDINO. Leave it to me; sealing letters is just my job. No one will ever know anything.

SMERALDINA. Then let us open it.

TRUFFALDINO. Can you read?

SMERALDINA. A little. But you can read quite well, I'm sure.

TRUFFALDINO. Yes, I too can read just a little.

SMERALDINA. Then let us hear.

TRUFFALDINO. We must open it cleanly.

Tears off a piece.

SMERALDINA. Oh! What have you done?

TRUFFALDINO. Nothing. I've a secret way to mend it. Here it is, open.

SMERALDINA. Quick, read it.

TRUFFALDINO. *You* read it. You will know your young lady's handwriting better than I do.

SMERALDINA, *looking at the letter*. Really, I can't make out a word.

TRUFFALDINO, *same business*. Nor I neither.

SMERALDINA. Then what was the good of opening it?

TRUFFALDINO, *takes the letter*. Wait; let me think; I can make out some of it.

SMERALDINA. Oh I know some of the letters too.

TRUFFALDINO. Let us try one by one. Isn't that an M?

SMERALDINA. No! That's an R!

TRUFFALDINO. Between R and M there is very little difference.

SMERALDINA. *Ri, ri, o.* No, no; keep quiet; I think it *is* an M— *Mi, mi, o—mio!*

TRUFFALDINO. It's not *mio*, it's *mia*.

SMERALDINA. But it is, there's the hook——

TRUFFALDINO. That proves it is *mia*.

BEATRICE *comes out of the inn with* PANTALONE.

PANTALONE, *to* SMERALDINA. What are you doing here?

SMERALDINA, *frightened*. Nothing, sir; I came to look for *you*.

PANTALONE, *to* SMERALDINA. What do you want with me?

SMERALDINA. The mistress wants you, sir.

BEATRICE, *to* TRUFFALDINO. What is this paper?

TRUFFALDINO, *frightened*. Nothing, just a bit of paper——

BEATRICE. Let me see.

TRUFFALDINO, *gives paper, trembling*. Yes, sir.

BEATRICE. What? This is a letter addressed to me. Villain, will you open all my letters?

TRUFFALDINO. I know nothing about it, sir——

BEATRICE. Look, Signor Pantalone, here is a letter from Si-

gnora Clarice, in which she tells me of Silvio's insane jealousy—and this rascal has the impudence to open it!

PANTALONE, *to* SMERALDINA. And you helped him to do so?

SMERALDINA. I know nothing about it, sir.

BEATRICE. Who opened this letter?

TRUFFALDINO. Not I.

SMERALDINA. Nor I.

PANTALONE. Well, who brought it?

SMERALDINA. Truffaldino brought it to his master.

TRUFFALDINO. And Smeraldina brought it to Truffaldino.

SMERALDINA, *aside.* Sneak! I don't like you any more.

PANTALONE. You meddlesome little hussy, so you are the
cause of all this trouble, are you? I've a good mind to smack
your face.

SMERALDINA. I've never had my face smacked by any man;
I'm surprised at you.

PANTALONE, *coming near her.* Is that the way you answer me?

SMERALDINA. You won't catch me. You're too rheumatic, you
can't run.

Exit running.

PANTALONE. You saucy minx, I'll show you if I can run; I'll
catch you.

Runs after her.

TRUFFALDINO, *aside.* If I only knew how to get out of this!

BEATRICE, *looking at the letter, aside.* Poor Clarice! She is in
despair over Silvio's jealousy; 'twill be best for me to discover myself and set her mind at rest.

TRUFFALDINO, *tries to steal away quietly.* I don't think he is
looking. I'll try to get away.

BEATRICE. Where are you off to?

TRUFFALDINO. Nowhere.

Stops.

BEATRICE. Why did you open this letter?

TRUFFALDINO. It was Smeraldina; I had nothing to do with it.

BEATRICE. Smeraldina, forsooth! You did it, you rascal. One

and one make two. That's the second letter of mine you have opened today. Come here.

TRUFFALDINO, *approaching timidly*. Oh, for mercy's sake, sir——

BEATRICE. Come here, I say.

TRUFFALDINO, *same business*. Oh, for the love of Heaven——

BEATRICE *takes the stick which* TRUFFALDINO *has at his flank (i.e., Harlequin's wooden sword or baton) and beats him well, she standing with her back to the inn.* FLORINDO *appears at the window and sees the beating.*

FLORINDO. What's this? Beating my servant?

Leaves window.

TRUFFALDINO. Stop, stop, sir, for pity's sake.

BEATRICE. Take that, rascal, and learn to open my letters.

Throws stick on the ground, and exit to street.

TRUFFALDINO, *after* BEATRICE *has gone*. My blood! My body! Is that the way to treat a man of my sort? Beat a man like me? If a servant is no good, you can send him away, but you don't beat him.

FLORINDO *comes out, unseen by* TRUFFALDINO.

FLORINDO. What's that?

TRUFFALDINO, *seeing* FLORINDO. Oh! I said people had no business to beat other people's servants like that. This is an insult to my master.

Looking toward direction of BEATRICE's *exit*.

FLORINDO. Yes, 'tis an affront put upon *me*. Who was it gave you a thrashing?

TRUFFALDINO. I couldn't say, sir; I do not know him.

FLORINDO. Why did he thrash you?

TRUFFALDINO. Because I—I spat on his shoe.

FLORINDO. And you let yourself be beaten like that? Did nothing? Made no attempt to defend yourself? And you expose your master to insult, with perhaps serious consequences? Ass! Poltroon!

Picks up the stick.

Since you enjoy being thrashed, I'll give you your pleasure, I'll thrash you myself as well.

Thrashes him and exit into inn.

TRUFFALDINO. Well, there's no mistake about my being the servant of two masters. They have both paid me my wages.

Exit into the inn.

ACT III

SCENE 1

A *Room in* BRIGHELLA's *Inn*

TRUFFALDINO *solus*

TRUFFALDINO. I don't care that for my beating! I have eaten well, I've dined well, and this evening I shall sup still better; and as long as I can serve two masters, there's this at least, that I draw double wages.

And now what's to be done? Master number one is out of doors, master number two is fast asleep; why, it's just the moment to give those clothes an airing—take them out of the trunks and see if there's anything wants doing. Here are the keys. This room will do nicely. I'll get the trunks out and make a proper job of it. I must have someone to help me though.

Calls.

Waiter!

Enter WAITERS.

FIRST WAITER. What do you want?

TRUFFALDINO. I want you to lend a hand to bring some trunks out of those rooms, to give the clothes an airing.

FIRST WAITER, *to* SECOND WAITER. Go and help him.

TRUFFALDINO, *to* SECOND WAITER. Come along, and I'll give you a good handful of what my masters gave me.

TRUFFALDINO *and* SECOND WAITER *go into* BEATRICE's *room.*

FIRST WAITER. He looks like a rare good servant—quick, ready, and most attentive; but I'll warrant he has his faults somewhere. I've been a servant myself and I know the ropes. Nobody does anything just for love. Whatever they do, either they are robbing their masters or they are throwing dust in their eyes.

TRUFFALDINO *comes out of the room with the* SECOND WAITER *carrying a trunk.*

TRUFFALDINO. Gently! Let's put it down here.

They put the trunk in the middle of the room.

Now let's fetch the other. But quietly, for my master is in there asleep.

TRUFFALDINO *and* SECOND WAITER *go into* FLORINDO's *room.*

FIRST WAITER. Either he's a real first-rate fellow, or he's a real knave; I never saw anybody wait on two gentlemen at once like that. I shall just keep my eyes open; maybe, under the pretense of waiting on two gentlemen at once, he means to rob them both.

TRUFFALDINO *and* SECOND WAITER *re-enter with the other trunk.*

TRUFFALDINO. And we'll put this one here.

They put it down a little way off from the other.

To SECOND WAITER.

There! You can run along now, if you like. I don't want anything more.

FIRST WAITER, *to* SECOND WAITER. Go on; off with you to the kitchen.

Exit SECOND WAITER.

To TRUFFALDINO.

Can I help you?

TRUFFALDINO. No, thank you; I can do my work myself.

FIRST WAITER. I must say, you are a giant for work; it's a marvel to me how you get through it all.

Exit FIRST WAITER.

TRUFFALDINO. Now I'm going to do my work properly, in peace and quiet, with no one to worry me.

Takes a key out of his pocket.

Now which key is this, I wonder? Which trunk does it fit? Let's try.

Opens one trunk.

I guessed right at once. I'm the cleverest man on earth. And this other will open t'other trunk.

Takes out second key and opens second trunk.

Now they are both open. Let's take everything out.

He takes all the clothes out of both trunks and puts them on the table. In each trunk there must be a black suit, books and papers, and anything else ad lib.

I'll just see if there is anything in the pockets. You never know, sometimes they leave biscuits or sweets in them.

Searches the pockets of BEATRICE's *suit and finds a portrait.*

My word, what a pretty picture! There's a handsome man! Who can it be? A queer thing, I seem to know him, but yet I can't remember. He is just the least little bit like my other master; but no, *he* never wears clothes like that, nor that wig neither.

FLORINDO *calls from his room.*

FLORINDO. Truffaldino!

TRUFFALDINO. Oh, plague take him! He has woken up. If the devil tempts him to come out and he sees this other trunk, he'll want to know—quick, quick—I'll lock it up and say I don't know whose it is.

Begins putting clothes in again.

FLORINDO, *calling.* Truffaldino!

TRUFFALDINO. Coming, sir!

Aside.

I must put these things away first. But I can't remember which trunk this coat came from, nor these papers neither.

FLORINDO, *calling.* Come here, I say; or must I fetch a stick to you?

TRUFFALDINO. In a minute, sir.

Aside.

Quick, before he comes! I'll put all straight when he goes out.

Stuffs the things into the trunks anyhow and locks them. FLORINDO *comes out in a dressing gown.*

FLORINDO. What the devil are you doing?

TRUFFALDINO. Pray, sir, didn't you tell me to give your clothes an airing? I was just about to do it here.

FLORINDO. And this other trunk, whose is that?

TRUFFALDINO. I couldn't say, sir; 'twill belong to some other gentleman.

FLORINDO. Give me my black coat.

TRUFFALDINO. Very good, sir.

Opens FLORINDO's *trunk and gives him the black suit.* FLORINDO *takes off his dressing gown with* TRUFFALDINO's *help and puts on the black coat; then puts his hand into the pockets and finds the portrait.*

FLORINDO, *much surprised.* What is this?

TRUFFALDINO, *aside.* Oh Lord, I've made a mistake. I ought to have put it into the other gentleman's pocket. 'Tis the color made me go wrong.

FLORINDO, *aside.* Heavens! There can be no mistake. This is my own portrait; the one I gave to my beloved Beatrice.

To TRUFFALDINO.

Tell me, how ever did this portrait come to be in the pocket of my coat? It wasn't there before.

TRUFFALDINO, *aside.* Now what's the answer to that? I don't know. Let me think——

FLORINDO. Come on, out with it, answer me. How did this portrait come to be in my pocket?

TRUFFALDINO. Sir, be kind and forgive me for taking a liberty. The portrait belongs to me, and I hid it there for safety, for fear I might lose it.

FLORINDO. How did you come by this portrait?

TRUFFALDINO. My master left it to me.

FLORINDO. Left it to you?

TRUFFALDINO. Yes, sir; I had a master who died, and he left me a few trifles which I sold, all except this portrait, sir.

FLORINDO. Great heavens! And how long is it since this master of yours died?

TRUFFALDINO. 'Twill be just about a week ago, sir.

Aside.

I say the first thing that comes into my head.

FLORINDO. What was your master's name?

TRUFFALDINO. I do not know, sir; he lived incognito.

FLORINDO. Incognito? How long were you in his service?

TRUFFALDINO. Only a short time, sir; ten or twelve days.

FLORINDO, *aside*. Heavens! More and more do I fear that it was Beatrice. She escaped in man's dress; she concealed her name—— Oh, wretched me, if it be true!

TRUFFALDINO, *aside*. As he believes it all, I may as well go on with the fairy tale.

FLORINDO, *despairingly*. Tell me, was your master young?

TRUFFALDINO. Yes, sir, quite a young gentleman.

FLORINDO. Without a beard?

TRUFFALDINO. Without a beard, sir.

FLORINDO, *aside, with a sigh*. 'Twas she, doubtless.

TRUFFALDINO, *aside*. I hope I'm not in for another thrashing.

FLORINDO. At least, you know where your late master came from?

TRUFFALDINO. I did know, sir, but I can't now call it to mind.

FLORINDO. Was he from Turin?

TRUFFALDINO. Turin it was, sir.

FLORINDO, *aside*. Every word he speaks is a sword thrust in my heart.

To TRUFFALDINO.

Tell me again, this young gentleman from Turin, is he really dead?

TRUFFALDINO. He is dead indeed, sir.

FLORINDO. Of what did he die?

TRUFFALDINO. He met with an accident, and that was the end of him.

Aside.

That seems to be the best way out.

FLORINDO. Where was he buried?

TRUFFALDINO, *aside*. I wasn't ready for that one.

To FLORINDO.

He wasn't buried, sir.

FLORINDO. What!

TRUFFALDINO. No, sir, another servant from the same place got permission to have him put into a coffin and sent home, sir.

FLORINDO. And was it, by any chance, the same servant who got you to fetch his letters for him from the Post this morning?

TRUFFALDINO. Exactly so, sir; it was Pasqual'.

FLORINDO, *aside*. Then all hope is lost. Beatrice is dead. Unhappy Beatrice! The discomforts of the journey and the tortures of her heart must have killed her. Oh! I can no longer endure the agony of my grief!

Exit into his room.

TRUFFALDINO. That portrait has touched him in the guts. He must have known the gentleman. Well, I had better take the trunks back to the rooms again, or I shall be in for more trouble of the same sort. Oh dear! Here comes my other master.

Enter BEATRICE *and* PANTALONE.

BEATRICE. I assure you, Signor Pantalone, the last consignment of mirrors and wax candles has been put down twice over.

PANTALONE. Maybe my young men have made a mistake. We will go through the books again, and then we shall find out exactly how things stand.

BEATRICE. I too have a list copied from my own books. We will compare them. Perhaps that may decide the point either in your favor or mine. Truffaldino!

TRUFFALDINO. Here, sir.

BEATRICE. Have you the key of my trunk?

TRUFFALDINO. Yes, sir; here it is.

BEATRICE. Why have you brought my trunk in here?

TRUFFALDINO. To air your clothes, sir.

BEATRICE. Have you aired them?

TRUFFALDINO. I have, sir.

BEATRICE. Open the trunk and give me—— Whose is that other trunk?

TRUFFALDINO. It belongs to another gentleman who has just come.

BEATRICE. Give me the memorandum book which you will find there.

TRUFFALDINO. Yes, sir.

Aside.

The Lord help me this time!

Opens trunk and looks for the book.

PANTALONE. As I say, they may have made a mistake; of course, if there is a mistake, you will not have to pay.

BEATRICE. We may find that all is in order; we shall see.

TRUFFALDINO. Is this the book, sir?

Holding out a book to BEATRICE.

BEATRICE. I expect so.

Takes the book without looking carefully and opens it.

No, this is not it—— Whose is this book?

TRUFFALDINO, *aside.* I've done it now!

BEATRICE, *aside.* These are two letters which I wrote to Florindo. Alas, these notes, these accounts belong to him. I tremble, I am in a cold sweat, I know not where I am.

PANTALONE. What ails you, Signor Federigo? Are you unwell?

BEATRICE. 'Tis nothing.

Aside to TRUFFALDINO.

Truffaldino, how did this book come to be in my trunk? It is not mine.

TRUFFALDINO. I hardly know, sir——

BEATRICE. Come, out with it—tell me the truth.

TRUFFALDINO. I ask your pardon for the liberty I took, sir, putting the book into your trunk. It belongs to me, and I put it there for safety.

Aside.

That was a good enough story for the other gentleman, I hope 'twill do for this one too.

BEATRICE. The book is your own, you say, and yet you gave it to me instead of mine, without noticing?

TRUFFALDINO, *aside*. He's much too clever.

To BEATRICE.

I'll tell you, sir; I have only had the book a very short time, so I did not recognize it at once.

BEATRICE. And how came you by this book?

TRUFFALDINO. I was in service with a gentleman at Venice, and he died and left the book to me.

BEATRICE. How long ago?

TRUFFALDINO. I don't remember exactly—ten or twelve days.

BEATRICE. How can that be, when I met you at Verona?

TRUFFALDINO. I had just come away from Venice on account of my poor master's death.

BEATRICE, *aside*. Alas for me!

To TRUFFALDINO.

Your master—was his name—Florindo?

TRUFFALDINO. Yes, sir; Florindo.

BEATRICE. And his family name Aretusi?

TRUFFALDINO. That was it, sir; Aretusi.

BEATRICE. And you are sure he is dead?

TRUFFALDINO. As sure as I stand here.

BEATRICE. Of what did he die? Where was he buried?

TRUFFALDINO. He tumbled into the canal and was drowned and never seen again.

BEATRICE. Oh, wretched that I am! Florindo is dead, my beloved is dead; my one and only hope is dead. All is lost. Love's stratagems are fruitless! I leave my home, I leave my relatives, I dress as a man, I confront danger, I hazard my very life, all for Florindo—and Florindo is dead. Unhappy Beatrice! Was the loss of my brother so little to me that Fate must make me lose my lover as well? Oh! Grief overwhelms me, I can no longer bear the light of day. My adored one, my beloved, I will follow you to the tomb.

Exit into her room, raving.

PANTALONE, *who has listened to her speech with astonishment.* Truffaldino!

TRUFFALDINO. Si'or Pantalon'?

PANTALONE. A woman!

TRUFFALDINO. A female!

PANTALONE. Most extraordinary!

TRUFFALDINO. Who'd have thought it?

PANTALONE. I'm struck all of a heap.

TRUFFALDINO. You might knock me down with a feather.

PANTALONE. I shall go straight home and tell my daughter.

Exit.

TRUFFALDINO. It seems I am not the servant of two masters but of a master and a mistress.

Exit.

SCENE 2

A Street

Enter DR. LOMBARDI *meeting* PANTALONE.

DR. LOMBARDI, *aside.* This doddering old villain Pantalone sticks in my gizzard. The more I think about him, the more I abominate him.

PANTALONE, *cheerfully.* Good day, my dear Doctor, your servant.

DR. LOMBARDI. I am surprised that you have the effrontery to address me.

PANTALONE. I have news for you. Do you know——

DR. LOMBARDI. You are going to tell me that the marriage has already been performed? I care not a fig if it has.

PANTALONE. The whole story is untrue. Let me speak, plague take you.

DR. LOMBARDI. Speak on then, pox on you.

PANTALONE, *aside.* I should like to give him a good doctoring with my fists.

To DR. LOMBARDI.

My daughter shall marry your son whenever you please.

DR. LOMBARDI. I am vastly obliged to you. Pray do not put yourself to inconvenience. My son is not prepared to stomach that, sir. You may give her to the Turin gentleman.

PANTALONE. If you knew who the Turin gentleman is, you would say differently.

DR. LOMBARDI. He may be who he will. Your daughter has been seen with him, *et hoc sufficit*.

PANTALONE. But 'tis not true that he is——

DR. LOMBARDI. I will not hear another word.

PANTALONE. If you won't hear me, 'twill be the worse for you.

DR. LOMBARDI. We shall see for whom it will be the worse.

PANTALONE. My daughter is a girl of unblemished reputation, and——

DR. LOMBARDI. The devil take you.

PANTALONE. The devil take you, sir.

DR. LOMBARDI. You disreputable old villain!

Exit DR. LOMBARDI.

PANTALONE. Damn you! He is more like a beast than a man. Why, how could I ever tell him that the man was a woman? Not a bit of it, he wouldn't let me speak. But here comes that young lout of a son of his; now I shall be in for more impertinence.

Enter SILVIO.

SILVIO, *aside*. There is Pantalone. I should like to run a sword through his paunch.

PANTALONE. Signor Silvio, if you will give me leave, I should like to give you a piece of good news, if you will condescend to allow me to speak, and not behave like that windmill of a father of yours.

SILVIO. What have you to say to me? Pray speak, sir.

PANTALONE. You must know, sir, that the marriage of my daughter to Signor Federigo has come to nothing.

SILVIO. Indeed? Do not deceive me.

PANTALONE. 'Tis true indeed, and if you are still of your former mind, my daughter is ready to give you her hand.

SILVIO. Oh, heavens! You bring me back from death to life.

PANTALONE, *aside*. Well, well, he is not quite such a bear as his father.

SILVIO. But heavens! How can I clasp to my bosom her who has for so long been the bride of another?

PANTALONE. To cut a long story short, Federigo Rasponi has turned into Beatrice his sister.

SILVIO. What? I do not understand you.

PANTALONE. Then you are very thickheaded. The person whom we thought to be Federigo has been discovered to be Beatrice.

SILVIO. Dressed as a man?

PANTALONE. Dressed as a man.

SILVIO. At last I understand.

PANTALONE. About time you did.

SILVIO. How did it happen? Tell me.

PANTALONE. Let us go to my house. My daughter knows nothing of it. I need only tell the story once to satisfy you both.

SILVIO. I will come, sir; and I most humbly beg your forgiveness, for having allowed myself to be transported by passion——

PANTALONE. 'Twas a mere nothing; I appreciate your feelings. I know what love is. Now, my dear boy, come along with me.

Going.

SILVIO, *aside*. Who is happier than I am? What heart could be more contented?

Exit with PANTALONE.

SCENE 3

A Room in BRIGHELLA's *Inn*

BEATRICE *and* FLORINDO *come out of their rooms simultaneously; each holds a sword or dagger and is on the point of committing suicide.* BRIGHELLA *is restraining* BEATRICE *and the* FIRST WAITER *restraining* FLORINDO. *They all come forward in such a way that* BEATRICE *and* FLORINDO *are unaware of each other's presence.*

BRIGHELLA, *seizing* BEATRICE'S *hand.* Stop, stop!

BEATRICE, *trying to break loose.* For pity's sake, let me go.

FIRST WAITER, *holding* FLORINDO. This is madness.

FLORINDO, *breaks away from* WAITER. Go to the devil.

BEATRICE, *breaking away from* BRIGHELLA. You shall not hinder me.

Both come forward, determined to kill themselves, they see each other, recognize each other, and stand dazed.

FLORINDO. What do I see?

BEATRICE. Florindo!

FLORINDO. Beatrice!

BEATRICE. Are you alive?

FLORINDO. Are you too living?

BEATRICE. Oh, destiny!

FLORINDO. Oh, my adored one!

They drop their weapons and embrace.

BRIGHELLA, *jokingly to the* WAITER. You had better mop up the blood; we don't want a mess here.

Exit BRIGHELLA.

FIRST WAITER, *aside.* Anyway I'll pick up the weapons and I shall not give them back again.

Picks up the daggers and exit.

FLORINDO. What brought you to attempt such an act of madness?

BEATRICE. The false news of your death.

FLORINDO. Who told you that I was dead?

BEATRICE. My servant.

FLORINDO. And mine gave me to believe that you were dead; and I too, carried away by the same agony of grief, intended to take my life.

BEATRICE. It was this book caused me to believe the story.

FLORINDO. That book was in my trunk. How came it into your hands? Ah, now I know. By the same means, no doubt, as the portrait I found in my coat pocket. Here it is. The one I gave you at Turin.

BEATRICE. Those rascally servants of ours— Heaven only knows what they have been up to.

FLORINDO. Where are they, I wonder?

BEATRICE. Nowhere to be seen.

FLORINDO. Let us find them and confront them.

Calling.

Ho there! Is nobody there?

Enter BRIGHELLA.

BRIGHELLA. Did you call, sir?

FLORINDO. Where are our servants?

BRIGHELLA. I don't know, sir. Shall I send to look for them?

FLORINDO. Find them at once if you can and send them to us here.

BRIGHELLA. For myself I only know one of them; I will ask the waiters, they will know them both. I congratulate you, sir, and madam, on having made such a satisfactory end of yourselves; if you want to get yourselves buried, you must try some other establishment; that's more than *we* can undertake. Your servant, madam and sir.

Exit BRIGHELLA.

FLORINDO. Then you too are lodged in this inn?

BEATRICE. I arrived this morning.

FLORINDO. I too this morning. And yet we never saw each other.

BEATRICE. Fate has been pleased to torment us a little.

FLORINDO. Tell me: your brother Federigo—is he dead?

BEATRICE. Have you any doubt? He died on the spot.

FLORINDO. I was told he was alive and here in Venice.

BEATRICE. It was I who traveled in his name and in these clothes to follow——

FLORINDO. To follow me—I know, my dearest; I read it in a letter from your servant at Turin.

BEATRICE. How came it into your hands?

FLORINDO. My servant gave it me by mistake and seeing it was addressed to you, I could not help opening it.

BEATRICE. I suppose a lover's curiosity is always legitimate.

FLORINDO. But where are these servants of ours? Ah!

Sees TRUFFALDINO *approaching.*

Here is one.

BEATRICE. He looks like the worse knave of the two.

FLORINDO. I think you are not far wrong.

Enter TRUFFALDINO *brought in by force by* BRIGHELLA *and the* FIRST WAITER.

FLORINDO. Come here, come here, don't be frightened.

BEATRICE. We shall do you no harm.

TRUFFALDINO, *aside.* H'm, I still remember the thrashing.

BRIGHELLA. We have found this one; if we can find the other, we will bring him.

FLORINDO. Yes, we *must* have them both here together.

BRIGHELLA, *aside to* WAITER. Do you know the other?

FIRST WAITER, *to* BRIGHELLA. Not I.

BRIGHELLA. We'll ask in the kitchen. Someone there will know him.

FIRST WAITER. If he had been there, I should have known him too.

Exeunt FIRST WAITER *and* BRIGHELLA.

FLORINDO, *to* TRUFFALDINO. Come, now, tell us what happened about that changing of the portrait and the book, and why you and that other rascal conspired to drive us distracted.

TRUFFALDINO, *signs to both with his finger to keep silence.* Hush!

To FLORINDO.

Pray, sir, a word with you in private.

To BEATRICE *just as he turns to speak to* FLORINDO.

I will tell you everything directly.

To FLORINDO.

You must know, sir, I am not to blame for anything that

has happened; it's all Pasqual's fault, the servant of that lady there.

Cautiously pointing at BEATRICE.

It was he mixed up the things, and put into one trunk what belonged to the other, without my knowledge. The poor man begged and prayed me to take the blame, for fear his master should send him away, and as I am a kindhearted fellow that would let himself be drawn and quartered for his friends, I made up all these stories to see if I could help him. I never dreamed it was a portrait of you or that you would be so much upset at hearing of the death of the owner. Now I have told you the whole truth, sir, as an honest man and a faithful servant.

BEATRICE, *aside.* 'Tis a very long story he is telling. I am curious to know what the mystery is about.

FLORINDO, *aside to* TRUFFALDINO. Then the man who got you to fetch that letter from the Post was the servant of Signora Beatrice?

TRUFFALDINO, *aside to* FLORINDO. Yes, sir, that was Pasqual'.

FLORINDO. Then why conceal from me a fact I so urgently desired to know?

TRUFFALDINO. He begged me not to tell anyone, sir.

FLORINDO. Who?

TRUFFALDINO. Pasqual'.

FLORINDO. Why didn't you obey your master?

TRUFFALDINO. For the love of Pasqual'.

FLORINDO. You and Pasquale deserve a sound thrashing together.

TRUFFALDINO, *aside to himself.* In that case I should get both.

BEATRICE. Have you not yet finished this long cross-examination?

FLORINDO. This fellow has been telling me——

TRUFFALDINO, *aside to* FLORINDO. For the love of Heaven, your honor, do not say it was Pasqual'. I'd rather you told the lady it was me. You can give me a beating if you like, but don't, don't let any trouble come to Pasqual'.

FLORINDO, *aside to* TRUFFALDINO. Are you so devoted a friend to Pasquale?

TRUFFALDINO. I love him as if he were my very own self. Now I am going to the lady, and I am going to tell her that it was all my fault; she may scold me as she pleases and do what she will to me, but I *will* protect Pasqual'.

TRUFFALDINO *moves toward* BEATRICE.

FLORINDO, *aside.* Well, he's certainly a very loyal and affectionate character.

TRUFFALDINO, *to* BEATRICE. Here I am, madam.

BEATRICE, *aside to* TRUFFALDINO. What is all this long story you've been telling Signor Florindo?

TRUFFALDINO, *aside to* BEATRICE. You must know, madam, that that gentleman has a servant called Pasqual'; he is the most arrant noddy in the world; it was he made all that mess of things; but because the poor man was afraid his master would send him away, I made up all the story about the book and the master who was dead and drowned, and all the rest of it. And just now I've been telling Si'or Florindo that I was the cause of it all.

BEATRICE. But why accuse yourself of faults which you have never committed?

TRUFFALDINO. Madam, 'tis all for the love I bear Pasqual'.

FLORINDO, *aside.* This seems a very long business.

TRUFFALDINO, *to* BEATRICE *as before.* Dear madam, I beg of you, don't get him into trouble.

BEATRICE. Whom?

TRUFFALDINO. Pasqual'.

BEATRICE. Pasquale and you are a pretty pair of rascals.

TRUFFALDINO, *aside to himself.* I fear I'm the only one.

FLORINDO. Come. That's enough. Signora Beatrice, our servants certainly deserve to be punished; but in consideration of our own great happiness, we surely may forgive what is past.

BEATRICE. True; but your servant——

TRUFFALDINO, *aside to* BEATRICE. For the love of Heaven don't mention Pasqual'.

BEATRICE, *to* FLORINDO. Well, I must go and call upon Signor Pantalone dei Bisognosi; will you accompany me?

FLORINDO. I would do so with pleasure, but I have to wait here and see my banker. I will come later, if you are in haste.

BEATRICE. I am, I must go at once. I shall expect you at Signor Pantalone's; and shall stay there till you come.

FLORINDO. I don't know where he lives.

TRUFFALDINO. I know, sir, I'll show you the way.

BEATRICE. Very well, and now I must go to my room and tidy myself up.

TRUFFALDINO, *aside to* BEATRICE. Very good, madam; I am at your service directly.

BEATRICE. Dear Florindo! What torments have I not endured for love of you!

BEATRICE *goes into her room.*

FLORINDO. Mine have been no less.

TRUFFALDINO. Sir, Pasqual' is not here, and Si'ora Beatrice has no one to help her dress; will you give me leave to wait upon her instead of Pasqual'?

FLORINDO. Yes, by all means. Wait upon her with diligence; I am delighted.

TRUFFALDINO, *aside.* For invention, for promptness and for intrigue I will challenge the attorney general.

TRUFFALDINO *goes into* BEATRICE'S *room.*

FLORINDO. What strange things have happened in the course of this one day! Tears, lamentations, and anguish, and then at last consolation and happiness. From tears to laughter is a happy step, which makes us forget our agonies, but when we pass from pleasure to pain the change is even yet more acutely perceptible.

Re-enter BEATRICE *followed by* TRUFFALDINO.

BEATRICE. Here I am, have I not been quick?

FLORINDO. When will you change these clothes?

BEATRICE. Do I not look well in them?

FLORINDO. I long to see you in a woman's dress. Your beauties ought not to be so completely disguised.

BEATRICE. Well, I shall expect you at Signor Pantalone's; make Truffaldino show you the way.

FLORINDO. I must wait for the banker; if he does not come soon another time will do.

BEATRICE. Show me your love in your anxiety to attend me.
About to go.

TRUFFALDINO, *aside to* BEATRICE. Do you wish me to stay and wait upon this gentleman?

BEATRICE. Yes, you will show him the way to Signor Pantalone's.

TRUFFALDINO. Yes, madam, certainly, as Pasqual' is not here.

BEATRICE. Wait upon him, I shall be pleased indeed.
Aside to herself.
I love him more than my very self.
Exit BEATRICE.

TRUFFALDINO. The fellow's nowhere to be seen. His master wants to dress, and he goes out on his own and is nowhere to be found.

FLORINDO. Of whom are you speaking?

TRUFFALDINO. Of Pasqual'. I love him, he is a good friend of mine, but he's a lazy dog. Now I am a servant worth two.

FLORINDO. Come and dress my wig. The banker will be here directly.

TRUFFALDINO. Please your honor, I hear your honor has to go to Si'or Pantalon's.

FLORINDO. Yes, what then?

TRUFFALDINO. I want to ask a favor of you.

FLORINDO. Well, you deserve it after all you have done.

TRUFFALDINO. If there has been any trouble, you know, sir, 'tis all the fault of Pasqual'.

FLORINDO. But where on earth *is* this cursed Pasquale? Can't one see him?

TRUFFALDINO. He'll come, the knave. And so, sir, I want to ask you this favor.

FLORINDO. What do you want?

TRUFFALDINO. You see, sir, I'm in love too.

FLORINDO. In love?

TRUFFALDINO. Yes, sir, and my young woman is maidserv-

ant to Si'or Pantalon'; and it would be very kind if your
honor——

FLORINDO. How do I come into it?

TRUFFALDINO. I won't say, sir, that you come into it; but I
being your servant, you might say a word for me to Si'or
Pantalon'.

FLORINDO. We must see first whether the girl wants you.

TRUFFALDINO. The girl wants me, no mistake. All I want is
a word to Si'or Pantalon'; I beg you, sir, of your charity.

FLORINDO. Certainly, I will speak for you, but how can you
keep a wife?

TRUFFALDINO. I shall do what I can. I shall ask for help from
Pasqual'.

FLORINDO. You had better ask help from someone with more
sense.

FLORINDO *goes into his room.*

TRUFFALDINO. Well, if I don't show sense this time, I shall
never show it again.

TRUFFALDINO *follows* FLORINDO *into his room.*

SCENE 4

A Room in the House of PANTALONE

PANTALONE, *the* DOCTOR, CLARICE, SILVIO *and*
SMERALDINA

PANTALONE. Come, Clarice, pull yourself together. You see
that Signor Silvio has repented and asks your forgiveness.
If he acted foolishly, it was all for love of you; I have forgiven him his extravagances, you ought to forgive him too.

SILVIO. Measure my agony by your own, Signora Clarice, and
rest assured that I most truly love you, since 'twas the fear
of losing you that rendered me distracted. Heaven desires
our happiness; do not be ungrateful for the blessings of

Providence. Do not let the idea of revenge spoil the most beautiful day of your life.

DR. LOMBARDI. I join my prayers to those of my son; Signora Clarice, my dear daughter-in-law, have pity on the poor young man; he nearly went out of his mind.

SMERALDINA. Come, dear madam, what would you? Men are all cruel to us, some more, some less. They demand the most absolute fidelity, and on the least shadow of suspicion they bully us, ill-treat us and are like to murder us. Well, you have got to marry one or another of them some day, so I say to you as one says to sick people—since you have got to take your nasty medicine, take it.

PANTALONE. There, do you hear that? Smeraldina calls matrimony medicine. You must not think it is poison.

Aside to DR. LOMBARDI.

We must try to cheer her up.

DR. LOMBARDI. Certainly, 'tis not poison, nor even nasty medicine. Matrimony is a lollipop, a jujube, a lozenge!

SILVIO. But dear Clarice, won't you say a word? I know I deserve to be punished by you, but, of your mercy, punish me with hard words rather than with silence. Behold me at your feet; have pity upon me.

CLARICE, *to* SILVIO *with a sigh.* Cruel!

PANTALONE, *aside to* DR. LOMBARDI. You heard that little sigh? A good sign.

DR. LOMBARDI, *aside to* SILVIO. Strike while the iron is hot.

SMERALDINA, *aside.* A sigh is like lightning; it promises rainfall.

SILVIO. If I could think that you desired my blood to avenge my supposed cruelty, I give it you with all my heart. But, oh God! instead of the blood of my veins, accept, I beg you, that which gushes from my eyes.

Weeps.

PANTALONE. Bravo! Bravo! Well said!

DR. LOMBARDI. Capital! Capital!

CLARICE, *sighing as before, but more tenderly.* Cruel!

DR. LOMBARDI, *aside to* PANTALONE. She's done to a turn.

PANTALONE. Here, come up with you.

He raises SILVIO, *takes him by the hand.*

Stand over there.

Takes CLARICE'S *hand.*

And you come here too, madam. Now, join your hands together again; and make peace. So no more tears, be happy, no more nonsense and Heaven bless you both.

DR. LOMBARDI. There; 'tis done.

SMERALDINA. 'Tis done, 'tis done.

SILVIO, *holding* CLARICE'S *hand.* Oh, Signora Clarice, for pity's sake——

CLARICE. Ungrateful!

SILVIO. Dearest!

CLARICE. Inhuman!

SILVIO. Beloved!

CLARICE. Monster!

SILVIO. Angel!

CLARICE, *sighs.* Ah!

PANTALONE, *aside.* Going, going——

SILVIO. Forgive me, for the love of Heaven.

CLARICE, *sighs.* I forgive you.

PANTALONE, *aside.* Gone!

DR. LOMBARDI. Come, Silvio, she has forgiven you.

SMERALDINA. The patient is ready; give her her medicine.

Enter BRIGHELLA.

BRIGHELLA. By your leave, sir, may I come in?

PANTALONE. Pray come in, good friend Brighella. 'Twas you, was it not, that told me all these pretty stories, who assured me that that party was Signor Federigo—eh?

BRIGHELLA. My dear sir, who would not have been deceived? They were twin brother and sister, as like as two peas. In those clothes I would have wagered my head that it was he.

PANTALONE. Enough. That's all done with. What is the news?

BRIGHELLA. Signora Beatrice is here, and desires to pay her respects.

PANTALONE. Let her come in; she is most welcome.

CLARICE. Poor Signora Beatrice, I am happy to think that her troubles are over.

SILVIO. You are sorry for her?

CLARICE. I am indeed.

SILVIO. And for me?

CLARICE. Oh, cruel!

PANTALONE, *aside to* DR. LOMBARDI. You hear these loving words?

DR. LOMBARDI, *aside to* PANTALONE. Ah, my son has a way with him.

PANTALONE. My daughter, poor dear child, has a very good heart.

SMERALDINA. Yes, they will both of them do their duty by each other.

Enter BEATRICE.

BEATRICE. Ladies and gentlemen, I come to ask your pardon and forgiveness, that you should on my account have been put to inconvenience——

CLARICE. No, no, my dear; come to me.

Embraces her.

SILVIO, *annoyed at the embrace.* How now?

BEATRICE, *to* SILVIO. What! May she not even embrace a woman?

SILVIO, *aside.* 'Tis those clothes again.

PANTALONE. Well, well, Signora Beatrice, I must say, for a young woman of your age you have a wonderful courage.

DR. LOMBARDI, *to* BEATRICE. Too much spirit, madam.

BEATRICE. Love makes one do great things.

PANTALONE. And you have found your young gentleman at last? So I hear.

BEATRICE. Yes, Heaven has made us happy.

DR. LOMBARDI. A nice reputation you have made yourself!

BEATRICE. Sir, you have no business with my affairs.

SILVIO, *to* DR. LOMBARDI. Sir, I beg you, let everyone do as they will; do not be so put out about it. Now that I am happy,

I want all the world to be happy too. Is anyone else going to be married? Let them all get married!

SMERALDINA, *to* SILVIO. What about me, sir?

SILVIO. Whom are you going to marry?

SMERALDINA. The first man that comes along, sir.

SILVIO. Find him then, here am I.

CLARICE, *to* SILVIO. You? What for?

SILVIO. To give her a wedding present.

CLARICE. That is no affair of yours.

SMERALDINA, *aside.* She's afraid everybody will eat him. She likes the taste of him, I see.

Enter TRUFFALDINO.

TRUFFALDINO. My respects to the company.

BEATRICE, *to* TRUFFALDINO. Where is Signor Florindo?

TRUFFALDINO. He is here and would like to come in, by your leave.

BEATRICE. Signor Pantalone, will you give Signor Florindo leave?

PANTALONE. Is that your young gentleman?

BEATRICE. He is going to marry me.

PANTALONE. I shall be pleased to meet him.

BEATRICE, *to* TRUFFALDINO. Show him in.

TRUFFALDINO, *aside to* SMERALDINA. Young woman, my respects to you.

SMERALDINA, *aside to* TRUFFALDINO. Pleased to see you, my little darkie.

TRUFFALDINO. We will have a talk.

SMERALDINA. What about?

TRUFFALDINO, *makes as though giving her a wedding ring.* Are you willing?

SMERALDINA. Why not?

TRUFFALDINO. We'll have a talk.

Exit TRUFFALDINO.

SMERALDINA, *to* CLARICE. Madam, with the company's leave, I want a favor of you.

CLARICE, *going aside to listen to* SMERALDINA. What is it?

SMERALDINA, *to* CLARICE. I too am a poor young girl that would like to settle myself; there's the servant of Signora Beatrice who wants to marry me; now if you would say a kind word to his mistress, and get her to allow him to take me to wife, I should be the happiest girl in the world.

CLARICE. Dear Smeraldina, with all the pleasure in life; as soon as I can speak freely to Beatrice, I will certainly do so.

PANTALONE, *to* CLARICE. What is all this whispering about?

CLARICE. Nothing, sir. She had something to say to me.

SILVIO, *to* CLARICE. May I not know?

CLARICE. How inquisitive they all are! And then they talk about us women!

Enter FLORINDO *shown in by* TRUFFALDINO.

FLORINDO. Your most humble servant, ladies and gentlemen.

All bow and curtsy.

To PANTALONE.

Are you the master of the house, sir?

PANTALONE. Yours to command, sir.

FLORINDO. Allow me, sir, to have the honor of waiting upon you this evening; I present myself by command of the Signora Beatrice, whose adventures will be known to you, and mine too.

PANTALONE. I am happy to know you, sir, and to see you here; I congratulate you most heartily on your good fortune.

FLORINDO. Signora Beatrice is to be my wife, and if you will not disdain to do us the honor, I hope you will give away the bride.

PANTALONE. Whatever has to be done, let it be done at once. Give her your hand.

FLORINDO. Signora Beatrice, I am willing.

BEATRICE. Here is my hand, Signor Florindo.

SMERALDINA, *aside. They* don't want pressing.

PANTALONE. Afterward we will settle up our accounts. You will put yours in order; then we will settle ours.

CLARICE, *to* BEATRICE. Dear friend, I congratulate you.

BEATRICE, *to* CLARICE. And I you, with all my heart.

SILVIO, *to* FLORINDO. Sir, do you know me again?

FLORINDO, *to* SILVIO. Indeed I do, sir; you would have provoked me to a duel.

SILVIO. 'Twas to my own disaster. Here is the adversary

Pointing to BEATRICE.

who disarmed me and very nearly killed me.

BEATRICE. And gave you your life too, you might say.

SILVIO. 'Tis true.

CLARICE. At my entreaty.

SILVIO. That is very true.

PANTALONE. Everything is in order, everything is settled.

TRUFFALDINO. The best is yet to come, ladies and gentlemen.

PANTALONE. What is yet to come?

TRUFFALDINO, *to* FLORINDO, *taking him apart.* With your good leave, sir, one word.

FLORINDO. What do you want?

TRUFFALDINO. You remember what you promised me, sir?

FLORINDO. What did I promise? I do not recollect.

TRUFFALDINO. To ask Si'or Pantalon' for Smeraldina as my wife.

FLORINDO. Of course, now I remember; I will do so at once.

TRUFFALDINO, *aside.* I, too, poor man, want to put myself right with the world.

FLORINDO. Signor Pantalone, although this is the first occasion on which I have had the honor of knowing you, I make bold to desire a favor of you.

PANTALONE. You may command me, sir; I will serve you to the best of my powers.

FLORINDO. My manservant desires to marry your maid; have you any objection to giving your consent?

SMERALDINA, *aside.* Wonderful! Here's another who wants to marry me! Who the devil can he be? I wish I knew him.

PANTALONE. For my part I am agreed.

To SMERALDINA.

What say you, girl?

SMERALDINA. If I thought he would make a good husband——

PANTALONE. Is he a good honest man, this servant of yours?

FLORINDO. For the short time he has been with me he has certainly proved himself trusty, and he seems to be intelligent.

CLARICE. Signor Florindo, you have anticipated me in something that *I* ought to have done. I was to propose the marriage of my maid with the manservant of Signora Beatrice. You have asked for her for *your* servant, I can say no more.

FLORINDO. No, no; since you so earnestly desire this, I withdraw altogether and leave you completely free.

CLARICE. Indeed, sir, I could never permit myself to have my own wishes preferred to yours. Besides, I must admit that I am not fully authorized. Pray continue in your proposal.

FLORINDO. You say so out of courtesy, madam. Signor Pantalone, I withdraw all that I have said. I will not say another word on behalf of my servant; on the contrary, I am absolutely opposed to his marrying her.

CLARICE. If *your* man is not to marry her, no more shall the other man. We must be fair on both sides.

TRUFFALDINO, *aside.* Here's a state of things! They pay each other compliments, and meanwhile I am left without a wife at all.

SMERALDINA, *aside.* It looks as if I should have neither one nor the other.

PANTALONE. Come, we *must* settle it somehow; this poor girl wants to get married, let us give her either to the one or the other.

FLORINDO. Not to *my* man. Nothing shall induce me to do Signora Clarice an injustice.

CLARICE. Nor will I ever tolerate an injustice to Signor Florindo.

TRUFFALDINO. Sir, madam, I can settle the matter myself.

With his usual air of great ingenuity.

Si'or Florindo, did you not ask the hand of Smeraldina for your servant?

FLORINDO. I did; did you not hear me?

TRUFFALDINO. And you, Si'ora Clarice, did you not intend Smeraldina to marry the servant of Si'ora Beatrice?

CLARICE. Most certainly I was to do so.

TRUFFALDINO. Good; then if that is so, give me your hand, Smeraldina.

PANTALONE. And pray what right have *you* to ask for her hand?

TRUFFALDINO. Because I am the servant of Si'or Florindo and of Si'ora Beatrice too.

FLORINDO. What?

BEATRICE. What do you say?

TRUFFALDINO. Pray be calm. Si'or Florindo, who asked you to ask Si'or Pantalon' for Smeraldina?

FLORINDO. You did.

TRUFFALDINO. And you, Si'ora Clarice, whom had you in mind as the intended husband of Smeraldina?

CLARICE. Yourself.

TRUFFALDINO. *Ergo,* Smeraldina is mine.

FLORINDO. Signora Beatrice, where is your servant?

BEATRICE. Why, here! Truffaldino, of course.

FLORINDO. Truffaldino? He is *my* servant!

BEATRICE. Is not yours called Pasquale?

FLORINDO. Pasquale? I thought Pasquale was *yours!*

BEATRICE, *to* TRUFFALDINO. How do you explain this?

TRUFFALDINO *makes silent gestures asking for forgiveness.*

FLORINDO. You rascal!

BEATRICE. You knave!

FLORINDO. So you waited on two masters at once?

TRUFFALDINO. Yes, sir, I did, that was the very trick. I took on the job without thinking; just to see what I could do. It did not last long, 'tis true; but at any rate I can boast that nobody would ever have found me out, if I had not given myself away for love of this girl here. I have done a hard day's work, and I dare say I had my shortcomings, but I hope that in consideration of the fun of the thing, all these ladies and gentlemen will forgive me.

MIRANDOLINA

[LA LOCANDIERA]

Carlo Goldoni

English Version by Lady Augusta Gregory

PERSONS

MARQUIS OF FORLIPOPOLI
COUNT OF ALBAFIORITA
CAPTAIN RIPAFRATTA
MIRANDOLINA, *an innkeeper*
FABRIZIO, *servant at the inn*
CAPTAIN'S SERVANT

The scene is laid in Florence.

ACT I

SCENE 1

Large room at an inn, with rough furniture and three doors.
COUNT *and* MARQUIS.

MARQUIS. There is some difference, Count, between you and myself!

COUNT. How do you make that out?

MARQUIS. Are you setting yourself up to be my equal?

COUNT. My money is worth as much as yours . . . at an inn.

MARQUIS. I am the Marquis of Forlipopoli!

COUNT. And I am the Count of Albafiorita!

MARQUIS. You only got your title through buying an estate.

COUNT. If I bought my estate, you sold yours.

MARQUIS. I should be treated with respect.

COUNT. Who is showing you disrespect?

MARQUIS. What is keeping you at this inn?

COUNT. The same thing that keeps yourself.

MARQUIS. I don't know what you're talking about.

COUNT. I am talking of Mirandolina.

MARQUIS. Mirandolina! The innkeeper! What have you to do with her?

COUNT. That's a good joke! You think no one but yourself may look at Mirandolina!

MARQUIS. She will never look at you while she has a chance of a marquis.

COUNT. What is a marquis against money? In these times a handle to the name counts less than pence in the pocket.

MARQUIS. I'll back my rank against your riches.

COUNT. It isn't riches I think of, but what they will buy.

MARQUIS. Go on buying till you break your neck! You won't

be able to do anything with her. She doesn't care *that* for you.

Snaps his fingers.

COUNT, *sarcastically.* I won't, and you will!

MARQUIS. I am what I am!

COUNT. I have what I have! She sees more of my money than of yours.

MARQUIS. I don't go about talking of what I do.

COUNT. Everybody knows what you *don't* do. Even the servants are talking about it.

MARQUIS. Servants! I suppose you mean that low fellow Fabrizio. . . . I have my suspicions of him.

COUNT. I think I hear him outside.

Opens the door and calls.

Fabrizio!

FABRIZIO, *coming in.* What is it you are wanting, sir?

COUNT. What way is the little missis today?

FABRIZIO. She is well, sir.

MARQUIS. Is she in the house?

FABRIZIO. She is, sir.

COUNT. Ask her to come here. I want to speak to her.

FABRIZIO. I will, sir.

Goes.

MARQUIS. What do you want with her?

COUNT. Don't you know it's her birthday? Mirandolina comes of age today.

MARQUIS. What's that to you?

COUNT. I'm going to give her a birthday present . . . aren't you?

MARQUIS. It's worth more to her than presents that I patronize her inn: I bring it into fashion.

COUNT, *tossing a handful of money.* I bring it what is better!

MARQUIS. You don't understand what you're talking about.

COUNT. You are talking nonsense.

MARQUIS. Hold your tongue, sir.

COUNT. Hold your own!

CAPTAIN, *coming in.* What's all this noise about? Are you quarreling?

COUNT. Only arguing.

CAPTAIN. What on earth about?

COUNT. Something you would laugh at.

MARQUIS. It's no laughing matter!

COUNT. The marquis has taken a fancy to our landlady.

MARQUIS. I am only thinking of her interests.

COUNT. He thinks of them. . . . I spend for them.

CAPTAIN. I never heard of anything so little worth a quarrel. To grow angry about a woman! To lose one's temper about a woman! Whoever heard of such a thing? I will never have words with anyone about a woman. I have never looked at one, and never thought much of any one of them. A weakness for woman is a ridiculous thing.

MARQUIS. For all that, there is something very taking about Mirandolina.

COUNT. The marquis is right. Our landlady is a very charming little thing.

MARQUIS. You may be sure any woman *I* lose my heart to must be something out of the common.

CAPTAIN. Stuff and nonsense! What could there be out of the common in a woman of that sort?

MARQUIS. She has a very taking manner.

COUNT. She is pretty and very conversable; she dresses with very good taste.

CAPTAIN. All things that are not worth twopence. I have been three days in this inn and I give you my word I wouldn't know her if I met her in the street.

COUNT. Take a look at her, and she may make an impression on you yet.

CAPTAIN. Rubbish: I've seen her well enough; she's like any other woman.

MARQUIS. She is not like any other woman. She is something more than others. I have known ladies in the best society, and I give you my word I've never met her equal.

COUNT. I know women well enough. I know them and their follies. But I tell you in spite of the length of time I have been running after Mirandolina and all the money I have spent, I haven't so much as touched her little finger.

CAPTAIN. Tricks, all tricks. You are fools to be taken in by her. She would never try her tricks on me! Believe me, all women are the same in the long run. They don't know anything. They are no use, and I don't like them.

COUNT. You have never been in love.

CAPTAIN. Never, and never will be. My people have worked heaven and earth to make me marry, but I never would give in to it.

MARQUIS. But you are the only one of your family. Don't you think it a pity your property should go to strangers?

CAPTAIN. I do think it. But whenever I remember that to have an heir I must put up with a wife, I banish the thought quickly enough.

COUNT. And what will you do with all your money?

CAPTAIN. I'll enjoy spending it in my own way.

COUNT. And you will spend nothing at all on women?

CAPTAIN. Not a penny. I will never give a woman the chance to come nibbling at it.

COUNT, *looking from door.* Here she is coming. Here is Mirandolina. Look at her! Isn't she adorable?

CAPTAIN. Oh, a great beauty! I would think a great deal more of a good greyhound.

MARQUIS. If you don't think much of her, I do.

CAPTAIN. I would leave her there if she was handsomer than Venus.

MIRANDOLINA *comes in.*

MIRANDOLINA, *curtsies.* Good morning to you, gentlemen. Do you want anything of me?

MARQUIS. I have something to ask of you but not now . . . by and by . . . but not here.

MIRANDOLINA. If you want anything from me, I will send a servant with it.

MARQUIS, *aside to* CAPTAIN. What do you think of that now?

CAPTAIN. What you call behavior I call impudence.

The MARQUIS *takes a silk handkerchief from his pocket, opens it and shows it to her.*

MIRANDOLINA. That's a pretty handkerchief, sir.

MARQUIS, *to* MIRANDOLINA. Ah! It's a fine one! I have good taste—aye?

MIRANDOLINA. It is certainly very tasty.

MARQUIS. It is from London.

MIRANDOLINA. Is it indeed?

MARQUIS, *folding up his handkerchief carefully.* It must be properly folded, that it may not be creased. A thing of this sort should be taken great care of.

Gives it to MIRANDOLINA.

Take it.

MIRANDOLINA. Do you want it sent to your room?

MARQUIS. No, to yours.

MIRANDOLINA. Why to mine?

MARQUIS. Because I am making you a present of it. A birthday present.

MIRANDOLINA. But I won't take it.

MARQUIS. Don't make me angry.

MIRANDOLINA. Oh! If it comes to that, you know, sir, I don't wish to disoblige anyone. So, just to keep you from losing your temper, I will take it.

COUNT. Dear Mirandolina, look at these earrings. Do you like them?

MIRANDOLINA. They are beautiful.

COUNT. Those are diamonds, do you know?

MIRANDOLINA. Oh, I know that. I know what diamonds are.

COUNT. And they are for you.

CAPTAIN, *aside to* COUNT. A fool and his money are soon parted!

MIRANDOLINA. Why are you giving them to me?

MARQUIS. A great present, indeed! In its own way the handkerchief is in better taste.

COUNT. Maybe so, but from way to way there is a good distance. These are set in the fashion. I want you to take them for my sake.

CAPTAIN. He has lost his wits!

MIRANDOLINA. No, indeed, sir.

COUNT. It is for your birthday. If you refuse you will vex me.

MIRANDOLINA. I don't know what to say. I would wish to be friendly with my guests. Not to vex the count, I *will* take them.

CAPTAIN. What a schemer!

COUNT, *to* CAPTAIN. Hasn't she a ready wit?

CAPTAIN. Very ready indeed. She will eat you up and never say thank you.

MARQUIS. Now, Mirandolina, *I* have a word to say to you. I am a nobleman.

MIRANDOLINA, *aside to* COUNT. What a fiery declaration! It won't burn him up altogether. If there is nothing else wanted, I will go.

CAPTAIN. Here, ma'am, I don't think much of the table linen you have given me.

Angrily.

If you have none better I will send out for some.

MIRANDOLINA. I will give you better, sir; it shall be sent up to you, but I think you might have asked it with a little more politeness.

CAPTAIN. Where I am spending my own money, there is no need of paying compliments.

COUNT, *to* MIRANDOLINA. You should pity him. He is a great enemy of all women.

CAPTAIN. What's that? I don't want to be pitied by her.

MIRANDOLINA. Poor women! What way have they treated him? Why are you so hard on us, sir?

CAPTAIN. That will do. There is no more to be said about it. Change the cloth for me, I will send my servant to fetch it. *Goes.*

MIRANDOLINA. That man is no better than a bear.

COUNT. Dear Mirandolina, if he knew you he would be at your feet.

MIRANDOLINA. I don't want him at my feet, but I don't like to be made little of.

COUNT. He is a woman hater. He can't bear the sight of them.

MIRANDOLINA. The poor foolish creature! He hasn't met yet with the woman who knows how to manage him—but he'll find her—he'll find her or maybe . . . maybe . . . he *has* found her! I hope she will punish him and put him down . . . and conquer him and get the better of him and teach him not to run down the best thing Mother Nature ever put a hand to!

COUNT. Don't waste another thought on him.

MIRANDOLINA. Indeed, I am so put out by his bad manners I will give him notice to leave the inn.

MARQUIS. Do so, and if he refuses to go, tell me and I will send him about his business. Make what use you will of my protection.

COUNT. And as to any money you may lose by it, you must allow me to make it up to you.

Aside.

Listen, send away the marquis along with him, and I promise I will make up for his loss.

MIRANDOLINA. Thank you, gentlemen, many thanks; but I am well able to tell a guest when I don't want him. And as to business, there is never an empty room in the house.

FABRIZIO, *coming in, to* COUNT. There is someone wanting you, sir.

COUNT. Do you know who it is?

FABRIZIO. I think he is a jeweler.

Aside to MIRANDOLINA.

Have sense, Mirandolina; this is no company for you.
Goes.

COUNT. Oh yes, he has an ornament to show me. I want it to go with these earrings, Mirandolina.

MIRANDOLINA. Oh no, sir.

COUNT. You deserve the best of everything, and I don't care a straw what it costs. I am going to take a look at it.
Goes out.

MARQUIS. That count is a nuisance with all his money!

MIRANDOLINA. Indeed, the count is giving himself too much trouble.

MARQUIS. There are some people who have no more than two-pence and will spend it for a show off! I know them; I know the ways of the world.

MIRANDOLINA. I know the ways of the world myself.

MARQUIS. They think a woman like you can be come round with presents!

MIRANDOLINA. Presents don't disagree with me at all.

MARQUIS. I would be afraid of offending you if I pressed things on you.

MIRANDOLINA. Indeed, sir, you have never offended me in that way.

MARQUIS. And I never will.

MIRANDOLINA. I believe that indeed.

MARQUIS. But if there is anything I can do for you, tell me of it.

MIRANDOLINA. But I should have to know first in what way you could help me.

MARQUIS. In every way.

MIRANDOLINA. But, tell me, for instance . . .

MARQUIS. By Jove, you are a wonder of a woman.

MIRANDOLINA. You are too kind, Your Excellency.

MARQUIS. Ah, I could almost commit a folly; I could almost curse my nobility.

MIRANDOLINA. Why is that, sir?

MARQUIS. There are times when I wish I could change places with the count.

MIRANDOLINA. I suppose because he is so rich?

MARQUIS. Rich! I don't care a pin for that! But if I were like him . . . a mere count . . .

MIRANDOLINA. What would you do then, sir?

MARQUIS. By all that's damnable . . . I would marry you! *Goes out.*

MIRANDOLINA, *looking out of door after him.* Oh! What is it he said? Your High Excellency the Marquis Misery would think of marrying me! But if you should wish to marry me, there is one little bar in the way . . . I myself would not wish it.

FABRIZIO, *enters.* Are you there, ma'am?

MIRANDOLINA. What is it?

FABRIZIO. That Captain Ripafratta in the middle room is crying out against the tablecloths; he says they are common and that he won't use them.

MIRANDOLINA. I know, I know; he told me about it and I'll change them.

FABRIZIO. All right. Come and put out whatever you have for him, and I'll carry them up.

MIRANDOLINA. Never mind . . . that will do . . . I will give them to him myself.

FABRIZIO. You will bring them to him yourself!

MIRANDOLINA. Just so, myself.

FABRIZIO. That is showing him great attention.

MIRANDOLINA. I pay attention to everything. Mind your own business.

FABRIZIO. It is quite plain to me, you will do nothing for me . . . you lead me on just to make a fool of me.

MIRANDOLINA. You are a goose, but you are a very honest servant.

FABRIZIO. It is always the custom that I should attend the lodgers.

MIRANDOLINA. You are a little too rough for them.

FABRIZIO. And you are maybe a little too smooth.

MIRANDOLINA. I know very well what I am doing. I want no advice.

FABRIZIO. All right. You may look for another servingman.

MIRANDOLINA. Why so, Mr. Fabrizio? Are you out with me? *Takes his hands.*

FABRIZIO. Do you remember what your father said to the two of us at the time of his death?

MIRANDOLINA. I do . . . and whenever I think of marrying I will bring it to mind.

FABRIZIO. But I am someway thin-skinned. There are some things I cannot put up with. Sometimes it seems as if you will have me, and other times that you will not have me. You say you are not giddy but you always take your own way.

MIRANDOLINA. But what sort of an owl do you take me for? A bit of vanity? A fool? I'm astonished at you. What are strangers to me, that are here today and gone tomorrow? If I treat them well it is for my own interest and the credit of the house. I live honestly and I like my freedom; I amuse myself with everybody but I fall in love with nobody. But I know who suits me and who is worth while. And when my time comes for marriage I will not forget my father. And whoever has served me well won't have to complain of me. I am not ungrateful. I know him, but he doesn't know me. That is enough, Fabrizio. You may understand me, if you can.

Goes.

FABRIZIO. Whoever can understand her is a very clever man. But, after all, if lodgers come, they go away again, and I am here always. The best chance will always be with me!

Goes.

SCENE 2

CAPTAIN's *Parlor.* CAPTAIN *sitting. His* SERVANT *comes in with a letter.*

SERVANT. If you please, sir, this letter has come for you.

CAPTAIN, *opening letter.* Who is writing to me? "The sincere friendship I have for you." It's another of these meddling friends of mine wants me to marry an heiress . . . £ 10,000. I can do without that while I am a bachelor. If I were married, that and as much again wouldn't be enough. *I* take a wife . . . I'd sooner take an ague. Bring in the chocolate.

SERVANT *goes out.*

MARQUIS, *coming in.* May I come in for a minute?

CAPTAIN. Certainly.

MARQUIS. You and I can have a sensible talk. That donkey of a count is not fit to join in with us at all. You know my way, I try to get on with everyone, but as to that man, I cannot stand him.

CAPTAIN. You can't stand him because he is your rival. For shame! A man of your rank in love with an innkeeper! A sensible man like you.

MARQUIS. My dear sir, she has bewitched me!

CAPTAIN. All folly! Weakness! What bewitchments? How is it that women don't bewitch me? Their bewitchings are in their humbug and flatteries. Anyone keeping out of their way as I do is in no danger of finding himself bewitched.

MARQUIS. I agree with you, and I don't agree . . . but what is worrying me more than that, just now, is that agent of mine in the country.

CAPTAIN. Has he robbed you?

MARQUIS. He has broken his word to me.

SERVANT *enters with chocolate.*

MARQUIS. Ha! What's this? Chocolate?

CAPTAIN, *to* MARQUIS. Perhaps you will take it?

MARQUIS, *takes and sips chocolate without ceremony, talking and drinking.* This agent of mine, as I was saying . . .
Drinks.
He promised to send me my money as usual . . .
Sipping.
but he has not sent it.

CAPTAIN. He'll send it another time.

MARQUIS. The fact is . . . the fact is
Finishes chocolate.
that I am in a great difficulty, and I don't know what to do.

CAPTAIN. Oh, a week more or less . . .

MARQUIS. But you, who are a man of position and breeding, know what a trying thing it is to have to break one's word. I am in a difficulty. Good God! What am I to do?

CAPTAIN. I am sorry to see you so much put out.

Aside.

If I could but escape with decency!

MARQUIS. You would not be able to oblige me? For a week . . . ?

CAPTAIN. My dear Marquis, if I could, you should make use of me with the greatest pleasure. I would have offered it to you at once if I had it. I am looking out for my own supplies, but they have not come in yet.

MARQUIS. Surely *you* are not short of money?

CAPTAIN. See here; this is all I have . . . it doesn't amount to much.

Shows him a gold piece and some change.

Yes, it is the last I have left.

MARQUIS. Lend it to me . . .

CAPTAIN. But what am I to do?

MARQUIS. I will pay you back.

CAPTAIN. I don't know what to say . . . well . . . take it.

Gives coin.

MARQUIS. I have to keep an appointment. I must be off. We shall meet again at dinner.

Goes.

CAPTAIN, *to* SERVANT. Bravo! He was in hopes of borrowing ten guineas and contented himself with one in the end. Well, if he doesn't pay, it will keep him from bothering me. I think worse of his having drunk my chocolate!

MIRANDOLINA *comes to door with linen.*

MIRANDOLINA. May I come in, sir?

CAPTAIN, *harshly.* What do you want?

MIRANDOLINA, *coming a little further.* Here is some finer linen.

CAPTAIN, *pointing to table.* All right, leave it there.

MIRANDOLINA. Will you see, if you please, sir, if it is what you like?

CAPTAIN. What sort is it?

MIRANDOLINA. There are cambric sheets.

CAPTAIN. Sheets?

MIRANDOLINA. Yes, sir, the very finest; look at them.

CAPTAIN. I did not ask that. . . . I only asked for some better cloths than what you gave me.

MIRANDOLINA. I got this linen for those I should think worthy of it, who would know the difference. I give it to you because you are yourself . . . but I would give it to no other one.

CAPTAIN. "Because you are yourself." I don't know what you mean——

MIRANDOLINA. Look at this tablecloth . . . it is from Flanders.

CAPTAIN. It's a pity to use it at all.

MIRANDOLINA. I would not grudge so small a thing to a gentleman of your quality. I have napkins of the same; they are here for you.

CAPTAIN, *turns his back.* Give the things to my servant, or leave them there. You need not put yourself to so much trouble.

MIRANDOLINA, *making a grimace behind him, mimicking his manner.* Oh, it is no trouble at all, when it is for someone like you.

CAPTAIN. Well, well, that will do; I don't want anything more.

MIRANDOLINA. I will put it in the cupboard.

CAPTAIN. Wherever you like.

MIRANDOLINA, *having arranged linen.* What would you like, sir, for your dinner?

CAPTAIN. Whatever there is will do.

MIRANDOLINA. I would wish to know your tastes, sir. If there is any dish you have a liking for more than another, tell me of it.

CAPTAIN. If I want anything I will tell the waiter.

MIRANDOLINA. Men don't give the same attention to these things as we do. If there is any dish you have a fancy for, or any dressing, tell me what it is, if you please.

CAPTAIN. I am obliged to you. But even this civility will not help you to do with me what you have done with the marquis and the count.

MIRANDOLINA. Oh, why should you talk of that folly? If people who come to an inn pretend to have fallen in love with

the landlady . . . we have something else to think of than
to give heed to their nonsense. We try to serve our own interest. If they give us soft words, we turn it to the good of
the business. As for myself, when I hear them beginning
their flatteries I laugh myself tired.

CAPTAIN. Well done! I like to hear you speak the truth.

MIRANDOLINA. I always do. That is the only good thing about
me.

CAPTAIN. For all that you are ready enough to make believe
with your admirers.

MIRANDOLINA. I, to make believe! Heaven preserve me from
any such thing! Go and ask those two gentlemen who are
making love to me if I have ever given them any sign of
liking at all, or if I have amused myself with them in any
way that could deceive them. I don't drive them away, because it would not be to my interest to do that, but I sometimes come very near it. I hate the sight of men of that sort.
Look here, I am not a young girl, I have left some years
behind me; I'm no great beauty, but I have had good
chances, but I never had a mind to marry, because I think
it a fine thing to be free.

CAPTAIN. Yes, indeed; freedom is a treasure well worth
having.

MIRANDOLINA. And there are many who are foolish enough to
part with it.

CAPTAIN. I know what suits me best; liberty suits me.

MIRANDOLINA. Has Your Excellency a wife?

CAPTAIN. God forbid! I don't want one.

MIRANDOLINA. That's right, keep to that always; as to women
. . . No, that's enough . . . I have no mind to speak ill of
them.

CAPTAIN. You are the first woman I ever heard say that.

MIRANDOLINA. I tell you, we innkeepers see plenty and hear
plenty, and I pity those men that are taken in by any
woman at all.

CAPTAIN. That is an odd thing for you to say.

MIRANDOLINA. With your leave, sir.

Is going.

CAPTAIN. You are in a hurry.

MIRANDOLINA. I don't want to be troublesome.

CAPTAIN. Not at all; you amuse me.

MIRANDOLINA. You see now for yourself, sir, that is the way I go on with others . . . I keep them in chat for a few minutes. I joke a little to entertain them . . . and then all of a minute—you understand me, sir?—they begin to make love to me.

CAPTAIN. That happens because you have a taking manner.

MIRANDOLINA, *with a curtsy.* You are too kind, sir.

CAPTAIN. And then they lose their hearts.

MIRANDOLINA. What folly to be in such a hurry to lose their hearts!

CAPTAIN. It is a thing I never could understand.

MIRANDOLINA. Talk of strength, indeed! Fine strong men they are.

CAPTAIN. Their weakness is a disgrace to humanity——

MIRANDOLINA. That is right talk for a man. . . . I would like, sir, to shake you by the hand.

CAPTAIN. Why do you want to shake hands with me?

MIRANDOLINA. If you would condescend, sir. See . . . mine is clean.

CAPTAIN. Here is my hand.

MIRANDOLINA. This is the first time I ever had the honor to touch the hand of a man who had the real mind of a man. . . .

CAPTAIN. That will do.

MIRANDOLINA. Look now, if I had held out my hand to either one of that featherbrained pair downstairs, he would have been full sure I was dying for him. He would have lost his heart then and there! I would not have taken any such liberty with them for all the gold of the world. They have no understanding; oh, it's a blessing to be able to say things out without raising suspicion or doing mischief! I beg your pardon, sir, for my forwardness. Whenever I can serve you, just give the order, and I will pay more attention to it than I have ever done for anyone in the whole world.

CAPTAIN. Why should you think so well of me?

MIRANDOLINA. Because you being a well-reared gentleman, I know I can say out my mind to you and have no fear you will think I have an object, or that you will torment me with follies and absurdities.

CAPTAIN. Now, if you want to attend to your business, don't let me keep you here.

MIRANDOLINA. Yes, sir, I will go and look after the housework. That is my delight and my joy. In case you should want anything I will send the servingman.

CAPTAIN. All right. But you might look in at some other time.

MIRANDOLINA. I am not in the habit of attending on my guests . . . but it will be different with you.

CAPTAIN. Why so?

MIRANDOLINA. Because, sir, I like you.

CAPTAIN. You like me!

MIRANDOLINA. I like you because you are not weak, you are not a fool, you are a strong man, you will never give in to love!

Goes.

ACT II

SCENE:

The CAPTAIN's *room, with a table laid for dinner.* CAPTAIN *is walking with a book.* SERVANT *standing near door.* FABRIZIO *brings in soup.*

FABRIZIO, *to* SERVANT. Tell your master the soup is on the table.

SERVANT. You can tell him as easy as myself.

FABRIZIO. He is so queer, I don't like to be speaking to him.

SERVANT. He is not altogether bad for all that. He can't bear the sight of a woman, but he is civil enough with men.

FABRIZIO. Your dinner is on the table, sir.

Goes.

CAPTAIN *puts down book and comes to sit at table. The* SERVANT *stands behind his chair with a plate under his arm.*

CAPTAIN, *eating, to* SERVANT. It seems to me dinner is earlier than usual today.

SERVANT. This room was served before the others, sir; the Count of Albafiorita made a great noise when he was not served the first, but the mistress would not give in to putting you after him.

CAPTAIN. I am obliged to her for that.

SERVANT. She is a very perfect woman, sir. I never saw so civil a one in any part of the world I traveled.

CAPTAIN. You admire her then?

Turning a little.

SERVANT. If it was not for disobliging my master I would come and take service with Mirandolina.

CAPTAIN. You are a fool. What am I to do with you?

Gives him plate and he changes it.

SERVANT. Such a woman! I would obey her just the same as a little lapdog she would have.

Goes for a dish.

CAPTAIN. By Jove! She puts her enchantment on you all. It would be a very laughable thing if she should put it on me! I think tomorrow I'll go on to Livorno.

SERVANT, *bringing boiled fowl and another dish.* The mistress says if you do not like the pullet she will send you a pigeon.

CAPTAIN. I like everything so far. . . . What is this?

SERVANT. The mistress says I am to say to Your Excellency she hopes you will like this sauce she has made with her own hands.

CAPTAIN. She is doing a great deal for me.

Takes it.

It is excellent. It is a capital sauce . . . I have never tasted a better. If Mirandolina goes on like this she will never be in want of guests. A good table, a good laundry . . . and there's no denying she is pleasing . . . but what I think most of is her truthfulness; that is the great thing.

SERVANT. It is, sir.

CAPTAIN, *taking more sauce.* Tell her I am enjoying this sauce and much obliged to her.

SERVANT. I will, sir.

CAPTAIN. Go and tell her at once.

SERVANT. At once, sir.

Goes.

CAPTAIN *goes on eating.*

SERVANT, *coming back.* She thanks Your Excellency for receiving her poor attempt so kindly. She is at this moment making ready another dish with her own hands, but I don't know what it is.

CAPTAIN. She is making it herself?

SERVANT. Yes, sir.

CAPTAIN. Give me something to drink.

SERVANT, *goes to sideboard, brings bottle.* Here it is, sir.

Brings it to table.

CAPTAIN. I must make a return for all this . . . it is too much. I must pay double . . . I will treat her well; but I'll go to Livorno.

Servant gives him wine.

The count has gone to dinner?

Drinks.

SERVANT. He went out, sir; he is not back yet.

MIRANDOLINA *comes to the door with a plate in her hand.*

MIRANDOLINA. May I come in?

CAPTAIN. Who is there?

SERVANT. Come in, ma'am; let me have it.

CAPTAIN. Take the dish from her.

MIRANDOLINA. No . . . let me have the pleasure of putting it on the table myself.

Does so.

CAPTAIN. You ought not to do that.

MIRANDOLINA. Ah, sir, who am I? Am I a lady? I am the servant of whoever comes into my inn.

CAPTAIN. What humility!

MIRANDOLINA. To tell the truth, it would be no trouble to me to attend all my guests at table, but I don't do it for certain reasons. I don't know if you understand me. But I have no scruple in coming to you, quite simply.

CAPTAIN. I am obliged to you. What dish is this?

MIRANDOLINA. It is a haricot made with my own hands.

CAPTAIN. Very good. If it is made by you it is sure to be good.

MIRANDOLINA. Oh, you are too kind, sir; I don't know how to do anything right. But I would wish to give so good a gentleman something to his liking.

CAPTAIN, *aside to* SERVANT. To Livorno tomorrow. . . . If you have anything to do now don't waste your time on me.

MIRANDOLINA. It doesn't matter, sir, the house is well provided with servants. I would be glad to know if this dish is to your taste.

CAPTAIN. Certainly. . . . I will try it.

Tastes.

Good! It couldn't be better. What a flavor! What is it?

MIRANDOLINA. I have secrets of my own, sir. This hand knows how to make good things.

CAPTAIN, *to* SERVANT *with some passion.* Give me some wine.

MIRANDOLINA. After this dish, sir, you ought to drink something good.

CAPTAIN, *to* SERVANT. Give me some Burgundy.

MIRANDOLINA. *Bravissimo!* Burgundy is a splendid wine. In my opinion it is the best of all at dinner.

SERVANT *puts down bottle and glass.*

CAPTAIN. You are a good judge of everything.

MIRANDOLINA. Sure enough, I don't often make a mistake.

CAPTAIN. But this time you are making a mistake.

MIRANDOLINA. In what way, sir?

CAPTAIN. In thinking I deserve to be made much of by you.

MIRANDOLINA, *sighing.* Ah! Sir.

CAPTAIN, *altered.* What is it? What do these sighs mean?

MIRANDOLINA. I will tell you. I show these little attentions to everybody, and I am sorry to think they displease you.

CAPTAIN, *quietly.* I will not be ungrateful to you.

MIRANDOLINA. I do not want to win gratitude from you . . . I am doing no more than my duty.

CAPTAIN. No, no, I know that very well. I am not so bad as you think. You will not have to complain of me.

Pours wine in his glass.

MIRANDOLINA. But . . . sir . . . I don't understand.

CAPTAIN. Your good health!

Drinks.

MIRANDOLINA. I am greatly obliged . . . it is too much honor.

CAPTAIN. This wine is beyond praise.

MIRANDOLINA. Burgundy is my favorite.

CAPTAIN. Take some and welcome.

MIRANDOLINA. Oh! No, thank you, sir.

CAPTAIN. Have you had your dinner?

MIRANDOLINA. Yes, sir.

CAPTAIN. Won't you try a little glass?

MIRANDOLINA. I don't deserve such a favor.

CAPTAIN. You are very welcome.

MIRANDOLINA. I don't know what to say . . . I am not worthy of your kindness.

CAPTAIN, *to* SERVANT. Bring a glass.

MIRANDOLINA. No, no; if you will allow me I will take this. *Takes the* CAPTAIN's *glass.*

CAPTAIN. Oh, but I have used that one.

MIRANDOLINA, *smiling.* I drink to your good looks, sir.

The SERVANT *puts another glass on the tray.*

CAPTAIN. Eh! By Jove!

Pours out wine.

MIRANDOLINA. But it is some time since I have eaten anything. I'm afraid it might go to my head.

CAPTAIN. There's no danger.

MIRANDOLINA. If you would favor me with a mouthful of bread.

CAPTAIN. Certainly.

Gives her a piece.

Take it.

MIRANDOLINA *with the glass in one hand and a piece of bread in the other, stands awkwardly as if not able to drink.*

CAPTAIN. You will be more comfortable if you sit down.

MIRANDOLINA. Oh! That is too much, sir.

CAPTAIN. Come, come; there is no one here.

To SERVANT.

Put a chair.

SERVANT, *aside.* The master must be near his death. I never saw him this way before.

Goes for a chair.

MIRANDOLINA. If the count should hear this . . . or the marquis . . . woe betide me.

CAPTAIN. Why so?

MIRANDOLINA. A hundred times they have pressed me to eat or drink something with them and I would not.

CAPTAIN. Come, sit down.

She sits down and sips the wine.

To SERVANT.

Listen . . .

Speaking low.

Don't mention to anyone that our landlady has been sitting at my table.

SERVANT. Never fear, sir.

MIRANDOLINA. May the captain have his heart's desire!

CAPTAIN. Thank you, my polite little landlady.

MIRANDOLINA. This toast has nothing to do with women.

CAPTAIN. No, and why?

MIRANDOLINA. Because I know you hate the sight of women.

CAPTAIN. That is true. I never wish to see one.

MIRANDOLINA. Is it so with you still?

CAPTAIN. I don't want . . .

Looks at SERVANT.

MIRANDOLINA. What don't you want?

CAPTAIN. Listen.

Leans across table.

I don't want you to make me change my nature.

MIRANDOLINA. I, sir? How could I do that?

CAPTAIN, *to* SERVANT. You may go and have a couple of eggs cooked for me and bring them up when they are ready.

SERVANT. What way should the eggs be done?

CAPTAIN. Whatever way you like, you fool!

SERVANT, *aside.* I understand, sir.

Goes.

CAPTAIN. Mirandolina, you are a very pretty young person.

MIRANDOLINA. Oh, sir! You are making fun of me.

CAPTAIN. Listen . . . I am going to say a true word . . . a very true word that will be to your honor.

MIRANDOLINA. I shall be well pleased hearing it.

CAPTAIN. You are the first woman I have ever enjoyed talking to in this world.

MIRANDOLINA. I will tell you why, sir; not that I would make too much of myself, but people that have something akin know one another when they meet; this sympathy, this feeling for one another is sometimes to be found even between people who have never met. I myself feel for you what I have felt for no other.

CAPTAIN. I am afraid you want to take away my peace of mind.

MIRANDOLINA. Oh, sir, you are a sensible man; you would never give in to the weaknesses others fall into. Indeed if I saw any sign of it I would never come in here again. I myself feel . . . as well as you . . . I don't know what . . . inside me . . . something I never felt before . . . but I will not give in to being foolish about a man . . . much less for one who is against us all . . . and he maybe . . . maybe, to try me, and then to laugh at me, has been talking in a way to lead me on . . . if you please, sir, give me another drop of Burgundy.

CAPTAIN. Eh? I know, I know . . .

Pours out wine. Giving her the glass of wine.

Take it.

MIRANDOLINA. Thank you, sir, but you yourself are not taking any.

CAPTAIN. Yes. I will take some.

Aside.

The one devil may drive out the other!

Pours wine into his glass.

And tell me, do you dislike men?

MIRANDOLINA. As you detest women.

CAPTAIN. My enemies are getting their revenge.

MIRANDOLINA. How is that, sir?

CAPTAIN. Ah, you little humbug, you know very well.

MARQUIS *heard calling, "Captain."*

Drinks.

MIRANDOLINA, *caressingly.* Captain!

CAPTAIN. What is it?

MIRANDOLINA. Touch it . . .

Makes her glass touch his.

To those who live in good fellowship!

CAPTAIN, *languidly.* In good fellowship.

MARQUIS calls nearer, "Captain."

MIRANDOLINA. With no ill thought!

CAPTAIN. I drink to that.

MARQUIS comes in.

MARQUIS. Here I am. Whose health are you drinking?

CAPTAIN, *changing manner.* What do you want to know?

MARQUIS. Excuse me, my dear sir. I had been calling out, and no one answered.

MIRANDOLINA. With your leave.

Is going.

CAPTAIN, *to* MIRANDOLINA. Don't go.

To MARQUIS.

I don't take such liberties with you.

MARQUIS. I beg pardon. I thought you were alone. I am delighted to see our admirable hostess here . . . ah! What do you say? Isn't she perfection?

MIRANDOLINA. I had brought up some things for the captain . . . a little faintness came over me and he came to my help with a glass of Burgundy.

MARQUIS, *to* CAPTAIN. Is that Burgundy?

CAPTAIN. Yes, it is Burgundy.

MARQUIS. Is it really?

CAPTAIN. At least I paid for it as such.

MARQUIS. I am a judge. Let me try it and I'll tell you if it is or not.

CAPTAIN, *calls at door.* Here!

SERVANT enters.

A glass for the marquis.

SERVANT gives it and goes.

MARQUIS. That glass is too small; Burgundy is not a liqueur; one can't judge without getting enough to judge by.

Takes a larger glass.

SERVANT, *comes in with plate.* Here are the eggs, sir.

Puts them on the table.

CAPTAIN. I don't want anything more.

MARQUIS. What have you there?

CAPTAIN. Eggs.

MARQUIS. I don't care about eggs.

SERVANT *takes them away to sideboard.*

MIRANDOLINA. Marquis, if the captain will allow me . . . will you taste this haricot . . . made with my own hands.

MARQUIS. Oh, very well, here . . . a chair . . .

SERVANT *hands him a chair and puts glass on tray.*

A fork . . .

CAPTAIN. Lay a place there.

SERVANT *does so.*

MIRANDOLINA. I am feeling better now, sir. . . . I will go.

Gets up.

MARQUIS. Do me the pleasure of stopping a little longer.

MIRANDOLINA. But I have my own business to attend to; and then, the captain . . .

MARQUIS, *to* CAPTAIN. You will allow her to stay a little longer.

CAPTAIN. Why do you want her to stay?

MARQUIS. I will ask you to taste a glass of Cyprus wine, the equal of which you have never tasted in this world, and I would wish Mirandolina to try it also and to give her opinion.

CAPTAIN, *to* MIRANDOLINA. You must stay to oblige the marquis.

MIRANDOLINA. The marquis will excuse me.

MARQUIS. Won't you just taste it?

MIRANDOLINA. Another time, Your Excellency.

CAPTAIN. Oh, you had better stay.

MIRANDOLINA, *to* CAPTAIN. Is that a command?

CAPTAIN. I say you are to stay here.

MIRANDOLINA, *sitting down.* I obey.

MARQUIS, *eating.* Oh, what a good dish! What a savory smell! What a flavor! Your health, Captain.

Drinks Burgundy.

CAPTAIN. Well, what do you think of it?

MARQUIS. With all due respect, it is very poor. Try my Cyprus wine. . . .

CAPTAIN. But where is this Cyprus wine?

MARQUIS. I have it here . . . I brought it with me. We must enjoy it together; there's no mistake about it.

Takes from pocket a very small bottle.

MIRANDOLINA. By what I see, sir, you don't want your wine to go to our heads.

MARQUIS. This! It should be tasted drop by drop like Tokay. Where are the glasses?

Opens bottle; SERVANT *brings glasses.*

Eh! Those are too big . . . have you no smaller?

He covers the bottle with his hand.

CAPTAIN, *to* SERVANT. Bring the liqueur glasses.

MIRANDOLINA. I think smelling it will be enough.

MARQUIS, *smelling it.* Oh dear! It has a very comforting smell.

SERVANT *brings three glasses on the tray, the* MARQUIS *very slowly fills the glasses, giving one to the* CAPTAIN, *one to* MIRANDOLINA *and keeping one, carefully recorking the bottle.*

What nectar!

Takes a sip.

What ambrosia! What distilled manna!

CAPTAIN, *aside to* MIRANDOLINA. What do you think of this filth?

MIRANDOLINA, *aside to* CAPTAIN. Bottle rinsings.

MARQUIS, *to* CAPTAIN. Eh! What do you think?

CAPTAIN. Very good! Delicious!

MARQUIS. Do you like it, Mirandolina?

MIRANDOLINA. Well, sir, as you ask me, I can't make a pretense. I think it nasty and I won't say it's nice. Let whoever

pleases pretend to like it, but I won't. To deceive in one
thing is to be ready to deceive in other things.

CAPTAIN. You say that as a reproach to me and I don't know
why.

MARQUIS. Mirandolina, you are no judge at all of wine of this
sort; I am sorry for you. You were able to understand the
handkerchief I gave you, and to admire it——

Rises.

—but you know nothing at all about Cyprus wine.

Finishes his glass.

May I call your servant?

Goes to door and talks to SERVANT.

MIRANDOLINA, *moves nearer to* CAPTAIN. It is amusing to hear
him praise his own goods.

CAPTAIN, *aside to* MIRANDOLINA. That is not my habit.

MIRANDOLINA, *aside to* CAPTAIN. Your boasting is of your contempt for us poor women.

CAPTAIN, *aside to* MIRANDOLINA. And yours in bringing to your
feet every man.

MIRANDOLINA, *carelessly.* Not all men.

CAPTAIN, *with some passion.* Yes, all.

MARQUIS, *returning from door.* Here is a clean glass.

SERVANT *brings them on a tray.*

MIRANDOLINA. I don't want any more.

MARQUIS. No, never fear, it's not for you. . . . Here, my man,
with your master's leave, go to the Count of Albafiorita and
tell him out *loud,* so that anyone may hear, that I beg him
to try a little of this.

SERVANT. I will, sir.

CAPTAIN. Marquis, you are very generous.

MIRANDOLINA. Take care it doesn't upset him, sir.

MARQUIS, *to* MIRANDOLINA. Do you know what it is upsets me?

MIRANDOLINA. What is it?

MARQUIS. Your beautiful eyes.

MIRANDOLINA. Is that so, indeed?

MARQUIS. Captain, I have entirely lost my heart to her. And I am as jealous as a bear. I don't mind her being here, because I know what you are, but otherwise I wouldn't let her near you for a hundred thousand pounds.

Exit.

CAPTAIN. The poor marquis is going crazy.

MIRANDOLINA. He has taken away his little bottle to comfort him.

CAPTAIN. He is mad, I tell you, and it is you who have driven him mad.

MIRANDOLINA. Am I one of those who make men mad?

CAPTAIN, *troubled.* Yes, you are.

MIRANDOLINA, *getting up.* Sir . . . with your leave . . .

CAPTAIN. Stay here.

MIRANDOLINA, *going.* I beg pardon, I don't trouble the wits of anyone.

Goes toward door.

CAPTAIN. Listen to me . . .

He gets up but stands before her.

MIRANDOLINA, *tries to brush past him.* Excuse me.

CAPTAIN, *imperiously.* Stay here, I tell you.

MIRANDOLINA, *turning, with pride.* What do you want with me?

CAPTAIN. Nothing . . .

Is confused.

Take another glass of Burgundy.

MIRANDOLINA. Well, be quick, for I am going.

CAPTAIN. Sit down.

MIRANDOLINA. Standing, standing!

CAPTAIN, *giving her the glass gently.* Take it.

MIRANDOLINA. I will give a toast, and then I will be off . . . a toast my nurse taught me:

> Wine comes in at the mouth,
> And Love comes in at the eye,
> That's all we shall know for truth,

Before we grow old and die;
I lift the glass to my mouth
I look at you and I sigh.

Goes.

CAPTAIN. Well done . . . Come back! Ah, the wretch, she has
made off . . . and she has left a hundred devils to torment
me! "I lift the glass to my mouth, I look at you and I sigh."
What does that mean? Ah! You little villain. I know what
you are at! You want to put me down, to get the better of
me. But you do it so charmingly; you know so well how to
wind yourself in. The devil, the devil, you can do as you
like with me. No, I will go away. I will never see her again.
Let her not come in my way again; my curse upon women!
I never will set foot again in any place where there is one
to be found.

SERVANT, *coming in.* Shall I put the fruit on the table, sir?

CAPTAIN. Go to the devil!

SERVANT. Are you speaking to me, sir?

CAPTAIN. I'll leave this tomorrow.

SERVANT. Very well, sir.

CAPTAIN. Yes, or tonight.

SERVANT. It will be hard to be ready, sir.

CAPTAIN. I will not stay here another night. I am determined.
I have made up my mind like a man. Go to Fabrizio and
tell him to bring my bill.

SERVANT. I will do that, sir.

CAPTAIN. Listen—have the luggage ready within two hours.
What's the matter? Do you hear me . . . ?

SERVANT. Oh, sir, my heart is broken going away, on account
of Mirandolina!

Goes.

CAPTAIN, *walking to door and returning as if undecided.* For
all that, I feel a sort of unwillingness to leave that is quite
new to me. So much the worse for me if I should stay;
Mirandolina might get hold of me. I ought to set out. I
am determined to get away this very minute.

FABRIZIO *coming in, meets him at door.*

FABRIZIO. Is it true, sir, that you are wanting your bill?

CAPTAIN. Yes, have you brought it?

FABRIZIO. The mistress is just making it out.

CAPTAIN. She makes up the accounts?

FABRIZIO. She does always. She did it living with her father. She can write and can make up figures better than any young fellow in business.

CAPTAIN. She is a wonderful woman.

FABRIZIO. And will you be going so soon from us?

CAPTAIN. Yes, I've business to attend to.

FABRIZIO. I hope you will remember the waiter.

CAPTAIN. Bring the bill and I'll know what I should do.

FABRIZIO. Is it here you want the bill brought? I'll bring it without any delay.

Goes.

CAPTAIN. You are all bewitched by Mirandolina! It is no wonder if even I myself catch fire . . . but I'll make my escape! I will go away. Who do I see? Mirandolina? What does she want with me? She has a sheet of paper in her hand. She is bringing the bill. What can I do! I must put up with this last attack. In two hours from this I set out.

MIRANDOLINA, *coming in with bill. Sadly.* Sir . . .

CAPTAIN. What is it, Mirandolina?

MIRANDOLINA, *standing in background.* I beg your pardon.

CAPTAIN. Come over here.

MIRANDOLINA, *sadly.* You asked for your bill. I have brought it.

CAPTAIN. Give it here.

MIRANDOLINA. Here it is.

Wipes her eyes with her apron as she is giving it.

CAPTAIN. What is the matter? You are crying.

MIRANDOLINA. Nothing, sir. The smoke has got into my eyes.

CAPTAIN. The smoke got into your eyes? Ah, that will do. What does the bill matter.

Reads it.

Two guineas in four days! Such a liberal table . . . only two guineas!

MIRANDOLINA. That is your account, sir.

CAPTAIN. And those two special dishes you gave me this morning? They are not put down.

MIRANDOLINA. I beg your pardon, sir. What I give I do not charge for.

CAPTAIN. You've been feasting me for nothing.

MIRANDOLINA. Forgive the liberty. I thank you for an act of kindness.

Covers her face appearing to cry.

CAPTAIN. But what is the matter?

MIRANDOLINA. I don't know if it's the smoke or if it's some weakness of the eyes.

CAPTAIN. I would not like you to suffer through cooking those two priceless dishes for me.

MIRANDOLINA. If it was for that, I would suffer very willingly.

She falls as if unconscious into a chair.

CAPTAIN. Mirandolina! Oh, my dear Mirandolina! She has fainted. Have you fallen in love with me? But so quickly . . . And why not? Am I not in love with you? Dear Mirandolina! I, saying "dear" to a woman! But it is for my sake you have fainted. Oh, how beautiful you are! If I had but something to bring you round . . . ! I, not being used to weak women, have no salts or scent bottles. Who is there? Nobody. Quick, I will go. Bless you, my poor little thing.

He goes.

MIRANDOLINA, *sitting up.* I've got him this time! I thought a faint would do it. Back to it now.

Falls as before.

CAPTAIN, *coming back with a glass of water.* Here I am! Here I am. She has not come to herself yet. Ah! There can be no doubt she likes me. I will sprinkle the water on her face. She ought to awake.

He sprinkles and she moves.

Courage, courage . . . I am here, my dear. I will not·go away now or ever.

SERVANT, *with sword and belt*. Here are the sword and the belt.

CAPTAIN, *to* SERVANT. Go away.

SERVANT. The portmanteaus.

CAPTAIN. Get away; confound you!

SERVANT. Mirandolina!

Comes toward her.

CAPTAIN, *seizing sword*. Go or I'll split your head!

SERVANT *goes.*

Not come round yet? Her forehead is moist. Come, dear Mirandolina, take courage. Open your eyes. . . . Tell me everything.

MARQUIS *and* COUNT *come in.*

MARQUIS. Captain!

COUNT. What on earth!

CAPTAIN. Oh, confound it.

MARQUIS, *excitedly*. Mirandolina!

MIRANDOLINA, *getting up*. Ah, dear me.

MARQUIS. It was my voice that brought her round.

COUNT. I am glad, Captain . . .

MARQUIS. Well done. Sir . . . after all your talk!

CAPTAIN. That's impertinence.

COUNT. Have you given in at last?

CAPTAIN. Go to the devil, the two of you!

He throws jug at them and goes toward them in a fury.

COUNT. He has gone mad!

They rush out, followed by CAPTAIN.

MIRANDOLINA, *getting up*. I've done it! His heart is on fire, in flames, in cinders. I have but to carry through my victory to teach a lesson to all unmannerly men!

ACT III

SCENE 1

Room with three doors, as in Act I, with a table, and linen to be ironed. MIRANDOLINA *alone.*

MIRANDOLINA. Eh, Fabrizio!

FABRIZIO, *coming in.* Ma'am?

MIRANDOLINA. Do something for me; bring me the hot iron.

FABRIZIO, *gravely, as he is going.* Yes, ma'am.

MIRANDOLINA. You must excuse me for giving you this trouble.

FABRIZIO. Not at all, ma'am. So long as I am eating your bread it is my duty to obey you.

Is going.

MIRANDOLINA. Stop, listen; you are not bound to obey me in these things . . . but I know you do it willingly for me, and I . . . that's enough, I'll say no more.

FABRIZIO. As for me, I would do the world and all for you . . . but I see all I can do is but thrown away.

MIRANDOLINA. How is it thrown away? Am I so ungrateful?

FABRIZIO. You have no respect for poor men . . . you are too much taken up with the quality.

MIRANDOLINA. Ah, you poor goose! If I could but tell you all . . . ! Come, come . . . go and get me the iron.

FABRIZIO. But what I have seen with my own eyes . . .

MIRANDOLINA. Come along . . . not so much chattering; get the iron.

FABRIZIO, *going.* All right, all right. I will do your bidding but not for long.

MIRANDOLINA, *pretending to speak to herself, but meaning to be heard*. With these men, the more one wants to please them, the less one succeeds.

FABRIZIO, *with tenderness, turning round*. What did you say?

MIRANDOLINA. Go away; bring me that smoothing iron.

FABRIZIO. I'll bring it. I don't understand you at all; one time you are for putting me up; another time for knocking me down. I don't understand it at all.

Goes.

MIRANDOLINA. You poor silly! You have to obey me in spite of yourself.

SERVANT, *coming in*. Mistress Mirandolina . . .

MIRANDOLINA. What is it, friend?

SERVANT. My master sends his compliments . . . and to know how you are.

MIRANDOLINA. Tell him I am very well.

SERVANT, *giving her a smelling bottle*. He says that if you will smell these salts, they will be very serviceable to you.

MIRANDOLINA. This bottle seems to be made of gold.

SERVANT. It is, ma'am, of gold; I can answer for that.

MIRANDOLINA. Why didn't he give me his smelling salts when I was in that terrible faint?

SERVANT. He had not the little bottle at that time.

MIRANDOLINA. And where did he get it now?

SERVANT. Listen, and I will tell you a secret: he sent me just now to bring a goldsmith and he bought it, and he paid seven guineas for it . . . and after that he sent me to an apothecary for the salts.

MIRANDOLINA. Ah! Ah! Ah!

SERVANT. Are you laughing?

MIRANDOLINA. I am laughing because he is so ready to cure me now the faint is over.

SERVANT. It will be good for another time.

MIRANDOLINA. Well, I'll smell it as a safeguard.

She smells it and gives him back the bottle.

Take it and say I am obliged to him.

SERVANT. Oh, the bottle is your own.

MIRANDOLINA. How is it mine?

SERVANT. The master bought it on purpose.

MIRANDOLINA. On purpose for me?

SERVANT. For you; but hush, be quiet.

MIRANDOLINA. Take him back his bottle and say I am obliged to him.

SERVANT. Ah, that won't do.

MIRANDOLINA. Give it to him, I tell you . . . I don't want it.

SERVANT. Would you wish to offend him?

MIRANDOLINA. Not so much talk. Do as I bid you; take it.

SERVANT. I suppose I must. I will bring it to him. Oh, what a woman! To refuse pure gold! I never met your equal, ma'am. And I should travel far to find it!
Goes.

MIRANDOLINA. He is boiled, baked, and roasted!

FABRIZIO, *comes in stiffly, with an iron in his hand.* Here is the smoothing iron.

MIRANDOLINA. Is it very hot?

FABRIZIO. It is, ma'am. It is so hot it might have scorched me.

MIRANDOLINA. Is there any new grievance?

FABRIZIO. This gentleman of a captain has sent you messages and has sent you presents by his servant.

MIRANDOLINA. Yes, Mr. High-and-Mighty . . . he sent me a little smelling bottle and I sent it back to him.

FABRIZIO. You sent it back to him?

MIRANDOLINA. I did . . . you can ask the same servant.

FABRIZIO. Why, now, did you do that?

MIRANDOLINA. Because, Fabrizio . . . I can't tell you. . . . Let us talk of some other thing.

FABRIZIO. My dear Mirandolina, you should have pity on me.

MIRANDOLINA. Go away. . . . Have done. Let me do my ironing.

FABRIZIO. I'm not stopping you from doing it.

MIRANDOLINA. Go and heat another iron, and, when it's hot, bring it to me.

FABRIZIO. I will. Believe now what I am saying . . .

MIRANDOLINA. Don't say another word; I am getting vexed.

FABRIZIO. I'll say nothing. You have a flighty little head, but I like you all the same.

Goes.

MIRANDOLINA. That is all right. I'm getting credit with Fabrizio for having refused the captain's gift. That shows I know how to live and what to do.

CAPTAIN, *coming in at back.* There she is. I didn't want to come . . . it's the devil that has dragged me.

MIRANDOLINA, *seeing him with the corner of her eye, and ironing.* There he is, there he is.

CAPTAIN. Mirandolina?

MIRANDOLINA, *ironing.* Oh, sir! I beg your pardon.

CAPTAIN. How are you?

MIRANDOLINA, *stepping back without looking at him.* Very well, thank you, sir.

CAPTAIN. I have reason to complain of you.

MIRANDOLINA, *looking at him a moment.* Why so, sir?

CAPTAIN. Because you have refused the smelling bottle I sent you.

MIRANDOLINA, *ironing.* What would you have me do?

CAPTAIN. I would have you accept what was offered to you.

MIRANDOLINA. Thank Heaven I am not subject to fainting fits.

Ironing.

What happened to me today is a thing that will never happen to me again.

CAPTAIN. Dear Mirandolina, I hope I was not the cause of it.

MIRANDOLINA, *ironing.* But I am afraid it is you yourself who were the cause of it.

CAPTAIN, *with passion.* I? Is that so?

MIRANDOLINA, *ironing with fury.* You made me drink that unlucky wine and it upset me.

CAPTAIN, *mortified.* What! Is it possible?

MIRANDOLINA. It was that and no other thing. I will never go near your parlor again.

CAPTAIN, *tenderly.* I understand; you will not come near me; I understand the mystery. Yes, I understand it. But come, my dear, and you will not regret it.

MIRANDOLINA. This iron is getting cold. Here, Fabrizio!
Calls very loud from the door.
If the other iron is heated, bring it in.

CAPTAIN. Do me this kindness now. Take this bottle.
Holds it out.

MIRANDOLINA, *with displeasure . . . ironing.* Indeed, sir, I don't accept presents.

CAPTAIN. But you took one from the count.

MIRANDOLINA, *ironing.* I was forced to take it, not to offend him.

CAPTAIN. And you would offend and disoblige me?

MIRANDOLINA. What does it matter to you if a woman offends you? You can't dislike them more than you do.

CAPTAIN. Ah! Mirandolina, I cannot say that now.

MIRANDOLINA. Tell me, sir, when will there be a new moon?

CAPTAIN. It is not the moon that has worked the change; it is your own beauty and your own charm.

MIRANDOLINA, *laughing out and ironing.* Ha! Ha! Ha!

CAPTAIN. You are laughing?

MIRANDOLINA. You don't want me to laugh? You make fun of me and then you don't want me to laugh!

CAPTAIN. That's all nonsense; here, take it.

MIRANDOLINA, *ironing.* No, thank you; no, thank you.

CAPTAIN. Take it . . . or you'll make me angry.

MIRANDOLINA, *ironing with exaggeration.* Fabrizio! The iron!

CAPTAIN, *angrily.* Will you take it, or will you not take it?

MIRANDOLINA. Oh! Fie! Temper, temper!
Takes bottle and throws it contemptuously into linen basket. Loud as before.
Fabrizio!

FABRIZIO, *comes in with the iron.* Here I am.
Seeing the CAPTAIN, *he grows jealous.*

MIRANDOLINA, *taking the iron.* Is it very hot?

FABRIZIO, *dignified.* It is, ma'am.

MIRANDOLINA, *tenderly to* FABRIZIO. What is the matter with you? You seem to be put out?

FABRIZIO. Nothing, ma'am; nothing at all.

MIRANDOLINA, *as before.* Are you not well?

FABRIZIO. Give me the other iron if you want it brought to the fire.

MIRANDOLINA, *as before.* Indeed I am afraid there is something wrong with you.

CAPTAIN. Give him the iron and let him go.

MIRANDOLINA, *to* CAPTAIN. I think a great deal of him, as you know. He is my good helper.

CAPTAIN, *aside, furious.* I can stand no more of this.

MIRANDOLINA, *giving the iron to* FABRIZIO. Take it, my dear, and heat it.

FABRIZIO, *tenderly.* Ah! Ma'am.

MIRANDOLINA, *driving him away.* Get along, hurry.

FABRIZIO. What a life this is; I can stand no more of it. *Goes.*

CAPTAIN. Great civility to your own servant.

MIRANDOLINA. Well, what have you to say about it?

CAPTAIN. I say you are in love with him.

MIRANDOLINA. In love with a servingman! You are paying me a fine compliment, sir. . . . I have not such bad taste as you think. When I want to fall in love I won't throw myself away foolishly.

CAPTAIN. You are worthy of a king's love.

MIRANDOLINA. The King of Spades or the King of Hearts?

CAPTAIN. Let us leave joking, Mirandolina, and talk sense.

MIRANDOLINA, *ironing.* Talk on then and I'll listen.

CAPTAIN. Can't you leave off your ironing for a few minutes?

MIRANDOLINA. Oh no, I must get ready this linen for to-morrow.

CAPTAIN. You think more of it than of me?

MIRANDOLINA. To be sure I do.

CAPTAIN. Can you say that?

MIRANDOLINA. Certainly. This linen is useful to me, and I see no use at all I can put you to.

CAPTAIN. On the contrary, you can do what you like with me.

MIRANDOLINA. Eh? You woman hater?

CAPTAIN. Don't torment me any more . . . you have had your full revenge. . . . I think well of you; I would think well of any woman like you if she were to be found . . . I admire you, I love you, and I ask your pity.

MIRANDOLINA. Oh yes, sir, I understand.

She lets a sleeve drop.

CAPTAIN. You may believe me.

Picks up sleeve and gives it to her.

MIRANDOLINA. Don't take that trouble.

CAPTAIN. You are well worth waiting on.

MIRANDOLINA. Ha! Ha! Ha!

CAPTAIN. Why are you laughing?

MIRANDOLINA. Because you are talking nonsense.

CAPTAIN. Mirandolina, I can bear no more.

MIRANDOLINA. Are you feeling ill?

CAPTAIN. Yes, I can't stand it.

MIRANDOLINA, *throwing him the bottle, with contempt.* Take a sniff of your own salts!

CAPTAIN. Don't treat me so harshly.

Tries to take her hand but she touches him with the iron. Damn!

MIRANDOLINA. I beg your pardon. I didn't do it on purpose.

CAPTAIN. Never mind . . . this is nothing. You have given me a worse wound than that.

MIRANDOLINA. Where, sir?

CAPTAIN. In the heart.

MIRANDOLINA, *calls laughingly.* Fabrizio!

CAPTAIN. For pity sake, don't call that man.

MIRANDOLINA. But I want the other iron.

CAPTAIN. Wait and I will call my servant.

MIRANDOLINA. Eh! Fabrizio!

CAPTAIN. I swear to Heaven if that man comes in, I will break his head.

MIRANDOLINA. Oh, that's a good joke! I am not to be attended by my own servant!

CAPTAIN. Call someone else. . . . I won't have that fellow come here.

MIRANDOLINA. It seems to me, sir, you are going a little too far.

She draws back from table with the iron in her hand.

CAPTAIN. Oh, forgive me! I am outside myself.

MIRANDOLINA. I had better go into the kitchen.

CAPTAIN. No, my dear, stay here.

MIRANDOLINA, *moving on round table.* This is a strange thing to happen.

CAPTAIN, *following her.* Take pity on me.

MIRANDOLINA, *passing back.* I am not to call who I like?

CAPTAIN. I tell you I am jealous of that man. This is the first time I have known what love is.

MIRANDOLINA, *still walking.* No one has ever given me orders.

CAPTAIN, *following her.* I don't want to give you orders.

MIRANDOLINA, *turning, with a change of manner.* What do you want of me?

CAPTAIN. Love, compassion, pity.

MIRANDOLINA. A man that could not put up with me this very morning to be calling out for love and pity! It is all nonsense. I am not giving heed to you. I don't believe a word of it.

Goes.

CAPTAIN, *alone.* My curse upon the hour I first looked at her! There is no help for me now, I have tumbled into the net!

Goes.

COUNT, *coming in.* What do you say, Marquis, to the great news?

MARQUIS. To what news?

COUNT, *to* MARQUIS. That unmannerly captain, that woman hater, has fallen in love with Mirandolina!

MARQUIS. Likely enough. He saw that anyone I cast my eye upon must be worth admiring. But he will be well punished for his impudence.

COUNT. But if Mirandolina encourages him?

MARQUIS. That cannot happen. She would not think it right toward me. She knows who I am. She knows all I have done for her.

COUNT. I have done a great deal more for her. But it is all thrown away. Mirandolina is making up to Captain Ripafratta. She has shown him attention she has never shown to either of us. That's the way with women, the more you do for them, the less thanks you get, and they run off after somebody who has never thrown them a civil word.

MARQUIS. If it were true . . . but it cannot be.

COUNT. Why can it not be true?

MARQUIS. Would she put that man on a level with me?

COUNT. Didn't you see her yourself sitting at his table? Did she ever do as much as that for us? The best linen for him, his table served the first. Dishes made for him with her own hands; the servants all notice it and talk about it. Fabrizio is raging with jealousy. And that fainting fit, whether it was real or a pretense, what was that but a declaration of love?

MARQUIS. What! She herself made that delicious ragout for him and gave me a dish of leathery beef and potatoes? This is a great insult, indeed.

COUNT. I, who spent so much on her!

MARQUIS. And I, who was always giving her presents! Why, I gave her a glass of my Cyprus wine!

COUNT. I see she is a thankless creature. I have made up my mind to give her up. I will leave this wretched inn this very day.

MARQUIS. Yes, you will do well to go away.

COUNT. And you had better do the same.

MARQUIS. But . . . where can we go?

COUNT. Leave that to me.

MARQUIS. All right. I'll punish this fool of a woman. I will give up her inn!

Both go out.

SCENE 2

The same room. MIRANDOLINA *rushes in by center door—bangs and locks it.*

MIRANDOLINA, *panting.* What an escape!

CAPTAIN *heard rushing to door and knocking at it.*

CAPTAIN. Mirandolina! Let me in, Mirandolina.

MIRANDOLINA. What do you want, sir?

CAPTAIN. Open the door!

MIRANDOLINA. Wait a while. . . . I will be with you directly.

CAPTAIN. Why can't you let me in?

MIRANDOLINA. There are people coming. Go, if you please. I am coming at once.

CAPTAIN. I am going. If you don't come, it will be the worse for you.

Goes.

MIRANDOLINA, *looking through keyhole.* Yes, yes, he is gone. *Goes to another door.*

Here, Fabrizio!

FABRIZIO, *coming in.* Did you call?

MIRANDOLINA. Come here; I want to tell you something.

FABRIZIO. I'm here.

MIRANDOLINA. Do you know that the captain has fallen in love with me?

FABRIZIO. Oh, I know that.

MIRANDOLINA. What! You know it? But I myself didn't know it.

FABRIZIO. You poor innocent! You never knew it. You did not take notice, the time you were handling your smoothing irons, of the eyes he was throwing on you and the jealousy he was showing toward myself.

MIRANDOLINA. I was thinking of my work. I didn't think much of what he was doing.

Goes to door and listens.

But since then, Fabrizio, he has said things to me that make me blush.

FABRIZIO. Look here, now. That is because you are young, and you are alone without father or mother or anybody at all. If you had a husband things would not turn out that way.

MIRANDOLINA. Well, it may be you are saying what is true. I have been thinking of marrying.

FABRIZIO. Remember what your father said to you.

MIRANDOLINA. Yes, I remember.

CAPTAIN *heard again beating at door.*

MIRANDOLINA, *to* FABRIZIO. Listen . . . Listen!

FABRIZIO, *loud, toward door.* Who is that knocking?

CAPTAIN. Open the door!

MIRANDOLINA, *to* FABRIZIO. Don't let him in!

FABRIZIO, *goes nearer to door.* What do you want?

MIRANDOLINA. Wait till I go away.

FABRIZIO. What are you afraid of?

MIRANDOLINA. Dear Fabrizio, I don't know . . . I am afraid. . . .

FABRIZIO. Don't be uneasy. . . . I'll take care of you.

CAPTAIN. Let me in, I say!

MIRANDOLINA *goes.*

FABRIZIO. What do you want, sir? What is this noise? That is no behavior for a respectable inn.

CAPTAIN. Open the door.

He is heard trying to force it.

FABRIZIO. The devil! I am in no hurry to open it. Are any of the men about? There's nobody!

MARQUIS *and* COUNT *come in at third door.*

COUNT. What is it?

MARQUIS. What is this noise?

FABRIZIO, *low that the* CAPTAIN *may not hear.* I beg your pardon, gentlemen. This captain that wants to get in . . .

CAPTAIN. Open the door, or I'll break it open!

MARQUIS, *to* COUNT. Is he mad? Let us go away.

COUNT, *to* FABRIZIO. Open it; I have something to say to him.

FABRIZIO. I will open it, but I ask of you——

COUNT. Don't be afraid. You have us here.

FABRIZIO *opens door and the* CAPTAIN *comes in.*

CAPTAIN. The devil! Where is she?

FABRIZIO. Who are you looking for, sir?

CAPTAIN. Mirandolina. Where is she?

FABRIZIO. I don't know.

CAPTAIN. The good-for-nothing baggage! I'll find her!

Comes farther into the room and sees COUNT *and* MARQUIS.

COUNT, *to* CAPTAIN. What has gone wrong with you?

FABRIZIO. What do you want with the mistress, sir?

CAPTAIN. That is no business of yours. When I give orders I expect to be obeyed. That is what I pay for.

FABRIZIO. You pay your money to be served in straight things and honest things.

CAPTAIN. What are you saying? What do you know about it? Get out of that, you rascal, or I'll knock you down.

FABRIZIO. I wonder at you.

MARQUIS, *to* FABRIZIO. Be quiet.

COUNT, *to* FABRIZIO. Leave the room.

CAPTAIN, *to* FABRIZIO. Get away out of this.

FABRIZIO, *getting warm.* I tell you, gentlemen . . .

MARQUIS. Be off!

CAPTAIN. Making me wait in my room!

They all push him away—he goes.

MARQUIS. What the deuce ails you?

CAPTAIN. She has been talking with Fabrizio. Was she talking of marrying him?

COUNT. Well, your heart is very easy to touch, after all.

CAPTAIN. What do you mean by saying that?

COUNT. I know why you're angry.

CAPTAIN, *to* MARQUIS. Do you know what he is talking about?

MARQUIS. I don't know anything.

COUNT. I am talking about you. Under pretense of despising women you tried to come between me and Mirandolina.

CAPTAIN, *confused, to* MARQUIS. I?

COUNT. Look at me and answer me. Perhaps you are ashamed of your behavior.

CAPTAIN. I should be ashamed to listen to you any longer without saying that you are telling a lie.

COUNT. I, telling a lie?

MARQUIS. Things are getting worse.

CAPTAIN, *to* MARQUIS, *angrily.* The count doesn't know what he is talking about.

MARQUIS. I don't want to mix myself with it at all.

COUNT, *to* CAPTAIN. You yourself are a liar.

MARQUIS. I'm going away.

Tries to go.

CAPTAIN, *holding him by force.* Stop here.

COUNT. And you will account to me.

CAPTAIN. Yes, I will account to you. . . .

To MARQUIS.

Lend me your sword.

MARQUIS. Come now, quiet yourselves, both of you. My dear Count, what does it matter to you if the captain is in love with Mirandolina.

CAPTAIN. I, in love? That's not true . . . whoever says that is a liar.

MARQUIS. I, a liar? That does not refer to me . . . it was not I who said it.

CAPTAIN. Who says it, then?

COUNT. I say it, and hold to it, and I will not be put down by you.

CAPTAIN, *to* MARQUIS. Give me your sword.

MARQUIS. I will not, I say.

CAPTAIN. Are you another enemy?

MARQUIS. I am everybody's friend.

CAPTAIN. Damn!

Takes sword from MARQUIS, *who gives it with scabbard.*
To MARQUIS.

If you take offense I will settle with you as well.

MARQUIS. Go away! You are too hot-tempered and

Grumbles to himself.

I don't like it.

COUNT. I want satisfaction.

Puts himself on guard.

CAPTAIN. I will let you have it!

Tries to take sword out of scabbard but can't.

MARQUIS. That sword does not know you!

CAPTAIN, *trying to force it out.* Confound it!

MARQUIS. Captain, you will never do it.

COUNT. I am out of patience.

CAPTAIN. Here it is!

Draws sword, but sees it has no blade.

What is this?

MARQUIS. You have broken my sword.

CAPTAIN. Where is the rest of it? There is nothing in the
scabbard.

MARQUIS. Yes, that is true. . . . I broke it in my last duel.
I had forgotten.

COUNT. I swear to Heaven you shall not escape me.

CAPTAIN. Who wants to escape? I am not afraid to stand up
to you with nothing but this inch of blade.

MARQUIS. It is a Spanish blade. . . . It does not know fear.

CAPTAIN. Yes, with this blade.

Goes toward COUNT.

COUNT, *putting himself at defense.* Back!

MIRANDOLINA *and* FABRIZIO *come in.*

FABRIZIO. Stop, stop, gentlemen!

MIRANDOLINA. Stop, stop, sir!

COUNT. It is all your fault!

MIRANDOLINA. Oh, poor me!

MARQUIS. It is on your account.

COUNT, *pointing at the* CAPTAIN. He has fallen in love with you.

CAPTAIN. That's a lie.

MIRANDOLINA. The captain in love with me! He denies it, and his denying it mortifies me and makes little of me and makes me understand his politeness and my own weakness. . . . To tell the truth, if I had made him care for me I should have taken credit for the greatest victory in the world; a man who can't bear the sight of a woman, who despises them, and makes nothing of them—how could we ever expect to see such a one fall in love? Gentlemen, I am very straight and truthful; when I ought to speak I speak out, and I cannot hide the truth. I wanted to punish the captain for his scorn of us all. I tried to touch his heart, but I failed to do it.

To CAPTAIN.

Is not this true, sir? I tried and tried and didn't succeed after all.

CAPTAIN. What can I say . . . ? I can't say anything.

COUNT, *to* MIRANDOLINA. What do you think of him now?

MARQUIS, *to* MIRANDOLINA. He has not courage to say no.

CAPTAIN, *angrily to* MARQUIS. You don't know what you are talking about.

MIRANDOLINA. Oh, the captain didn't give way! He sees through all arts, he knows the roguery of women, he doesn't give heed to what they say, he is not taken in by their tears; if they faint, he only makes fun of it.

CAPTAIN. Are all women's tears a lie, then, and their faintings a cheat?

MIRANDOLINA. What! Don't you know, or are you making pretense not to know?

CAPTAIN. Good heavens! Such deceit deserves a knife across the throat!

MIRANDOLINA. Oh, sir, don't be angry because these gentlemen think you were really in love!

COUNT. You are still, you can't deny it.

MARQUIS. One can see it in your eyes.

CAPTAIN, *angrily to* MARQUIS. No, you can't!

MIRANDOLINA. No, gentlemen, I say he is not. I say it. I stick to it, and I am ready to prove it.

CAPTAIN. I can stand this no longer! Count, at some other time you will find me with a proper sword.

Throwing away MARQUIS' *half sword.*

MARQUIS, *picking it up.* Eh, the hilt is worth money.

MIRANDOLINA. Stay here, Captain, for your own sake. These gentlemen believe you are in love with me. You must undeceive them.

CAPTAIN. There is no need for that.

MIRANDOLINA. Oh yes, sir, there is. . . . Wait a minute.

CAPTAIN. What is she going to do?

MIRANDOLINA. The surest sign of love is jealousy; no one who does not know jealousy can have any knowledge of love. If this gentleman cared for me, he could not bear the thought that I was going to another . . . but, as you shall see, he will bear it.

CAPTAIN. Who are you going to marry?

MIRANDOLINA. The husband chosen for me by my father.

FABRIZIO. You are maybe speaking of me?

MIRANDOLINA. Yes, my dear Fabrizio, in the presence of all these gentlemen I give you my hand as a token.

CAPTAIN, *angrily to himself.* Marry *him!* I won't bear it.

COUNT. If she is marrying Fabrizio she has no fancy for the captain. . . . Yes, marry him, and I will give you what will pay for the wedding.

MARQUIS. Mirandolina, an egg today is worth more than a chicken tomorrow; marry him and I will give you—this very minute—my blessing.

MIRANDOLINA. Thank you, gentlemen, but I have no need of anything. I am but a poor woman, without graces, without liveliness, not able to kindle any love or any passion at all. But Fabrizio wants me and I will take him.

CAPTAIN. Yes, you wretched woman, marry whoever you will, I know that you deceived me. I know you are triumphing in yourself at having dragged me down. . . . But I will go away out of your sight. I leave my curse upon your cajoleries and your tears and your pretenses. You have made me know what an unlucky power you have over us, you have made me learn at my own expense that to get the better of you it is not enough to despise you, but to run away.

Goes.

COUNT. And you said just now that he was not in love!

MIRANDOLINA. Hush, hush. He is gone and he will not return, and if the matter is over now, I call myself very lucky. Poor man, I succeeded only too well in making him care for me, and I ran an ugly risk. I don't want to do it again. Fabrizio, come here, dear, and give me your hand.

FABRIZIO. Go gently, ma'am. You take delight in drawing men on in this way, and then you think that I am ready to take you all the same!

MIRANDOLINA. Ah, get along, you goose; it was a joke, a fancy, a play game. I was like a child having no one to keep me in order. When I am married I know what I will do.

FABRIZIO. What will you do?

CAPTAIN'S SERVANT *comes in.*

SERVANT. Mistress Mirandolina, I am come to pay my respects before I go. They are putting the horses to the carriage.

MIRANDOLINA, *gives him the gold bottle.* Good-by, take this little bottle as a remembrance, and forgive me for anything I may have done.

SERVANT. Good luck to you, ma'am. . . . Good-by.

Goes weeping.

MIRANDOLINA. Thank God, the captain is gone! I do feel sorry. I won't try any more of those tricks to the end of my life.

COUNT. Mirandolina, child, married or single, I will always be the same to you.

MARQUIS. You may always make use of my protection.

MIRANDOLINA. Dear gentlemen, now that I am marrying, I don't want patrons. I don't want amusement. I have been amusing myself up to this, and I was foolish and I ran into danger. I won't do so any more! This is my husband.

FABRIZIO. But go easy now.

MIRANDOLINA. Go easy! What are you talking about? What difficulties are there? What is to hinder us? Give me your hand.

FABRIZIO. We had best make out our contract first.

MIRANDOLINA. What contract? This is our contract. . . . Give me your hand or get away with you to your own district.

FABRIZIO. I will give you my hand . . . but after . . .

MIRANDOLINA. But after . . . yes, my dear, I will belong to you altogether. Don't be doubting me. I will always love you; you will be my very life.

FABRIZIO, *giving her his hand.* Take it, my dear. I cannot but give in.

MIRANDOLINA. That is another thing settled.

COUNT. Mirandolina, you are a great woman; you are able to bring men to whatever you will.

MIRANDOLINA. If that is so, I may make one request of you, there is just one last favor I will ask.

COUNT. You have but to tell it.

MARQUIS. Speak out.

FABRIZIO. What is she going to ask for this time?

MIRANDOLINA. I ask you as a favor to find for yourselves rooms at another inn.

FABRIZIO. Bravo! I see now you are in earnest.

MIRANDOLINA. I thank you very much for all your kind words. In changing my state I mean to change my manners, and you yourselves may also learn a lesson. If you are ever in danger of losing your hearts, think of the humbug you have seen practiced and the trickeries, and remember Mirandolina!

THE KING STAG

A FAIRY TALE

Carlo Gozzi

English Version by Carl Wildman

To the memory of
Edward J. Dent (1876–1957)
who graciously allowed perusal
of his literal English translation of
Il Re Cervo

c.w.

CHARACTERS

(In order of appearance)

CIGOLOTTI

A PARROT

FIRST GUARD

SECOND GUARD

SMERALDINA, *country cousin of*

BRIGHELLA, *King's butler*

TRUFFALDINO, *King's birdcatcher*

TARTAGLIA, *Prime Minister*

CLARISSA, *his daughter*

LEANDER, *son of Pantaloon*

PANTALOON, *Second Minister*

ANGELA, *his daughter*

DERAMO, *King of Serendip*

A BUST

FIRST HUNTSMAN

SECOND HUNTSMAN

A BEAR

KING STAG

ANOTHER STAG

AN OLD MAN

FIRST PEASANT

SECOND PEASANT

MUSICIAN

DURANDARTE, *Magician*

> *The action takes place in the oriental kingdom of Serendip: the royal palace and the nearby Forest of Roncislappe in the year 1762.*

ACT I

THE CHOICE OF A QUEEN

SCENE 1

PROLOGUE—INTRODUCING THE PARROT

It is early morning.

An ornamental lantern lights the forestage, in front of the curtain.

On either side of the forestage, there is a balcony, framed by two round pillars, over an opening which can become a doorway or window, as required.

Light, bantering music ends the Overture.

CIGOLOTTI's *voice, from the wings.* Polly! Polly!

CIGOLOTTI appears with an empty cage.

Polly! Polly! Come here! Oh, where are you, Polly?

A magnificent green PARROT appears on one of the balconies.

PARROT, *mocking.* Polly, Polly! Where are you?

The PARROT disappears before CIGOLOTTI sees him.

CIGOLOTTI. Polly!

PARROT *voices mock him from both sides of the stage.*

Oh, I can hear parrots everywhere! But not a sign of my own Poll.

He stamps.

Polly!

To the audience.

You've no idea what a life he leads me! The tantrums he went into last night . . . and the language . . . And when

I let him out he flew through the window, screaming: "Catch me! Catch me!" I've been chasing all over the town after him. Has any one there seen a parrot, a big green bird?

The PARROT *has meanwhile appeared between the curtains, center.*

CHILD's *voice, in the audience.* Yes, he's behind you!

CIGOLOTTI. Oh, thank you! Thanks very much! Phew! What a game! You see, this parrot . . .

PARROT. Come on, Cigolotti!

CIGOLOTTI. Yes, master parrot.

To audience.

Just wait a minute and I'll let you into a secret.

Going to the PARROT.

Where have you been?

He sets the cage down against the curtain.

PARROT. Scratch a Poll!

CIGOLOTTI, *after difficulty in catching him up the curtain.* You *have* led me a dance! Now, please come along with me! That's right!

CIGOLOTTI *carries the* PARROT *in his hand. He sits on the step of the tower on the right of the stage, with the* PARROT *on his knee. To the audience.*

Well, this is my tale. . . . A few years ago there came to the court of Serendip, here, a great magician called Durandarte. . . .

PARROT. Cigolotti!

CIGOLOTTI, *to the* PARROT. Yes, yes, I know.

To audience.

Durandarte was a master of black magic, blue magic, green magic—every sort of magic! And I, Cigolotti, was his servant. He performed many wonders at this court, and the King of Serendip was kind to him, so . . . on leaving the palace, Durandarte told the King two great magic secrets. Then Durandarte took me into a dark corner and said, he said . . .

PARROT, *interrupting.* Cigolotti, Cigolotti! What have I done?

CIGOLOTTI. That's right! He knows!

Continuing.

Oberon, King of the Fairies, he said, is going to punish me for revealing fairy secrets to a mortal, he's going to turn me into a parrot for talking too much. . . .

PARROT. Talking too much, Cigolotti!

CIGOLOTTI. Nice Polly, will you please be quiet till I get to the end of my story?

He strokes the PARROT, *who bites him.*

Ow! All right! You just go into your cage.

Business.

I've had enough of you, my lord, for one day! Now stand on your perch!

PARROT. On your perch, Cigolotti!

CIGOLOTTI. There!

Returning to the audience.

Now, where was I? Oh yes . . . Durandarte was saying . . . The more terrible of those two magic secrets will be put to evil use five years from hence, on the fifth day of January 1762. On that day, don't forget, Cigolotti, he said to me, you must take me to the Forest of Roncislappe, and leave me there. A birdcatcher will catch me; I shall then work great wonders, and the next day I shall be free!

PARROT, *turning in his cage.* Free! Free!

CIGOLOTTI. No sooner had he said this than, instead of my master Durandarte standing beside me, there appeared in a flash . . . a great green parrot!

Gesture.

Him!

PARROT, *turning.* Cigolotti, Cigolotti!

CIGOLOTTI, *aside, to the audience, laughing.* That's my master, the magician, Durandarte!

Glumly.

Aye, but what a time I've had . . . never a moment's peace since that day. Why, it must be well nigh . . .

PARROT. Five years!

CIGOLOTTI. What's that? Let me see: One, two, three . . .

PARROT. Five!

CIGOLOTTI. Five . . . five years!

PARROT. Today!

CIGOLOTTI. Today!

Clapping his hand to his forehead.

It's the fifth of January 1762 today!

PARROT. Come on, Cigolotti!

CIGOLOTTI. Oh, ye gods and little fishes! We must go!

He picks up the cage.

PARROT. Roncislappe!

CIGOLOTTI. Yes, Polly, yes, the Forest of Roncislappe, I know.
Ten miles for me to traipse. . . .

PARROT. Run, Cigolotti!

CIGOLOTTI. Yes, Master Durandarte!

To audience.

Phew! Who would be servant to a magician?

Exit.

Music.

*The curtain rises, revealing two guards, lounging sleepily
outside the closed privy chamber. They straighten up and
march off to either side.*

A bell rope has run down beside the left balcony.

SCENE 2

SMERALDINA COMES TO COURT

Enter SMERALDINA, *fantastically arrayed, followed by*
BRIGHELLA, *her cousin, the King's butler. Both are of comic
proportions.*

SMERALDINA. And this?

BRIGHELLA. The King's privy chamber!

SMERALDINA. Oh, so this is it?

BRIGHELLA. Yes, this is it, but don't hang about!

SMERALDINA. Oh, Brighella, I'm all of a twitter!

BRIGHELLA. Cousin, this is not the time or place for you to be all of a twitter.

SMERALDINA. What an entrancing chandelier! Just like the one we have in the drawing room at home. Better, of course.

BRIGHELLA. Smeraldina, for goodness' sake, listen to me for a moment. This is a very serious business—for both of us. . . .

SMERALDINA. I know.

Looking at the ornamental work on the doors of the privy chamber.

Is this real gold?

BRIGHELLA. Smeraldina, I warn you, if you carry on like an ignoramus you'll upset the whole applecart. You have to appear before the King. Oh, criminy! What a fright you look!

SMERALDINA. What? Listen, Brighella, you may be the royal butler and live at court, but I know how to make an impression. . . . The King will swoon to see me!

BRIGHELLA. That's what I'm afraid of! I can see myself remaining a butler for the rest of my born days. I know the King's taste, he prefers a less gaudy dish. He's one for style and distinction—not all these feathers and fripperies.

SMERALDINA. How silly you are, my dear. Keep to your kitchen matters. I fancy I'm arrayed fine enough to make a beast fall in love with me, let alone a king!

BRIGHELLA, *cleaning his ear with a finger.* What a vulgar way to go on! Listen, Smeraldina, your job is to appeal to His Majesty's fancy. Just think, if you become Queen, I shall be promoted from butler to commander in chief!

He salutes.

SMERALDINA. Oh, let me alone for appealing to the fancy! I have been studying all the best love scenes . . .

BRIGHELLA. What's the use of that, if you don't know how to conduct yourself? Look, cousin, I must at least show you how to appear before the King. . . . Lesson One: the curtsy!

He gives a demonstration, with SMERALDINA following and trying to follow suit.

Now! Head erect, arms draped loosely at your sides . . .
glide along . . . stop, right knee behind the left leg, and
. . . curtsy!

SMERALDINA *makes a quick, wobbly curtsy.*

Terrible! Go back and try again. Head erect, arms draped
loosely at the . . .

TRUFFALDINO, *who has appeared on the left balcony, slides
down the rope which hangs beside the balcony, repeating
BRIGHELLA's directions.*

TRUFFALDINO. . . . arms draped loosely at the side, glide
along, stop . . .

SMERALDINA *loses her balance and falls.* TRUFFALDINO *helps
her up.*

SMERALDINA. Have you lost control of yourself, Mister Birdcatcher?

TRUFFALDINO, *laughing.* Lost control of yourself? Ha! Ha! Ha!
Pulling the feathers in her headgear.

May one know what fancy-dress ball you're going to, noble
mistress?

BRIGHELLA, *parting them.* As a matter of fact, we are going
to the royal privy chamber for the competition. . . .

TRUFFALDINO. To become Queen?

SMERALDINA. Yes, fellow, to become Queen!

TRUFFALDINO. Seriously?

SMERALDINA. Seriously.

TRUFFALDINO, *to* BRIGHELLA. Seriously?

BRIGHELLA. Seriously!

TRUFFALDINO. Seriously?

BRIGHELLA *and* SMERALDINA, *together, shouting.* Seriously!

TRUFFALDINO, *running to* SMERALDINA. What about your engagement to me?

An ominous theme is played by the orchestra—the TAR-
TAGLIA *theme.* BRIGHELLA *and* TRUFFALDINO *are frozen still.*
TARTAGLIA's *voice is heard.*

BRIGHELLA. Sh!

TARTAGLIA's *voice is heard calling.* Clarissa!

BRIGHELLA. Tartaglia!

TRUFFALDINO. Tartaglia! Quick, Smeraldina, quick!

BRIGHELLA. Let's get out. I'd rather meet a wolf than that man!

SMERALDINA. But who are you talking about?

TRUFFALDINO, *scared, runs hither and thither.*

BRIGHELLA. Tartaglia, the Prime Minister.

SMERALDINA. The Prime Minister? Oh, what luck, I'm dying to see a Prime Minister close to!

TRUFFALDINO, *dancing up and down.* Smeraldina!

TARTAGLIA's *voice, nearer, calling.* Clarissa!

BRIGHELLA. Look out, here he is!

BRIGHELLA, *going out right, stops and turns in the doorway.* TRUFFALDINO *runs into him and is bounced back onto the stage.* BRIGHELLA *shuts the door in his face.* TRUFFALDINO *tries to climb the pillar beside the door.* BRIGHELLA *opens the door and lifts* TRUFFALDINO *in.*

SMERALDINA. The Prime Minister!

SCENE 3

TARTAGLIA'S AMBITION TO MAKE HIS DAUGHTER, CLARISSA, QUEEN

SMERALDINA *remains planted in the middle of the floor.*
TARTAGLIA *enters, followed by his daughter,* CLARISSA.
SMERALDINA *smirks and attempts a curtsy.*
TARTAGLIA *fixes her with an angry glance, and* SMERALDINA *runs off.*

CLARISSA. But, father, all this haste and secrecy—what does it mean?

TARTAGLIA. Clarissa, my child, this is a great moment. Thanks to my unremitting labors, our fortunes in the kingdom of

Serendip are in the ascendant. That is well. You are a lady in waiting and I am First Minister! That is well. But better is to come. Heed my words, Clarissa, and you shall be Queen!

CLARISSA, *surprised and not altogether pleased.* Me, Queen? Oh, father!

TARTAGLIA. Yes, Queen, my girl! King Deramo lacks a queen. You are not ignorant of the fact that he has already interviewed in his privy chamber 2748 princesses and ladies of high estate from all parts of the globe. But of all these, Deramo found not one to his liking.

CLARISSA, *relieved.* Then he would scarcely consider taking me for his wife.

TARTAGLIA, *angrily, and beginning to stutter.* P-paltry girl! When your father is speaking do not interrupt! The other day, with great tact and subtlety, I persuaded him that, for the sake of the happiness of his subjects, he should take a wife. He has agreed to interview two hundred young women, with a solemn pledge that he will choose one for his consort. The names of the candidates have been drawn from an urn to decide the order of interview, and your name came out first!

CLARISSA, *unhappily.* First?

TARTAGLIA. First! But wait. There remains one obstacle. I could not wean him from his obstinate resolve to submit the candidates to questioning in that devilish privy chamber! So, Clarissa, there we are. I am the King's favorite, you are my daughter, you are not ugly. Conduct yourself well at the interview and you will be Queen, and I . . . I will be the most glorious, most magnificent person in the world!

CLARISSA *turns away, silent.* TARTAGLIA *eyes her suspiciously.*

Tell me, my little Clarissa, you have nothing to be ashamed of, eh?—no peccadillo on your conscience which might be discovered at the interview?

CLARISSA. Father, I beg you as you are my father, release me from this ordeal.

LEANDER *appears on the left balcony.*

TARTAGLIA. What do I hear? You willful baggage! You little mewing puss! Would you oppose your father's will?

CLARISSA. No, father, no . . . but do not press me. . . .

CLARISSA *sees* LEANDER *on the balcony and waves to him when* TARTAGLIA *is not looking.*

TARTAGLIA. By all the jewels in the crown, I will press you! Are you my daughter, Tartaglia's daughter . . . or a quivering little toad?

CLARISSA, *determined.* I cannot undergo this trial!

TARTAGLIA, *coldly.* So you cannot, madam minx! Come to my room, we shall see your "cannots and your do-not-press-mes"! I will persuade you . . . even if I have to cut off your nose or bite off your ear . . . do you understand?

CLARISSA *runs off, followed by* TARTAGLIA.

LEANDER *leaves the balcony.*

SCENE 4

ANGELA'S FEARS

Enter PANTALOON, *a tottering and talkative old gentleman —the Second Minister—and* ANGELA, *his daughter.*

PANTALOON, *entering.* Nobody knows, my dearest Angela. Nobody knows. After all, it is called the King's privy chamber, and since *privy* means nothing more or less than *private,* it must follow that what takes place therein is, more or less, private. It would be more than impertinent to attempt to pry into what is, by nature, privy.

Seeing LEANDER, *who has come forward.*

Well, my son, do you wish to converse with me?

LEANDER. Father, may I speak to my sister for a moment?

PANTALOON. Yes, my boy, you may. But be brief, as I have more to say to her myself.

LEANDER. Thank you, sir.

PANTALOON, *who has been carrying a cushion, places it on the step, pats it and settles himself on it.*

ANGELA *and* LEANDER *go aside.*

I have just seen my beloved Clarissa dragged off by her father, who is in a towering rage. What can this mean?

ANGELA. Ah, Leander, we are all in trouble today. Clarissa has been selected to appear first before the King this morning—in the competition for the choice of a queen.

LEANDER. Clarissa—to take part in that competition! Oh, my heart, I shall lose my love!

ANGELA. Cheer yourself, dear brother. I feel we shall be rejected, all of us—and your Clarissa will be free.

LEANDER, *going.* Oh, Angela . . . I have little hope. . . . *Exit.*

ANGELA, *returning quickly to her father, and kneeling.* Dear father, if only we knew how the King makes his choice!

PANTALOON. My pet, there are in the world 2748 princesses and noble ladies who would join you in that sentiment. The King received them in that privy chamber, asked them three or four questions, and then politely bade them farewell. Maybe he disliked their wit, or their voice, or maybe he sees in their heart something he does not care for. In all my years of office I have always found him wise, intelligent and serious beyond his years. I venture to think that, in this particular instance, there is some mystery, black art . . . or I know not what.

ANGELA. Father, why have you exposed me to such mortification? If the King rejects me . . .

PANTALOON. My angel, I went down on my knees to him, I indulged in supplications, I implored him to exempt you, to no avail. You must undergo this ordeal, Angela, though it can but bring us shame and break my heart.

ANGELA. I am afraid to present myself because I know I am not worthy of such a rank.

Rising.

But if, by his questions, the King is seeking sincerity and faithfulness . . . if he looks for love . . .

PANTALOON. How, how? What do I hear? Are you already in love, my child?

ANGELA, *smiling*. Father . . . yes . . . I confess it. I have been bold enough to fall in love with my King! He will reject me, father, and I shall not wish to live. Not because I have been scorned by a monarch but because I am despised and rejected by the one who is my very life.

PANTALOON. Oh, poor dear me!

ANGELA. But more than anything else, I fear the opposition of Tartaglia. His first ambition is to see his own daughter on the throne, and his second—to make me his wife.

PANTALOON, *rising*. Tartaglia . . . after my daughter . . . That's very pretty! Tartaglia! That uncouth, uneducated upstart! The arrogant fellow, to have designs on my daughter! Rabble, that's what he is! Rabble!

He begins to shout.

ANGELA, *calming him*. Father!

PANTALOON. You are right, my dear. I am losing my head. We might be betrayed and he is a dangerous man.

ANGELA. But we are alone.

PANTALOON. In this palace, one never knows.

Loudly.

Tartaglia is a great minister!

To ANGELA.

Let us retire until your audience with the King. You are to be third, you know.

ANGELA, *at the door*. Cupid, I commend myself to you!

Exit.

TRUFFALDINO *enters*.

PANTALOON, *before going turns round and says even more loudly:* A very great minister!

Face to face with TRUFFALDINO, *who for a moment thinks* PANTALOON *is speaking to him.*

TRUFFALDINO. My . . . my lord Pantaloon . . . a word in your lordship's ear. I cannot find my chuck—my Smeraldina —anywhere.

PANTALOON *picks up his cushion.*

I dare not ask the First, the Third, or the Fourth Ministers —but Your Excellency the Second Minister is kind and knows the court . . .

PANTALOON. To the point, my friend!

TRUFFALDINO. Is it true my little hen, Smeraldina, is to be married today to the monarch of this realm?

PANTALOON, *faintly amused, but anxious to go.* Ah, my poor Birdcatcher to His Majesty, that I cannot say. All our fates hang on what passes in this privy chamber. Farewell!

Exit PANTALOON, *shutting the door.*

TRUFFALDINO, *mournfully.* My little country bumpkin! The King will certainly take you from me.

He gives vent to his feelings by suddenly sitting on the floor and blowing mournful notes on his pipes. Gradually he whistles more gaily.

If only I could catch her as easily as the birds in the Forest of Roncislappe!

He whistles and calls.

Pretty, pretty, pretty!—a goldfinch!

Enter SMERALDINA. TRUFFALDINO *sees her.*

Smeraldina!

She runs off pursued by TRUFFALDINO *calling her name.*

SCENE 5

SMERALDINA SETS OUT TO BE QUEEN

Re-enter SMERALDINA *running. She tries to hide.*
Re-enter TRUFFALDINO. *He sees her.*

TRUFFALDINO. Smeraldina!

He goes down on one knee to her.

SMERALDINA, *haughtily.* One does not dally with a bird-catcher when the King is agog to meet one.

TRUFFALDINO. No so fast, my little country sparrow! You promised to marry me!

SMERALDINA. A royal command overrules all promises.

TRUFFALDINO. No, no, no! His Majesty wouldn't play me such a dirty trick. I shall go down on my knees to him.

He goes down on his knees and takes SMERALDINA'S *hand. She listens resignedly.*

Your Majesty, I'll say, I, your humble servant . . . I'll say . . .

BRIGHELLA, *appearing on the right balcony.* Smeraldina!

SMERALDINA. Yes, my dear?

TRUFFALDINO. . . . having served . . .

BRIGHELLA. Come along!

SMERALDINA. I come.

TRUFFALDINO. . . . faithfully . . .

BRIGHELLA. Hurry, do!

SMERALDINA. I'm all haste!

TRUFFALDINO. . . . all these years . . .

Quickly, as SMERALDINA *starts to go.*

Please don't take Smeraldina from me.

He pulls her back by her skirts.

You shan't go. I forbid it, do you hear?

BRIGHELLA, *leaning over the balcony.* Listen, Truffaldino, a future queen does not toy with the idea of marrying a feather-brained birdcatcher!

TRUFFALDINO. I'd rather have feathers in my brain than suet! Keep your fingers out of this pudding, butler!

SMERALDINA. Gently, gently, gentlemen—or I shall faint!

BRIGHELLA *disappears from the balcony.*

Affectedly.

Oh, Truffaldino, I do well comprehend the depths of your sorrow, the irreparable damage to your heart, the acuteness of your grief . . .

TRUFFALDINO *has been pacing up and down.* SMERALDINA *stops him with a loud and vulgar*

. . . *But,* dear man,

Resuming her affected tone.

. . . if you lose a wife, you gain a queen!

TRUFFALDINO, *stamping.* But it's not the same thing!

BRIGHELLA, *entering, below.* Come on, we shall be late!

SMERALDINA. Hie to high fortune!

Exit SMERALDINA *with* BRIGHELLA. TRUFFALDINO *follows miserably.*

SCENE 6

TARTAGLIA THREATENS HIS DAUGHTER CLARISSA

Enter TARTAGLIA, *dragging on* CLARISSA.

TARTAGLIA. Clarissa, come here. It is almost the hour for your interview and you still persist in being as obstinate as a mule.

He shuts the door.

CLARISSA. Father dear, as I have tried to tell you already, I would like to please you, but I cannot go before the King.

TARTAGLIA. Cannot?

He pushes her.

You shall, and first!

CLARISSA. No, no, Father!

TARTAGLIA. So, you would disobey your father, minx. . . .

He threatens her with his staff of office.

CLARISSA. Well . . . since you force me to it, I must tell you that my heart is not free.

TARTAGLIA. Ha-ha!

CLARISSA. I am in love already . . . I love Leander. And it would be beyond my power to conceal my passion from the King.

TARTAGLIA, *recoiling in anger.* With Leander? With the son of Pantaloon? With the son of an inferior minister, a very inferior minister? You little tadpole! One more word of this abominable passion for Leander and it will be no more Tartaglia, father dear, but only Tartaglia, the tartar!

CLARISSA, *artfully*. Please listen, father. There is one more reason . . . I would not enter into competition with Angela, my dearest friend; I know that she is in love with the King.

TARTAGLIA, *taken aback*. Angela, Pantaloon's daughter, in love with the King?

Aside.

Oh, my lights! Angela, that pure jewel whom I had intended to be mine, by fair means or foul—in love with Deramo! My plans and secret will shall not thus be thwarted.

To CLARISSA.

Listen and quake!

Advancing on her step by step.

If you do not present yourself before the King, if your replies to him are not satisfactory, if you reveal your love for Leander, if you do not make the King choose you, and if you repeat a single word of what I have just said . . . poison is ready! You shall learn what it is to cross the will of Tartaglia! You shall be Queen, or you shall die!

TARTAGLIA *pulls her off and goes out*.

SCENE 7

KING DERAMO AND THE BUST

Music.

The inner chamber is opened by two guards, revealing the KING, *alone, and seated. He is looking away towards the ornamental palace grounds*.

Against the opened wing, on the right-hand side, stands a bust on a narrow-necked pedestal.

On the opposite wing hang two swords crossed, and a shield.

A golden cloth is draped over the head of the bust.

KING DERAMO's *opening words are spoken to a musical background.*

DERAMO, *turning toward the audience.* Today I must face the serious task of choosing me a wife. My wise and faithful Tartaglia, would I could take your word that I shall thus bring peace to my realm! If I choose according to my office I may wrong my heart, and if I choose according to my heart I may wrong my kingdom. In this most difficult of tasks, I cannot depend on my trusted Tartaglia. I cannot rely even on my own judgment.

The music ceases. DERAMO *rises.*

I must rely on a bloodless head! Bust, precious secret of a great magician, aid me once more with your faculty of laughing or of smiling when a woman is deceitful in your presence.

DERAMO *goes to the bust and uncovers it. He contemplates it.*

A head! No body, no heart—a mere head! A plaster shell! But five years we have lived together and you are like an old friend to me. I have relied on you and I have hated you!

Moving away.

For you made me realize to the full the loneliness of princes.

Four years ago you ruthlessly revealed, by a plaster smile, the traps and treachery beneath the graces of womankind. Yes, you made me despair of happiness and I hated you! From then on, I ceased to use your powers lest you should utterly destroy my faith in human kind.

Today, however, I shall make a last experiment!

Laugh, if you see treachery or untruth. But . . . I pray . . . may you yet remain as serious as a statue once; may I find a woman to rejoice my heart and grace my throne. So, my strange companion, I commend myself to you—and to your master, Durandarte, the great sage and magician of the East!

Durandarte, may I this time have cause to be grateful that you should have made this parting gift to help me rule —this revelation of the mysterious powers of a statue!

A door is opened by a guard.

But here comes Tartaglia's daughter. We shall see if she be truthful. Bust, play your part!

SCENE 8

THE KING CHOOSES A QUEEN

DERAMO. Come in, Clarissa, and be seated.

He indicates a heap of cushions.

CLARISSA. Your Majesty!

She curtsies.

DERAMO. You need not feel intimidated by the presence of your King. Be at ease and speak freely.

He sits.

Your father's great qualities in war and peace are well known, and too much humility would not befit his daughter.

CLARISSA. Your Majesty, your kindness overwhelms me, and it is only in obedience to your command that I sit in your presence.

She sits.

DERAMO. Clarissa, I have to choose a wife, and it is only natural that the daughter of the Minister I esteem most highly should make me a suitable partner. But first, I should like to hear from your own lips if such a match would please you.

CLARISSA. Can there be a single girl the world over who would not be proud of being united to so illustrious and virtuous a king?

DERAMO, *having looked at the bust, which remains impassive.* That is very flattering, Clarissa, but too vague. It may well be that a great number of women might be proud to marry a king, but, are you sure you are of that number? That is my question, and that is what I wish to know.

CLARISSA. You question me very closely, Your Majesty . . .

But how could you think that I should be the only one out of that number to be so foolish and disdain such good fortune?

DERAMO *glances at the bust, which gives no sign.*

DERAMO, *rising.* Clarissa, your replies are too cryptic. I am only interested in what *you* think and feel.

Going toward her.

Tell me plainly: would you be happy if you married me, or not?

CLARISSA, *distressed.* Oh, my life goes with my love.

Controlling herself.

Truly . . . I should be happy, beloved King . . .

The bust smiles and becomes impassive again.

DERAMO, *walking away.* You are a little overwrought. . . . Perhaps you do not dare to speak your mind for fear of offending your King—but surely, Clarissa, is not your heart already given to another?

CLARISSA, *protesting.* No, no, my King. . . . I love no one but you. I am well aware that I am not worthy of a royal hand —but, if I were, yours is the one I would desire . . . and I have never loved before.

The bust grins broadly, then becomes statuesque again.

DERAMO. Well, Clarissa, you may retire.

He pulls the bell rope.

I do not wish to keep you in suspense but I will first see the others before I give my decision.

CLARISSA *rises, curtsies, and exclaims as she leaves:*

CLARISSA. Please Heaven he reject me and I remain true to my Leander!

Exit.

DERAMO, *to the bust.* You see. . . . Is there a single woman, who speaks the truth? Thank you, Bust, I thought for a moment you were sulking . . . but, no, you are a marvel!

He sees SMERALDINA *approaching.*

But, who is this? . . . Come in. Please be seated.

SMERALDINA *enters, curtsies to the public, and seats herself with absurd airs and graces on the King's seat. He indicates the cushions. She goes to them with a titter. He goes to her.*

Let me see, are you not my butler's cousin from the country?

SMERALDINA. As you say, Your Majesty, as you say. We come of distinguished country stock . . . but, through calamities, misfortunes, you know . . . our circumstances are a trifle reduced. However, as Your Highness will be the first to appreciate—poverty does not pollute noble minds!

DERAMO *looks at the bust, which laughs broadly.*

DERAMO. Quite, quite! But, tell me, good lady, do you love me?

SMERALDINA. Ah, cruel tyrant! Enchanter! How could you ask me such a question? From my childhood days I have languished for you!

She says this, going toward him on her knees.

The bust laughs still more.

DERAMO. Pray, let me hear more! If I should choose you to be my consort, and, for example, I died before you, leaving you a widow, would you be easily consoled?

SMERALDINA, *with melodramatic gestures.* Oh, you claw my heart! You are a tiger in disguise! The very thought of it makes me swoon, oh, cruel . . .

She looks round to see where to fall and pretends to faint.

The bust laughs more and more.

DERAMO. How unfortunate!

He pretends to call the guards.

Guards! Come here and carry this poor lady away.

SMERALDINA *immediately revives.*

Madam, you love me too much.

Pause.

One more question. Are you a widow?

SMERALDINA. Your Majesty! Had I been a widow, would I have had the audacity to present myself as bride to such a king? The fresh bloom of youth on my cheeks is surely testimony enough . . . that for you . . . I have preserved my maidenly modesty!

Spoken with coy gestures with her fan.

The bust rocks with laughter. DERAMO *covers it hastily with the golden cloth.*

DERAMO. That is sufficient, Smeraldina! I can assure you that none of the women I have seen so far has given me so much pleasure. I shall shortly make my decision known.

He pulls the bell rope. SMERALDINA *pretends not to understand.*

You may go now.

SMERALDINA, *rising and following him about as he retreats.* My Lord! A great tide of affection was surging in my bosom, an ocean of tenderness was swelling in my throat, and I had on the tip of my tongue a thousand endearments and sweet nothings—but I shall keep them till I come arrayed in my white wedding gown to transport you into Heaven. Then you shall know how I love you.

She coquettishly tickles him with her fan. Then she attempts to curtsy and nearly falls.

. . . Farewell, my *sweet* King!

She blows him a kiss.

To the audience, from the door.

He's mine! I've hooked him! I'm Queen!

Exit.

DERAMO *bursts out laughing. He removes the cloth from the head of the bust.*

DERAMO, *to the bust.* Oh, my secret companion—with what hilarious entertainment you provide me!

He suddenly becomes serious.

How can I ever more believe in a woman's words . . . What hope have I? . . . and yet, I hope . . .

The guard opens the door.

. . . here comes Angela . . . and I hope, I hope madly, against all reason and all my unhappy experience.

With growing violence.

And I swear that if she prove false . . .

To the bust.

I hate your grinning mouth, this time you shall not smile. . . .

He draws a sword from the wall. He is going to destroy the bust, but he stops, as if charmed. He gazes at ANGELA.

How lovely and pure she looks. . . .

With sudden decision.

No suspicion must hang over her! Bust! Do your worst!

He lays down the sword.

ANGELA, *entering.* I came, Your Majesty, in obedience to your decree, though I cannot say if it be just.

DERAMO, *in a quiet but tense voice.* I, unjust? . . . Be seated, Angela . . .

ANGELA, *sitting on the cushions.* You are the King! No one would dare to criticize your decrees!

DERAMO. No one? Angela does not appear to me to lack that courage!

He sits.

But, in case you still have some scruple, I grant you complete liberty of speech. Speak frankly, I shall take no offence.

ANGELA. Then, though it be against my interest, allow me to ask you, sir: Where is the justice in compelling wretched girls to come and offer their hearts to you in this secret chamber? What a fond hope you have caused to be born in the minds of all women! Is it not a cruel game, then, to send them away, all of them, to weep at having failed to please you? I am not speaking for myself—but in the name of all those women who have gone before, of all those who will come tomorrow and the next day, and are now sadly waiting this affront—spare them, and let me be the last to suffer! Forgive me, my King, you gave me liberty to speak and perhaps I have abused that privilege.

He rises and looks at the bust, which has remained impassive.

DERAMO. No, Angela, I forgive you, in fact, I appreciate your candor.

He goes to the back of the privy chamber and gazes into the court gardens.

Though, if you knew the truth, you would not speak in this way. Four years ago I sought the woman who would love me truly. I did not find her! The necessity of having an heir, and a fond hope of happiness, compel me today to seek again—although I fear the search will be vain.

ANGELA. And how can you be sure that, out of all those who have entered here, not one is worthy of your love?

DERAMO, *turning toward her.* How can I be sure? That is a secret I cannot divulge. But, believe me, I know for certain.

Pause.

Angela, do you love me?

ANGELA, *in a cry, after a pause.* Would I did not, then your inevitable disdain would not kill me!

DERAMO *looks in amazement at the bust, which remains immobile.*

DERAMO. It is not possible!

To ANGELA.

Angela, is this true? . . . And would you love me forever?

ANGELA. Till death and beyond, I do believe! Oh, do not flatter innocent hopes with these vain questionings!

She sobs.

DERAMO *steps away, looking from the bust to* ANGELA, *from* ANGELA *to the bust.*

DERAMO. Love must be clouding my sight. Oh, Angela, if you do not love me—for pity's sake, tell me, before I set my heart on you!

ANGELA *throws herself at his feet.*

ANGELA. Oh, sir, cease these cruel flatteries! Give me your refusal now and try me no more! What pleasure can you derive from tearing the heart out of an innocent girl who knows she is unworthy of you? I can stand no more, Deramo, I can stand no more. . . . In pity let me go!

She bursts into tears.

DERAMO *is greatly moved. He looks once more at the bust, close to. The bust remains completely impassive.* DERAMO *goes to* ANGELA *and raises her up.*

DERAMO. Angela, my dear Angela, weep no more! My quest is ended! I have found the fair and noble soul I have been searching for! Ministers and guards, come in!

He pulls the bell rope. Chimes are heard.

Let the people rejoice!

He pulls the bell rope again. Double chimes are heard.

Here is the woman who loves me now and forever.

ANGELA, *softly and urgently.* Deramo, I am not worthy to be the wife of a king!

DERAMO. My Angela, you would be worthy of far greater a king than I. Before this moment I despaired of finding happiness, and if I had not pursued my quest until it appeared tyrannical, I should have remained in despair forever and become an embittered king, unfit for ruling! Angela, you are my salvation and the salvation of my kingdom!

The guards open the doors.

Come in, Ministers, come in.

Music.

Enter PANTALOON *and* TARTAGLIA *from opposite sides.*

At last I have chosen a wife. Here is your Queen!

SCENE 9

ANGELA IS PROCLAIMED QUEEN

PANTALOON. My little girl, Queen?

DERAMO. Your daughter, my good Pantaloon!

TARTAGLIA. Ah! I could burst with rage!

PANTALOON. Your Majesty, have you not already heaped enough benefactions upon my unworthy head without raising so poor a girl to such exalted rank?

DERAMO. I am merely raising virtue to her rightful position. Angela alone was worthy of this tribute.

TARTAGLIA, *with forced gaiety and much stuttering.* Viva! Viva! Hurrah! Your Majesty could not have chosen better!

He kisses the KING'S *hand.*

Angela, may you be very happy!

He kisses her hand.

Pantaloon, my hearty congratulations!

PANTALOON. Thank you, Tartaglia!

TARTAGLIA, *between his teeth.* I'll teach you who I am, you fawning old toady!

PANTALOON, *calling* ANGELA *to him.* My little one, never forget your humble birth, and don't become proud. . . . But, perhaps His Majesty will allow me to spend a couple of hours with my daughter to teach her a few useful maxims, and give her fatherly advice. . . .

DERAMO, *smiling.* Do not offend me.

He comes to the center.

Angela is my wife elect . . . if she is willing.

Music ceases.

ANGELA. My King, here is my hand and, with my hand, my heart and eternal faith.

They join hands and kiss.

CLARISSA *and* LEANDER *appear on the left balcony.*

SMERALDINA *and* BRIGHELLA *on the right balcony.*

A final flourish is played by the orchestra.

TARTAGLIA. Eternal fiddlesticks! May your oath burn your tongue!

Turning to the KING.

But, most beloved Monarch . . . ahem . . . could you not now perhaps divulge for what reason the other 2750 ladies . . . and princesses . . . ?

DERAMO. Sir, I will tell you. Five years ago, the great magician, Durandarte, who attended this court, made me a present of two great secrets, one of which is this . . .

He points to the bust.

. . . and the other . . . I am not revealing. This simple plaster bust possesses the faculty of divining when a woman lies, and showing it by a smile. Of all those women who came before me, only Angela proved sincere.

PANTALOON, *with pride.* There! And now she's a great lady!

TARTAGLIA, *furious.* And that bust laughed at Clarissa! Then my daughter is a liar! With your permission, I'm going to cut her throat!

CLARISSA, *on the balcony, hides behind* LEANDER.

DERAMO. Stop, rash Minister! Clarissa is in love with another. Her only fault was in fearing for some reason to disclose the fact.

Angela, I wish to give you a proof of my faith in you.

He picks up a sword and points it at the bust.

ANGELA *runs to* PANTALOON.

Let this infernal machine be destroyed and, with it, all temptation to suspect!

He strikes the bust with the sword. The bust falls to pieces with smoke and a flash.

To TARTAGLIA.

Do not scowl so, my faithful Tartaglia. You need not mope over your daughter. It is my royal pleasure. Let us revel!

Music.

A general holiday shall be declared! We will celebrate with a festive hunt in the Forest of Roncislappe! Tartaglia see to it.

TARTAGLIA *bows.*

Come, Angela.

ANGELA. I am coming, my King.

All bow. Exeunt ANGELA *and* DERAMO. *The balconies empty. Exeunt the guards.* PANTALOON *follows them, but stops at the door. He is as excited as a child. Unthinkingly he addresses* TARTAGLIA.

PANTALOON. My little girl, Queen! Well, Tartaglia, on my honor as a gentleman, I cannot believe it. I must send a word to the social gossip column of the Serendip *Gazette.* Of course, they will know already, but still, I'll send them word all the same.

Exit.

Music stops.

TARTAGLIA, *alone.* Angela lost! Lost! My daughter rejected.
'Sblood and death! Envy, jealousy and madness gnaw at my
vitals! But a man of my rank and fiber will not lightly support such mortal injury! A curse on my daughter, the King,
Pantaloon . . .

Going upstage, past the bust.

. . . and that infernal b-bust!

Mocking, as he paces up and down.

"Let us revel!" "A festive hunt at Roncislappe!" Is this the
moment? But not so fast. . . . Calm, Tartaglia, calm. The
Forest of Roncislappe! That is my cue! There I will wreak
such horrible revenge, posterity's eyes will p-pop!

Music: TARTAGLIA *theme.*

ACT II

THE PRIME MINISTER'S REVENGE

SCENE 1

TARTAGLIA QUARRELS WITH PANTALOON

Music: A gavotte.

The curtain rises, revealing the scene in front of the closed privy chamber as in ACT I, SCENES 1–6.

CLARISSA *enters laughing and running away from* LEANDER. *Then, she playfully tries to show him how to dance the gavotte with mock disapproval of his false steps.*

The TARTAGLIA *theme breaks into the gavotte.*

CLARISSA *signs to* LEANDER *to hide till she has spoken to her father.* LEANDER *hides.*

CLARISSA *finishes her gavotte with a curtsy, hiding her face from* TARTAGLIA *with her fan.*

TARTAGLIA, *striding in.* A famous hunt this will be! You empty-noddled chit of a girl! Is that all you can do after throwing away a crown I practically put in your hand!

CLARISSA *hides her face behind her fan again.*

You may well hide your face!

Raising his hand.

I could dislocate that little neck of yours with pleasure! Why did you go about boasting of your flirtation with Leander?

CLARISSA, *turning to him with affected innocence.* Oh, but father, I never breathed a word, I swear! It was the bust who gave away my secret!

TARTAGLIA. Oh, so it was the bust! And by whose leave did you go philandering? If you hadn't managed to fall in love with Leander you wouldn't have made the bust laugh, nincompoop!

CLARISSA. But . . . I didn't mean to . . . it just happened. . . . Leander is so charming and says such wonderful things —I had no time to ask your permission!

TARTAGLIA. Oh, so you had no time!

CLARISSA, *pretending to cry and be very upset.* Oh, father, don't scold me so! It is consolation I need! Since the King has chosen another wife, you should console me!

TARTAGLIA. Console you! What d'you mean, you brazen little hussy?

CLARISSA, *artfully.* Perhaps if I could marry Leander . . . After all, he's a lord in waiting and now he is brother to the Queen, he has a future!

TARTAGLIA. C-curse!

He splutters and chokes. Then aside.

My temper will give me away. I must not spoil my plans.

To CLARISSA.

Listen, daughter, forget what I have just said. I was angry. You see, Clarissa, I have had a great, great disappointment. You should sympathize with me and give me time to recover.

CLARISSA *pretends to make a fuss of him.*

Just let my anger pass and then I will give you consolation. But don't pester me!

CLARISSA. You are good, father.

TARTAGLIA. Am I, daughter? Well, just go to your room and leave me quiet a moment.

CLARISSA. Oh, thank you, thank you, father. . . .

She tries to put her arms round his neck. TARTAGLIA's *paunch is in the way.*

TARTAGLIA. Yes, yes, that will do!

CLARISSA *makes a sign to* LEANDER, *who comes out of hiding, then she goes.*

How can I keep calm till Roncislappe—and revenge! Enough

time wasted! I'll announce to the King we are ready for the hunt!

He is about to go, when LEANDER *comes forward and addresses him.*

LEANDER. Lord Tartaglia!

TARTAGLIA. What insolent nuisance is this? I'm on my way to the hunt!

LEANDER. One word with Your Excellency before you go. I . . . I . . .

TARTAGLIA. Well, out with it!

LEANDER. I do realize a Prime Minister has many cares . . . but as I have been lucky enough to have my sister chosen by the King—I would like to marry Clarissa!

TARTAGLIA. Not so fast, young man! I . . . I don't exactly refuse your offer, but . . . Just wait three or four days. I am busy with affairs of state . . .

Aside.

I'll show him what these affairs of state are, if the devil stand by me!

Enter PANTALOON.

LEANDER. Lord Tartaglia, how good you are! I'm too happy for words!

PANTALOON. What is this, my boy?

LEANDER. Clarissa's father has not refused me!

PANTALOON. Well, my dear Tartaglia, who would have thought that my children would make such good matches . . . ?

TARTAGLIA. He's a trifle familiar, since this morning!

PANTALOON. This is indeed a happy day, and . . .

Hunting horns are heard and dogs baying.

TARTAGLIA. The hunt is ready! His Majesty must be informed. Leander, see him mounted. Hurry up, young man!

LEANDER, *leaving.* Where is the hunt to be?

TARTAGLIA. In the Forest of Roncislappe . . .

Exit LEANDER.

. . . where I fancy *my* quarry will be a big one!

Now, my lord Pantaloon! I have been looking for this opportunity of speaking to you as man to man . . .

PANTALOON. It is a rare pleasure, indeed, and . . .

TARTAGLIA, *cutting him short.* I don't like your policy!

PANTALOON, *taken aback.* My policy?

TARTAGLIA, *walking round and away from* PANTALOON, *who is obliged to follow him.* I have no wish to know by what underhand means you managed to foist your daughter on the King. But you have tried to humiliate me by casting aspersions on my Clarissa, *and,* not content with that, you thrust that frail and defenceless young girl into the arms of your booby of a son!

PANTALOON. But this is sheer fabrication, Tartaglia. I have always held Clarissa in high esteem. It was the bust alone who decided against your daughter!

TARTAGLIA. I don't believe in fairy tales, Mr. Pantaloon!

PANTALOON, *going right up to* TARTAGLIA. But the King himself stated . . .

TARTAGLIA. A most unfortunate infirmity has taken possession of the King's mind—an infirmity from which you hope to benefit.

TARTAGLIA *pushes* PANTALOON *out of his path with his paunch.*

Take care, Mr. Pantaloon! If the people rise against a scoundrelly minister, I can do nothing to prevent it. And remember, you may be the future father-in-law to the King, but I am still Prime Minister, and—your humble servant!
Exit.

PANTALOON, *dumfounded.* Well!
With resolution.
His Majesty shall know of this!
More sounds of hunting.
LEANDER *and two huntsmen enter.*

LEANDER. Quick, father! The hunt is moving off!
They bear PANTALOON *away.*

SCENE 2

SMERALDINA TRIES TO CATCH THE BIRDCATCHER

Enter from a different side TRUFFALDINO, *dressed in his green harlequin suit as formerly and carrying his camouflage net for birdcatching. He stalks in as if making a stealthy departure.*

VOICE OF SMERALDINA. Truffaldino!

TRUFFALDINO stops with a pained expression, then runs off but loses his hat on the way. He reappears and enters cautiously to retrieve his hat. Just as he is about to pick it up, SMERALDINA's *voice is heard close to.* TRUFFALDINO *crouches down with his camouflage net thrown over him.*

VOICE OF SMERALDINA. Truffaldino!

Enter SMERALDINA, *holding her shoes in her hand, and looking for* TRUFFALDINO. *Not seeing him, she tries awkwardly to put her shoes on, looks for something to sit on, and sits on the crouching* TRUFFALDINO. *They both collapse.*

SMERALDINA, *pulling the net off* TRUFFALDINO. Truffaldino, sweetheart! Don't be horrid, I love you!

TRUFFALDINO gets up and tries to pass SMERALDINA, *who tries to stop him with his net, which she holds out as he runs up and down.*

TRUFFALDINO. Oh, leave me alone, will you! So I wasn't good enough for you! Well, now you're not good enough for me! I'd rather live with fifty screeching cockatoos! I don't want anything to do with you!

SMERALDINA. You don't know what you want!

TRUFFALDINO tries to dash past her. SMERALDINA *throws the net over him. He falls.*

You see, you need someone to look after you!

TRUFFALDINO, *under the net.* Oh, go to bath! You'd make a bust laugh like a yaffle!

He pulls off the net.

SMERALDINA, *bending over him.* Truffaldino, my little bird-catcher, the bust laughed at me because I was in love with you!

TRUFFALDINO, *rising, into her face.* It laughed because your hat was on crooked and your glass eye was squinting at your false teeth!

He goes to the exit.

SMERALDINA, *blubbering.* Oh, Truffaldino!

TRUFFALDINO. May you be stuffed and put in a glass case!

The stage becomes dark.

SMERALDINA. Where am I?

TRUFFALDINO leaps back behind SMERALDINA.

TRUFFALDINO. Boo!

SMERALDINA *screams and runs off.* TRUFFALDINO *disappears.*

Black out.

Music.

The scene changes to the Forest of Roncislappe.

SCENE 3

THE PARROT FLIES AWAY IN THE FOREST

With the music and lights appear rocks, flowers and vines. Two stags are seen browsing.

Hearing someone whistling in the distance, the two stags run off.

Enter CIGOLOTTI, *whistling to himself. He is tired. He sets down the cage with the* PARROT *and goes to sit on a rock.*

CIGOLOTTI. Phew! Ten miles!

PARROT. Roncislappe! Roncislappe!

CIGOLOTTI. Looks like a good place for hedgehogs. I could do with a nice fat hedgehog baked in clay!

He smacks his lips and peers about.

PARROT. Let me out, Cigolotti!

CIGOLOTTI. Yes, coming, Polly! Here, master?

PARROT. Here, Cigolotti!

CIGOLOTTI. Good!

To public.

Save me traipsing any more!

CIGOLOTTI *opens the cage and takes out the* PARROT.

CIGOLOTTI. There you are, master!

He strokes the PARROT.

Now, away you go!

PARROT, *flying.* Good-by, Cigolotti! Good-by, Cigolotti! . . .
Good-by, Cigolotti!

CIGOLOTTI. Good-by, Durandarte!

Watching him fly away.

Don't forget Cigolotti when you're a magician! I wonder if
I'll ever see him again.

He shrugs his shoulders.

Oh well!

*He picks up the empty cage, brightens up, and saunters to
the stream, whistling.*

And now for fat Mr. Hedgehog! . . . Oh, he's been for a
drink, I can see. Here are his tracks. . . .

CIGOLOTTI *goes out, following the tracks of the hedgehog.*

SCENE 4

TARTAGLIA LEARNS THE MAGIC SPELL

Hounds are heard baying, horns blowing.
The hunting party arrives. Each carries a harquebus.

BRIGHELLA. Lord Pantaloon, I fail to see . . .

FIRST HUNTSMAN, *from the rocks, spotting some quarry.* Hist!

The party moves off.

As KING DERAMO *is about to go with the party,* TARTAGLIA *lays a restraining hand on* DERAMO's *arm.*

DERAMO. What is it, Tartaglia?

TARTAGLIA. This is a likely spot, Your Majesty. We might have a better chance of finding game away from the others.

DERAMO, *looking into the auditorium.* Ah yes. This is where I killed a fine stag two years ago. Do you remember, Tartaglia?

He turns toward TARTAGLIA.

TARTAGLIA *has meanwhile levelled his gun at* DERAMO's *back. When* DERAMO *turns toward him* TARTAGLIA *pretends to be examining the lock.*

TARTAGLIA. Y-yes, Your Majesty! And an excellent place it is . . .

Aside.

. . . for my purpose, if you'd give me time.

TARTAGLIA *points off right.*

And over there is a good spot too!

He levels his gun at DERAMO.

DERAMO. Ah yes . . . but it would be more enjoyable if some game would come along. Don't you think so?

DERAMO *turns back to* TARTAGLIA.

TARTAGLIA *shoulders his harquebus.*

TARTAGLIA. It will, Your Majesty.

Aside.

If I can hit him, I'll throw his body into the stream . . . but my hand is sh-shaking!

DERAMO, *from the rocks.* I cannot see or hear the other hunters . . .

TARTAGLIA *has again levelled his harquebus. When* DERAMO *looks around he pretends to be pointing it to something in the sky.*

TARTAGLIA. Oh, they are a long way off by now.

Aside.

Ah! A second more and I'd have had him!

DERAMO, *sensing something wrong*. My dear Tartaglia, what is wrong? You seem to be sadly preoccupied and nervous. I should like to see you gay today, otherwise my pleasure will be spoiled. Sit down and we will have a friendly talk. Have you something on your mind? If so, tell me and I will do all I can to help you. For, today, of all days, I cannot bear to see you in that state.

TARTAGLIA, *hesitating*. I can't do it now . . . I must watch for another opportunity.

To DERAMO.

Your Majesty, there's nothing wrong.

DERAMO. Oh, but I can see there is. I insist. Be seated and unburden your mind.

Pause.

Perhaps you have a grudge for what happened today?

TARTAGLIA, *sitting*. Ah, nothing escapes Your Majesty. And it is no use my concealing that I have in fact been deeply humiliated.

DERAMO. You, Tartaglia? How?

TARTAGLIA. For thirty years, Your Majesty, I have served you faithfully, and I think I can say, without false modesty, that I have given you good counsel in war and peace.

DERAMO, *sitting*. True, Tartaglia; continue.

TARTAGLIA. How many times have I exposed myself to danger in furious battles on behalf of my King! I have spared neither my body nor my life. My wounds can vouch for that! But, thanks to the energy with which I conducted operations, Serendip has always been victorious.

DERAMO. Yes, you have served your King and country well, Tartaglia—and I am proud to have such a Prime Minister . . . but of what are you complaining?

TARTAGLIA. Your Majesty, I wish to tender my resignation!

DERAMO. Resignation? You are not serious, Tartaglia. What has so offended you?

TARTAGLIA. I no longer have your confidence, Your Majesty.

DERAMO. But that is untrue, Tartaglia. I have always been your friend, and, as you have just said, always found your counsels wise. . . .

TARTAGLIA. Your Majesty, you have possessed two secrets of the magician, Durandarte. Oh, no doubt, you have every reason not to reveal them to any one. But, surely, these secrets—which affect the security of the state—you could have confided them in your First Minister. I used to fancy I enjoyed your royal confidence. Today, I suddenly discover I do not. It is only fit I should resign.

DERAMO. No, my dear Prime Minister, do not take it so ill. It was perhaps unjust of me, after so many proofs of your loyalty, not to have explained the secret of the bust to you . . . and I could perhaps have exempted your daughter, Clarissa, from the test. . . .

TARTAGLIA. My daughter's disgrace is nothing to me beside the loss of confidence. I beg Your Majesty to accept my resignation.

DERAMO *rises and goes to* TARTAGLIA. *He speaks in a tense voice.*

DERAMO. Tartaglia, listen! I will give you proof that my trust in you is as complete as ever. I wish you to remain Prime Minister and, so that no shadow shall remain between us, to you I will reveal the second and greater secret which Durandarte taught me.

TARTAGLIA *rises.*

I myself have never tried it, as yet.

DERAMO *takes a piece of paper from his cuff and holds it for a moment between his two hands, without speaking.*

On this piece of paper is written a magic spell! And these are its powers: If you say these words aloud over the dead body of an animal, or man, you die . . . and, by enchantment, your spirit passes into the dead body and brings it to life!

TARTAGLIA *weighs up the possibilities of the spell. He leads the* KING *on.*

TARTAGLIA. Ha! Certainly rare and dangerous knowledge. But, what use can it be put to? If I recite these words, say, over . . . a dead donkey . . . I should bring it to life . . . and I should remain a donkey for the rest of my days! No,

my King, you are making fun of me, you want to make me
a laughingstock!

DERAMO. Tartaglia, you offend me!

He is going to put the paper away.

TARTAGLIA. No, no, Your Majesty. I spoke in jest.

DERAMO. Then, let me finish. The "donkey" has only to repeat the same words over the body you left behind, and
your own body springs back to life. You are yourself again!

TARTAGLIA, *sinister.* Ha! I think I see how it can serve.

DERAMO. Here are the magic words.

He gives the paper to TARTAGLIA.

Learn them by heart, and, if need be, we can both use this
charm.

Gaily.

Now, tell me, Tartaglia, am I your friend, and do I trust
you?

TARTAGLIA. My King, forgive my doubting of it for so much
as a second. I shall cherish this mark of your high esteem.
Much good may come of it in the Kingdom. Thank you,
thank you, Your Majesty. . . .

He goes to kneel.

DERAMO. Rise! One thing more I will do for you, Tartaglia.
To compensate your daughter for my refusal, let her marry
Leander and I will present him with three castles.

TARTAGLIA, *effusively.* Oh, generous King, how can I ever show
gratitude enough for your great bounty?

DERAMO. There is no need. Learn by heart the magic words
. . . and come further on to find some sport!

Exit.

TARTAGLIA. His great bounty! He gives castles to Pantaloon's
son and steals my Angela! He gives to others and takes away
from me. Pah!

He spits.

But let me look at these famous words.

He reads, stuttering.

"Crypto, Cra Cra Trif Traf, Crypto-concoid-syphonos-tamata!" Difficult enough to pronounce, let alone to learn. But I must master them to master him!

Hunting horns.

Exit TARTAGLIA, *saying the words to himself.*

SCENE 5

THE BEAR HUNT

Enter a bear. A shot rings out. The bear rolls over, gets up and lumbers off.

VOICE OF BRIGHELLA. Ah! Well missed! Your turn, Lord Pantaloon!

Enter PANTALOON, LEANDER, BRIGHELLA *and two huntsmen.*

PANTALOON. Oh, clumsy fellow! Let me try.

PANTALOON fires. The recoil causes him to sit. The bear escapes.

BRIGHELLA. Bravo . . . you've put him to flight!

PANTALOON. Your turn, my boy!

LEANDER, *from the top of the rocks.* Look out!

He fires.

I've hit him! I've hit him!

PANTALOON. He's hit! Hey, whippersnappers, you fire now!

The two huntsmen fire. A dog howls.

BRIGHELLA. Oh, the idiots, they've shot the dog!

LEANDER. Up to the hill! You this way, you that! Quick, after him, boys.

Exeunt.

SCENE 6

KING INTO STAG

Enter DERAMO, *then* TARTAGLIA, *running.*

DERAMO. What a cannonade that was! I do not see any one . . .

TARTAGLIA. I thought by the noise they'd caught an elephant! But they're away over the hill.

DERAMO, *looking into the distance.* Look! Two stags running this way! Quick! Hide!

TARTAGLIA. By Jove, what could be better!

They hide.

Enter a stag with a white mark on its forehead. Another stag follows.

DERAMO *shoots one,* TARTAGLIA *the other.*

Well done, Your Majesty.

DERAMO. Congratulations to you, Tartaglia!

They shake hands.

I shall give these two fine beasts to my sweet Angela.

TARTAGLIA. A splendid idea, Your Majesty, splendid.

Aside.

The devil help me. This is my last chance!

He lays down his harquebus. To DERAMO.

Here we have two dead stags . . .

He pushes one with his foot.

Well and truly dead!

DERAMO. Yes, they have stopped moving.

TARTAGLIA. As dead as doornails! We are alone, the hunters are a long way off . . . supposing we tried out the magic spell? We could turn ourselves into those stags—just long enough to run to the top of the hill, see the view, and come back here. I must say, it seems well-nigh impossible to me —not that I doubt Your Majesty's word—but it's so extraordinary I'd like to see it happen.

DERAMO. Well, all you need do is to recite the magic words over one of those stags. You will then see how it works.

TARTAGLIA, *retreating with a nervous laugh.* Hee! Hee! Your Majesty . . . I . . . er . . . I must confess I'm a bit scared . . . and not prepared . . . And perhaps I don't believe in it enough . . . well . . .

DERAMO. You mistrust me, do you?

TARTAGLIA. Oh no, Your Majesty, but . . .

DERAMO. Are you the brave Tartaglia of countless battles?

TARTAGLIA. Ah, but this is not natural. . . . I've never tried magic before. Now, Your Majesty, with the bust . . .

DERAMO, *putting down his harquebus.* Very well. I will show you.

Pause. Then very seriously.

And then you will do exactly the same . . . ?

TARTAGLIA, *significantly.* Yes, Majesty.

DERAMO, *leaning over the stag with a white mark on its forehead.* Crypto, Cra Cra Trif Traf, Crypto-concoid-syphonos-tamata!

Tremulous music.

DERAMO *gradually sinks down and dies, while the stag comes to life.*

The stag turns its head toward TARTAGLIA, *who looks from the stag to the body of the* KING. TARTAGLIA *makes as if to pick up his gun. The stag runs swiftly off.*

TARTAGLIA. O marvel! Tartaglia, my old Tartaglia, I could dance for joy!

He is beside himself, his hands quiver with excitement.

Tartaglia, now for revenge and your heart's desires. . . . I enter into the King's body, take possession of the kingdom —and marry Angela!

He goes to the KING's *body, but as he starts to recite the spell, hunting horns sound.* TARTAGLIA *hides off stage.*

The bear enters growling. He sniffs at the body of the sec-
ond stag, then hides in the rocks.

Two hunters cross the stage behind the rocks.

VOICE OF BRIGHELLA. Eh! Wait for me!

BRIGHELLA *runs past the* KING's *body without seeing it. His*
harquebus is over his shoulder.

BRIGHELLA. Not so fast! It's not dignified!

His harquebus goes off over his shoulder. He runs off with
a yell.

TARTAGLIA *re-enters and recites the spell.*

TARTAGLIA. Crypto, Cra Cra Trif Traf, Crypto-concoid-
syphonos-tamata!

Tremulous music.

TARTAGLIA *gradually sinks down and dies, while* DERAMO's
*body comes to life (*TARTAGLIA's *spirit having entered*
DERAMO's *body).*

The bear reappears from the rocks. A shot is heard.

DERAMO *picks up his harquebus and runs off.*

The bear disappears into another hole in the rocks.

BRIGHELLA, *re-entering.* Hey! Follow me! Now, we've got him
cornered.

He looks around for the bear. The bear appears behind him
with arms outstretched to give him a bear hug. BRIGHELLA
suddenly notices the bear beside him. He gives a yell and
runs off.

The bear makes off, with the two huntsmen in pursuit,
through and over the rocks.

BRIGHELLA *re-enters and retrieves his harquebus, which he*
had let fall when the bear appeared behind him.

TARTAGLIA, *resembling the* KING *exactly in dress and fea-*
tures, returns.

TARTAGLIA, *as* KING. Deramo, stay in your unhappy s-state!
Oh, c-curse this impediment of speech! Are you still to
plague me? But what is there to fear? I am King, master of
the realm, and of Angela! I shall know how to get rid of all
whom I suspect or hate.

Looking at the body of TARTAGLIA.

Ah, but the King Stag must not be able to get into *my* body. . . .

He kicks it.

You are no use to me now, so . . .

He drags it into bushes off stage.

. . . into the bushes you go!

TARTAGLIA *returns, wiping one hand against the other.*

TARTAGLIA. What could be simpler! Now I must destroy the King Stag . . . there lies the only danger. . . . Here comes the court! Now, dignity, Tartaglia, you are the K-King!

SCENE 7

THE KING STAG IS HUNTED

Enter PANTALOON, BRIGHELLA, LEANDER *and huntsmen.*
TARTAGLIA *greets them haughtily.*

TARTAGLIA. Make haste, gentlemen, make haste. Two stags came this way. I have just killed one of them, as you can see. The other made off toward the hill. It is the finer of the two, and you will know it by the white mark on its forehead. It is imperative it be tracked down. Whoever kills it will receive a big reward. Follow me!
Exit.

PANTALOON, *who has been sitting down.* Come on, young men. Do His Majesty's bidding.
Exit.

LEANDER. I'll see to it! If I kill the stag I shall ask for Clarissa as a reward.

BRIGHELLA. After it, then. . . . This will be like the bear hunt. No one will manage to put a grain of salt on his tail.
Exit.
Music.

The KING STAG *runs in and tries to hide among the rocks.*
Sound of hounds and horns.
Enter the hunting party.

FIRST HUNTSMAN. Here it is!

The stag runs to and fro.

PANTALOON. My shot!

He fires and misses.

LEANDER. My shot!

He fires and misses.

BRIGHELLA. My shot!

He fires and misses.

TARTAGLIA, *pushing his way through them, furiously.* Bah! You useless lot! Crazy loons!

Enter across the stream a ragged OLD MAN *of repulsive appearance.*

Tell me, old man, did you see which way the stag went that just passed here?

OLD MAN. I dinna see 'un, sir.

TARTAGLIA. Oh, so you didn't see one? Listen to me, you mangy dog.

He takes hold of the OLD MAN.

Think hard. You certainly did see it. Which way did it go?

OLD MAN. But I saw nowt, sir.

TARTAGLIA. You've seen n-nothing. Well, I'll show you something!

TARTAGLIA *looks round and sees the pistol in* LEANDER's *belt. He takes it and fires at the* OLD MAN *point blank.*
The OLD MAN *utters a cry and drops dead.*

TARTAGLIA. There's something for you!

LEANDER. What sort of tyranny is this?

TARTAGLIA, *rounding on them.* Country louts and base courtiers—useless crew—a curse on the lot of you! Whoever betrays me will suffer the same fate!

PANTALOON, *going over to the body of the* OLD MAN. This is sheer madness. . . . Whatever are you doing, Your Majesty? Are you feeling unwell?

TARTAGLIA. Father-in-law wants to preach me a sermon, does he? Have a care, or I shall make short shrift of you . . . and of all useless people!

LEANDER. Your Majesty, it is too late to hunt any more today. . . .

TARTAGLIA. Through your fault! Then, you can start tomorrow at dawn and surround the wood. That stag must be killed at first light. Announce immediately that whoever brings to the King a stag with a white mark on its forehead will receive ten thousand ducats reward. But where is Tarta-Tartaglia?

PANTALOON, *aside.* He has become a raging beast, I don't know him any more. Even his voice has changed and he's caught Tartaglia's stammer.

TARTAGLIA. Where is Tartaglia? What were you saying about him?

PANTALOON. Oh, nothing, nothing. Tartaglia was with Your Majesty.

TARTAGLIA. Yes, but I lost sight of him some time ago.

LEANDER. We are not so far from Serendip. He knows the way. Perhaps he's gone back.

TARTAGLIA. Don't talk nonsense, g-greenhorn. You know very well he is detested because I like him, and I shouldn't want him to be set on by any gang. Find him and tell him of my d-de-decision!

PANTALOON. What a terrible fit of stuttering!

TARTAGLIA. Huntsmen, take this stag with you, as a present to my dear Angela. And tomorrow, don't forget, everyone in the forest at the break of day.

Exit.

The second huntsman lifts the stag onto the first huntsman's back.

PANTALOON. Let us return to Serendip too. I am exhausted. I do not like leaving my daughter alone at the court. And Tartaglia's disappearance bodes no good.

LEANDER. Ah, Brighella, if I kill the stag, I could ask for Clarissa.

BRIGHELLA, *who has been looking aghast at the* OLD MAN'S *body*. His head is full of his Clarissa . . . and, as things go, I can almost feel a load of grapeshot in my head like the bunch that struck the old man.

Exit.

SCENE 8

KING STAG INTO OLD MAN

Music: DERAMO *theme.*

The KING STAG *enters timidly, with leaves caught in his antlers. He looks for his body. He scents the* OLD MAN'S *body, turns, and goes to it. He recites the spell over the* OLD MAN.

KING STAG. Crypto, Cra Cra Trif Traf, Crypto-concoid-sy-phonos-tamata!

Tremulous music.

The KING STAG *slowly sinks down and dies. The* OLD MAN *comes to life.*

OLD MAN (DERAMO). A man, Deramo, once again. Thank Heaven, I have escaped from the gravest peril.

He sits.

Now I no longer need to snatch a leaf or a few blades of grass among the rocks and trees, forever in dread of the hounds' cruel teeth and my hunters' guns.

Rising.

Durandarte, intoxicated by the happiness of the day, I used your dangerous secret to satisfy an idle curiosity—and I have been punished.

He kneels.

Durandarte, forgive me. Do not punish me more. Let me go to Serendip to save my crown and Angela from the clutches of the impious Tartaglia, now parading in my body.

Rising.

Vengeance, Deramo! How weak I feel . . . and thirsty . . .
Going to the stream.

All my strength has gone.

He bends over the stream. He recoils.

What a hideous creature! It is not me! It is not Deramo!
Where is *my* body? Oh that impious, faithless Tartaglia,
whom I protected and befriended, these are my thanks!

In a cry.

Angela! Angela no sooner found than lost! I must go to
Serendip and try and gain entry to the palace—but how will
Angela believe I am Deramo in this misshapen body? She
will have me chased from the palace like the beggar I appear to be! Angela, I am coming to save you from a usurper
—do not reject me!

He is almost overcome.

I must summon all my strength to drag my bones along.

He goes out, tottering.

SCENE 9

THE PARROT IS CAUGHT BY THE BIRDCATCHER

Music: Pastorale.

Enter TRUFFALDINO, *whistling, with his trap, his nets, his
cage, etc.*

TRUFFALDINO. This is just the spot for me! What an aviary!
He sets down his paraphernalia and inspects the scene.

Trees, rocks, a stream . . .

He prods the ground.

soft ground—bushes—all the birds will come here!

He hops up and down, and points off stage. To the public:
A hornbill hopping along a branch!

A whistling cadence is heard. He picks up his hand net.

Listen! A schoolboy thrush whistling among the rocks!

He imitates the call on his pipes. Then he comes downstage, following imaginary birds.

Honeybirds, playing hide-and-seek!

He mimes catching one and releasing it. He stalks another, catches it, and releases it, blowing a kiss after it.

Who wouldn't be a birdcatcher? Why, all the ministers of state could pass here, they wouldn't see a quarter of what I can see now! Where shall I put my trap? Ah, those rocks!

While talking, he fixes the trap on the rocks.

And to think I used to catch all these birds for Smeraldina— yes, and paradise flycatchers and golden orioles into the bargain! I must have been crazy! I should have sent her kites and crows and brain-fever birds!

He comes down to where he has left his cage, nets, etc.

Silly old cuckoo!

He picks up his camouflage net and hand net. To the public:

Now, sh!

He sits at the bottom of the rock, with the camouflage net over his head and whistles with his bird warbler. He brings around his net cautiously and catches a small bird against the rock.

A white-eye!

He disentangles it from his net and puts it in his hip basket. He sees two birds in the air, downstage. He stalks them.

Two weaverbirds!

They fly away. He sulks.

The PARROT *appears on the rocks.*

What's that, moving up there? A parrot! A great, green parrot!

Excitedly.

Polly! Polly! Pretty Poll! Come and have some sugar cane! Come on, Polly! Come and bite your uncle's ear!

To TRUFFALDINO'S *astonishment, the* PARROT *walks into the trap. He pulls away the stick and the* PARROT *is caught.*

Magnificent! What a day for Truffaldino!

PARROT. Truffaldino!

TRUFFALDINO, *alarmed.* What's that? An echo?

PARROT. Truffaldino!

TRUFFALDINO. Who's that?

PARROT. Truffaldino!

TRUFFALDINO. Oh dear!

He retreats upstage and comes across the body of
TARTAGLIA.

Ah! It's a dead body talking! Oh! Tartaglia! Quick, my nets,
I'm off! They'll say I did it!

Business.

PARROT. Truffaldino, come here! Don't be scared!

TRUFFALDINO. Who said that? . . . Could it be the parrot?
Surely not! Let's see!

Gingerly, to the PARROT.

Scratch a Poll!

PARROT. Take me to the Queen!

TRUFFALDINO, *taken aback.* Eh? What? Oh, a learned parrot!
What can I do for you, Mr. Parrot?

PARROT. Take me to the palace, I said.

TRUFFALDINO. To be sure, my lord Parrot. To the palace to
see the Queen!

PARROT. You'll be rich!

TRUFFALDINO, *going to the* PARROT. Rich? Oh, no doubt—if
you talk nicely to the Queen.

He takes the PARROT *out of the trap.*

I shall earn a lot of money!

He puts the PARROT *in the bird cage.*

Please enter your house! Mind your tail! There!

Fastening the cage.

Eh? Sh! Don't say that in front of the Queen!

PARROT. Rich!

TRUFFALDINO. Now I'll make my fortune!

Remembering the body of TARTAGLIA, *he makes a gesture
round his throat.*

. . . unless I'm hanged first! Quick, I've got my trap, my birds, my nets . . .

He sees the dead stag.

. . . but what is this?

Coming toward the public.

Oh, a stag come to die near the stream!

He stops.

Wait a minute!

He looks more closely at the stag.

A white mark on its forehead! Why, this must be the one there is a big reward for . . . I'm dreaming!

He pinches himself.

Ow! No, I'm not, and this is the king stag with the white mark! What luck!

He capers, then starts to collect his paraphernalia.

Oh, but I'll never manage all this.

PARROT. Come along!

TRUFFALDINO. I'm coming, as quick as I can, Mr. Parrot. I must get some help.

TRUFFALDINO *whistles.*

Answering whistle.

Hi there!

PARROT. Hi there!

TRUFFALDINO *looks at the* PARROT.

VOICE, *off.* Hi!

TRUFFALDINO, *calling.* This way! Can you give me a hand?

Enter two peasants.

FIRST PEASANT. What with?

TRUFFALDINO. I've got too much to carry.

FIRST PEASANT. Bit heavy all that . . .

TRUFFALDINO, *ordering, to* SECOND PEASANT. You're pretty hefty! Take this stag to the palace. . . .

SECOND PEASANT, *looking at* TRUFFALDINO. Eh?

TRUFFALDINO. . . . and I'll give you a big present.

The two peasants look at each other and nod their heads.

SECOND PEASANT. To palace? Aye, that we will, master.

They tie the stag by its feet to a pole.

TRUFFALDINO. Now I have everything.

He sees TARTAGLIA's *body again.*

Euh! Tartaglia's body . . . I don't want to be hanged, but I'd better spread the news before the crows and vultures get him.

To the peasants.

Let's go!

To the public.

Believe the word of a birdcatcher—we'll see some strange doings yet. . . .

Exeunt.

SCENE 10

ANGELA'S SONG

Music.

The stage darkens. ANGELA's *room appears, lighted from inside.*

Through curtained casements ANGELA *is perceived, reclining on a heap of cushions.*

At her feet, a MUSICIAN *with a lute.*

Two guards open the casements and retire.

In an alcove, at the back of the room, is a small table on which stands a bowl of flowers.

MUSICIAN, *singing.*

>   The first fine day of spring
>   The young and gay on holiday
>   At the fair were gathering.

Bis.

ANGELA, *speaking.* Will the hunt never be ended?

Pause.

Deramo is so long returning.

Singing.

> In the sun small birds I spied
> Who sang and twittered merrily!

MUSICIAN, *singing sadly.*

> In the sun I longed and sighed—
> Oh, my love, come back to me!

ANGELA, *singing.*

> I have waited at the window so
> From morning till the sunset glow!

MUSICIAN, *singing.*

> What was I waiting for now?
> What was I waiting for?

Faint sound of a horn.

ANGELA *runs to the window, which, in this scene and those following, replaces the door in the tower, downstage right.*

ANGELA's *face is lit by the glow of the setting sun.*

ANGELA, *speaking.* Oh, musician, is that not the hunt returning?

MUSICIAN, *rising and speaking.* Not yet, madam . . .

Pause.

But it will not be long. . . .

ANGELA, *singing as she gazes out of the window.*

> In the sun I longed and sighed—
> Oh, my love, come back to me!

The left-hand door opens silently. TARTAGLIA, *as* KING, *appears.*

MUSICIAN, *singing.*

> What was I waiting for now?

At a sign from TARTAGLIA, *the* MUSICIAN *begins to withdraw, singing.*

> What was I waiting for?

As he leaves, he finishes his song merrily.

> The first fine day of spring
> The young and gay on holiday
> At the fair were gathering.

Bis.
Exit.

SCENE 11

TARTAGLIA AS KING IN THE PALACE

While the MUSICIAN *is singing,* TARTAGLIA *silently approaches* ANGELA *till, on the last bar of the music, he is immediately behind her as she stands at the window.*

He places his hands over her eyes. ANGELA *utters a cry, then takes his hands.*

ANGELA. Is that you, Deramo? How long you have been!

A pause.

Do not move, my prince. I am so happy. I have waited all day for this minute when you return.

A pause.

Let this minute last!

A pause.

How strange! You are standing there behind me and I only seem to be holding two trembling hands—but they are trembling less than my heart!

She kisses his hand.

Deramo, my prince!

TARTAGLIA, *coming suddenly before her.* Angela!

ANGELA's *smile fades and she retreats from him.*

What is the m-matter?

ANGELA. I . . . I do not know, Deramo. . . . I had a sudden feeling of strangeness. I have been waiting for you all day, listening to every sound in the palace. A door opening—and my heart leaped in my breast. But when you came in just now I did not even recognize your footstep.

TARTAGLIA. You are overwrought. It's nothing, nothing at all. Tomorrow we'll have our wedding. Sit down and we'll talk about it.

ANGELA. No, no, please, leave me to myself!

TARTAGLIA. But I can't possibly leave you in such a state!

ANGELA. For pity's sake, let me go!

She bursts into tears and runs out.

TARTAGLIA. Bah! A silly girl's pique! But I'll persuade her yet! Who can resist me? The throne is mine; I've turned the King into a stag. . . . Though, if the king stag should not be killed . . . and return in some guise to overthrow me. . . . Never fear. Once I am wedded to Angela, no one would believe him, whatever his shape! We'd throw him into the deepest dungeon to rot in oblivion. My wedding is the thing. . . .

Enter PANTALOON. *He speaks from the door.*

PANTALOON. Your Majesty, I crave audience.

TARTAGLIA. This is not the day, Pantaloon, and scarcely the moment.

PANTALOON. That I know, Your Majesty, but a grave incident emboldens me to . . .

TARTAGLIA. In that case, speak, but be brief.

TARTAGLIA *sits on the window seat.*

PANTALOON. Thank you, Your Majesty.

PANTALOON *comes forward to impart his important news.*

I have to inform you, Tartaglia has not returned from the hunt!

TARTAGLIA *turns his head away.*

TARTAGLIA. The devil he hasn't! Has anything serious happened to him?

PANTALOON. This morning, maddened by Your Majesty's choice of my daughter, he uttered some imprudent remarks. Not only did Tartaglia openly accuse my son and me of plotting against him, but he threatened to arouse the people against me. He even suggested Your Majesty's mind was deranged! I felt it my duty to warn His Majesty, and to assure him he can count on my lifelong devotion.

PANTALOON *bows low.*

TARTAGLIA. Old man, your tales amuse me. I fear your brain is softening with age.

PANTALOON, *indignant.* On my honor, sir . . .

TARTAGLIA, *rising.* Yes, yes, I know. A lot of honor and few
brains. You're growing old. I have observed on several occasions you needed a rest. Mr. Pantaloon, from today you
will cease to be a Minister. I need a young man who is
clever, who has energy and authority. In short, some one
capable, not a feeble old man.

PANTALOON, *dumfounded.* Your Majesty has never once . . .

TARTAGLIA. Everything comes to an end—even my patience
and this audience.

TARTAGLIA *opens the door for* PANTALOON *to go.* PANTA-
LOON, *furious, stumps out.*

Guards! Stand at the door! Tell Angela the King awaits her.
He goes into the alcove.

Now I will impose my will!

ANGELA *enters. A guard bars the exit.*

TARTAGLIA *advances toward her.* ANGELA *looks around to
the door and sees the guard.*

ANGELA. No! No! Leave me in peace!

TARTAGLIA. But what is the m-matter? You look demented!
I'm beginning to think I was wrong in choosing you to be
my consort! Where is the great love you protested this morning and only a moment ago?

ANGELA, *in agitation.* Oh, Deramo, forgive me for what I am
about to say, but I cannot go on with this . . .

TARTAGLIA. Wh-What? Explain yourself!

ANGELA, *in agitation.* Your Majesty, I am suffering from a cruel
disillusion! I see my King in you—but not my Deramo!

TARTAGLIA. What do you mean? This is nonsense. I . . . I
am Deramo. Deramo is me!

ANGELA. This is Deramo's face, Deramo's bearing and noble
air I so admired, and yet—it is not you! Even your voice
has changed!

TARTAGLIA, *taken aback.* My—my voice?

ANGELA. Your sentiments, as well. I no longer find that gentleness of mind, of speech, that tenderness which so delighted
me and made me long to be your wife. My King, forgive

me, but it was not your face or mien that so affected me. It was a nature which I no longer find.

She flings herself on to the cushions, weeping.

TARTAGLIA, *nonplused.* Deramo's nature from Deramo's body cannot be divorced. No, no . . . it's you who have changed!

ANGELA, *between her tears.* No, my King, I have not changed, and permit me to tell you with the sincerity which pleased you so this morning: If I had seen you then as I see you now, I would have said: I do not love you and I do not wish to marry you!

She sobs.

TARTAGLIA *dismisses the guard, with a gesture.*

TARTAGLIA. This is mere childishness! A brain storm . . . madness that will—

He stamps.

that *must* pass!

ANGELA, *rising.* You are right. I am mad . . . with grief. You would not have spoken to me in this way before. Let me go, or my heart will break!

She makes toward the door. TARTAGLIA *intercepts her.*

TARTAGLIA. Where do you think you are going, you little stupid? I'll call a doctor and have you bled! Think of my heart!

ANGELA. In pity, let me pass!

TARTAGLIA. Very w-well . . . for the time being, but I'll soon have you yourself again, and . . .

ANGELA *goes and shuts the door.* TARTAGLIA *shouts after her.*

. . . we marry tomorrow!

Ah! I am in a rage with frustration! That little fiend resists me yet. The stag is still at large! . . . Calm, calm, tartar . . . After all, I am King—and I will stay King. If I cannot have my way by gentle methods, I'll use force. I will destroy all who stand in my path.

Going back to the alcove.

There is no lack of poison and of empty cells in the royal prisons. I'll put the kingdom to sack rather than fail!

CLARISSA, *running in.* Justice, justice, my gentle Highness!

CLARISSA *kneels, bursting into tears.*

TARTAGLIA. Why these tears, Clarissa?

CLARISSA. My dear father has been killed!

TARTAGLIA, *aside.* Hm! I hadn't thought of that. Poor child, I'm sorry for her.

To CLARISSA.

Ah, woe is me! Who are the assassins? Who killed my faithful T-Tartaglia?

CLARISSA. I only know I am the unhappiest creature alive.

TARTAGLIA, *aside.* She moves me to pity. If only I could tell her how great her father has become.

To CLARISSA.

Be comforted, Clarissa.

He raises her.

I will be a *second* father to you, and avenge the death of my dear friend, even if it means making blood to flow like w-water. I'll soon bring the murderer to book. Go now, Clarissa, and be comforted!

CLARISSA. I will, Your Majesty, and put my trust in you.

Enter PANTALOON *and* LEANDER *in haste.* CLARISSA *goes to* LEANDER.

LEANDER. Your Majesty, we bring most painful news . . .

PANTALOON. My affliction is greater, Your Majesty, for I sadly misjudged Tartaglia. I crave your pardon for my suspicion. The Prime Minister . . .

TARTAGLIA. . . . has been killed. I know already.

With affected sorrow.

My poor Tartaglia . . . my great and noble friend . . . dead . . .

With a sob in his voice.

. . . killed!

CLARISSA *can stand no more. She goes.* TARTAGLIA *says suddenly:*

Who brought this news?

LEANDER. Truffaldino, the court birdcatcher, Your Majesty.
He says he found the body in the Forest of Roncislappe,
in a thicket.

TARTAGLIA. Guards!

Enter two guards.

Have the body of my dear Prime Minister burned immediately, and his ashes put in a golden urn. Let the urn
be placed in my rooms in honor of the memory of so great
and worthy a man!

The guards salute.

Guards, these are my orders! Imprison Truffaldino and all
who accompanied me at today's hunt!

The guards salute.

LEANDER *and* PANTALOON, *who had listened to* TARTAGLIA'S
oration with bowed heads, are dumfounded.

LEANDER. Your Majesty, how can you . . . ?

TARTAGLIA, *in a terrible voice.* I have spoken! Disarm Leander
and Pantaloon and put them into the dungeon.

The guards salute and seize PANTALOON *and* LEANDER.

I'll begin my investigation with them.

PANTALOON. I do not understand, Your Majesty!

TARTAGLIA. You only have to obey! I know what treachery
and envy can do in the hearts of courtiers.

To LEANDER.

T-Tartaglia did not give you his daughter, Clarissa.

To PANTALOON.

And you, old dotard, told me yourself how you envied and
distrusted Tartaglia. That is enough for you to be hanged!
If I find you innocent, I shall acquit you!

Peremptorily.

To the tower, both of you!

LEANDER. Justice!

PANTALOON. We are innocent!

TARTAGLIA. Away with them!

Exeunt LEANDER *and* PANTALOON *with the guards.*

I lock up my Ministers and my rule is secured. No crown has ever been so firmly fixed on a head . . . unless the stag . . . but I shall have it destroyed tomorrow, by hook or by c-c-crook!

ACT III

THE RIGHTFUL KING RETURNS TO THE PALACE

SCENE 1

ANGELA'S DILEMMA

Next morning.

The curtain rises on ANGELA'S *room.*

In the alcove, instead of the flower bowl standing on the small table, there is the PARROT'S *cage, covered by a cloth.*

Music: DERAMO *theme.*

DERAMO, *as the* OLD MAN, *appears at the window.*

DERAMO. At last!

Climbing through the window.

I never thought I should get so far. My poor legs will not go any more . . .

He gets into a corner near the window.

In this palace I was King . . . and now . . . I must slip in here like a thief! How savagely my own hounds set on me. . . . Still, I have reached Angela's room. If only I can see her! I must tell her . . . But will she believe me in this wretched guise?

He starts to cross to the door opposite, when the door opens. He hides behind the casement curtains, left.

Enter ANGELA, *with a letter in her hand.*

ANGELA, *unfolding the letter.* What is this? My father writes to me from prison? My father in prison? What does this mean?

She sits on the cushions and reads.

"I am in prison and Leander is with me, awaiting His Majesty's pleasure . . ." My brother in prison, too?

Reading.

"Tartaglia is dead. May Heaven protect us . . . we are innocent. Do not grieve and take care of yourself, my darling daughter—your loving father." This is monstrous! My father and my brother too! Both taken away! What have they done, poor souls?

DERAMO, *calling softly from his hiding place.* Angela!

ANGELA. Deramo! How could he have done such a cruel act? He is too changed!

DERAMO, *calling, as before.* My Angela!

ANGELA. I am so bewildered, and yet, in my fancy, I can hear my name spoken as the Deramo I first knew used to say it. Such outrageous tyranny cannot be the sane act of a king who urges me to marry him this very morning!

DERAMO, *calling, as before.* My bride!

ANGELA, *rising.* A bride could wish for a less gruesome wedding gift!

Coming forward.

What a fearful dilemma I am in! How can I marry such a tyrant? But, if I do not, my father and Leander will most likely be left to rot in that foul prison. . . .

DERAMO, *calling, as before.* My wife!

DERAMO *begins to make his way through the curtains, but at this moment* TRUFFALDINO *enters* ANGELA'S *room and* DERAMO *is obliged to withdraw again.*

SCENE 2

THE BIRDCATCHER PRESENTS ANGELA WITH
THE PARROT

TRUFFALDINO *wants to address* ANGELA, *but is intimidated by her air. He returns to the door.*

ANGELA. What do you want, birdcatcher?

TRUFFALDINO *returns and speaks with deep bows and exaggerated gestures. He is showing off to the* QUEEN.

TRUFFALDINO. Gracious lady! Allow me to offer, in token of my homage, a gift of the rarest creature you have yet seen!

ANGELA. Truffaldino, at the moment I have other matters to think about than your gifts. What is it you want to give me? Tell me quickly, and then go.

ANGELA, *trying to be patient, sits on the window seat.*

TRUFFALDINO. It is a parrot, my lady, but not any old parrot. This one is a most accomplished specimen of the great green variety. He is more learned than all the professors at the university combined . . .

Aside, to the public.

. . . which is saying a lot for a parrot!

To ANGELA.

He . . . well, with Your Ladyship's permission, I will give a demonstration. I have been bold enough to have him brought by two hirelings into the alcove of Your Ladyship's apartments.

He goes to the cage and sets it on a cushion on the floor with elaborate gestures.

ANGELA. You are beginning to try my patience, birdcatcher, with all this nonsense. Take your parrot away!

TRUFFALDINO, *running back to* ANGELA. Ah, but my gracious lady, this parrot is most *erudite.* Just one moment and I will show you.

With a grand gesture, TRUFFALDINO *removes the cloth from the* PARROT's *cage.*

There! Isn't he a beauty? But listen to him!

He tries to encourage the PARROT *to talk.*

Hello, Polly! Had a nice breakfast, Polly?

The PARROT *remains silent.*

Polly, had a nice breakfast?

Silence. Menacingly.

Scratch a Poll!

The PARROT *does not budge.* TRUFFALDINO *shakes the cage.*

Well, are you going to talk, you little beast?

ANGELA. That will do. Do not try my patience any more. Leave me.

TRUFFALDINO. But, my lady, he will speak, he will. Good-for-nothing, are you going to say something? Eh?

Crawling round the cage.

Polly, have you had a nice breakfast—yes or no?

ANGELA, *rising*. I can see I shall have to have you taken away by force.

TRUFFALDINO. No, I'm going, Your Ladyship, I'm going.

TRUFFALDINO *puts the cage back on the table. To the* PARROT.

So these are the riches you promised me for bringing you all that road to see the Queen! You won't catch me again that way!

He trips over a cushion and falls.

I'll screw your neck!

He picks himself up and is about to go when a GUARD *enters and bars his way.*

GUARD. Allow me, Your Ladyship!

ANGELA. Who gave you permission to come here?

TRUFFALDINO, *running to* ANGELA. Oh, please don't be cross this time, my lady! The guard here has certainly been sent to pay the ten thousand ducats promised by the king to whoever valiantly slew the stag with the white mark. Now, I am that valiant man!

Crossing.

Isn't that right, soldier?

GUARD. Your Ladyship, the King has ordered that this man be thrown into the deepest cell of the dungeon. He is suspected of killing Tartaglia.

To TRUFFALDINO.

Come along with me, you rapscallion!

The GUARD *tries to seize* TRUFFALDINO, *who avoids him by an acrobatic trick.* TRUFFALDINO *throws a cushion at the*

GUARD, *and while the* GUARD *is returning it,* TRUFFALDINO *crawls through his legs, and, on all fours, makes for the door, where he finds himself face to face with the* SECOND GUARD. *He leaps back and is caught by the* FIRST GUARD.

ANGELA. How dare you, in my private rooms!

FIRST GUARD, *coming to attention.* The King's orders, Your Ladyship!

TRUFFALDINO *leaps back and is caught by the* FIRST GUARD. Now then, come on, no more clowning! Forward!

TRUFFALDINO, *being propelled forward by the collar.* Is this my reward? May the crows peck out that parrot's eyes and the kites eat the stag, and the vultures make a meal of Tartaglia!

His voice is drowned in the wings.
The SECOND GUARD *follows.*

SCENE 3

THE OLD MAN TELLS ANGELA HE IS THE KING

ANGELA *goes to the window.*

ANGELA. Where will this tyranny end? And what will become of me?

DERAMO, *still in hiding.* Do not weep, Angela!

ANGELA, *astonished and alarmed.* Who spoke?

DERAMO. Angela, you must not weep!

ANGELA. Deramo's voice . . .

DERAMO. It is, indeed . . .

ANGELA. Where did it come from?
Going to the alcove.
Was it the parrot? Surely not!

DERAMO, *leaving his hiding place and raising a trembling hand toward* ANGELA. Angela, do not be afraid, and, above all, try not to be aghast at my appearance.

ANGELA. Who brought you here? Who are you?

DERAMO. Angela . . .

ANGELA. You are a spy!

DERAMO *tries to speak, but* ANGELA *continues.*

You have slipped into my room to overhear what I say and inform the King! Go away, old man, or else I'll call my servants!

She runs to the door. DERAMO *makes his way after her.*

DERAMO. No, for mercy's sake! Angela! First, listen! Tell me, do you not find the King very different now from what he was yesterday morning?

ANGELA. Why do you ask that? Who sent you here to ask me that question?

DERAMO, *bent on convincing her.* Do you remember what your Deramo said when he broke the bust as a proof of his faith in you? "Five years ago, the magician, Durandarte, made me a present of two great secrets, one of which is this . . .

He takes his staff in his other hand to support himself while he makes the gesture to where the BUST *used to be.*

. . . and the other I am not revealing . . ."

ANGELA, *still more amazed.* Yes—yes, that is true. But, how do you know? Who told you?

DERAMO. Ah, you see!

Pursuing his advantage.

Then, you will remember that Deramo teased you about a birthmark on your neck. He said it was a blemish on your beauty . . .

ANGELA, *breathless.* But . . .

DERAMO. But Deramo himself is now covered from head to toe with hideous blemishes and is in agony of mind because his promised wife no longer knows him, and . . .

He sinks to the ground.

. . . he is deprived of his youth, his strength, and his kingdom!

ANGELA, *bewildered, going to him.* What are you saying, old man?

DERAMO. That I am Deramo! Yes, Angela, it is Deramo speaking to you in this repulsive shape. By a magic enchantment Tartaglia took possession of my real body and had me hunted by my own hounds. I believed in him too much!

ANGELA. Such a change is not possible! Why have you come to me with this incredible story?

DERAMO, *with outstretched arms.* Precisely because you are the only person in the world who could believe me!

ANGELA. I cannot believe you. My eyes cannot be deceived to that extent. . . .

DERAMO. I am not appealing to your eyes . . .

ANGELA, *in a hysterical cry, as she runs away toward the window.* Leave me in peace!

DERAMO, *raising himself with the help of his stick, and turning toward her.* Angela, my Angela! You are trembling . . . you are not sure! You doubt in your heart and that doubt is almost a confession—do not fight against your heart! I am your Deramo!

ANGELA, *beside herself.* Go away, you poor old madman!

ANGELA *turns her head away.* DERAMO *gazes at her tragically, then, bowed, he turns to go.*

Music: DERAMO *theme in a minor key.*

As DERAMO *reaches the door and opens it,* ANGELA *says, as in a dream:*

Deramo! . . . Deramo!

The music ceases.

DERAMO *stops. He looks around, closing the door.*

ANGELA, *still as in a dream.* Again that gentleness of speech; that tenderness I missed. That was my Deramo!

ANGELA *looks toward the door, and sees* DERAMO *is still there. She gazes at him as if seeing him for the first time.*

For a moment ANGELA *and* DERAMO, *on either side of the stage, stand with an outstretched arm. Then,* ANGELA *goes halfway across the intervening space and kneels with bowed head, as if asking forgiveness for not recognizing him immediately.*

DERAMO *goes to* ANGELA.

DERAMO. My Angela, your heart knows what your eyes cannot see.

ANGELA, *rising*. Deramo, who would believe such a thing could happen? You, like this—and Tartaglia, King!

DERAMO. Dry your eyes, we must be very brave.

ANGELA, *suddenly exclaims*. But we are lost! Tartaglia as King has proclaimed my wedding to him for this very morning! I tried to dissuade him, and in his fury he has thrown my father and my brother into prison . . . I shall *have* to marry him for fear of worse things to befall!

DERAMO. Oh, that blackest of traitors!

ANGELA. But no! I will reveal his treachery! I will run through Serendip and shout the truth to all the people.

She runs to the door.

They will rise against him. . . .

DERAMO. No, my little one. Who would believe such incredible things? No. We must be calm. We must find a plan to save us. Let us go, my sweet, where we cannot be overheard, and we will see what we can devise . . .

ANGELA *assists* DERAMO *through the casement curtains on the left.*

First and foremost . . . you must tell me everything that Tartaglia has told you. . . .

SCENE 4

SMERALDINA PLAGUES BRIGHELLA

As soon as DERAMO *and* ANGELA *have disappeared,* BRIGHELLA *pushes up the bottom half of the downstage right window, looks through, then climbs in.*

SMERALDINA, *from the outside, catches hold of his coat tail.*

BRIGHELLA. Oh, go away, don't plague me like this!

He slams down the bottom half of the window, nearly catching SMERALDINA's *fingers.*

I've . . .

Realizing the window is closed and SMERALDINA *cannot hear him, he stands on the window seat and pushes down the top half.*

I've just been told a guard is coming to throw me into jail. I've got something else to do than to bother my head about your capers. . . .

SMERALDINA *pushes up the top half of the window and pinches his fingers. He jumps down.* SMERALDINA *pushes up the bottom half of the window and climbs in.*

SMERALDINA. Yes, you wretch . . . your ambition to become commander in chief was the cause of my downfall!

BRIGHELLA. If you go on, I shall duck you in the pond, like the witch you are!

SMERALDINA, *screaming.* Help! Help! He's going to drown me!

BRIGHELLA, *who was peering out of the opposite door, in a thunderous voice.* Quiet, won't you!

SMERALDINA, *who only wants to tell her story. She goes to* BRIGHELLA *and sits on the step beside him.* Well then, cousin, listen to what happened next. One moment the bird-catcher was there, talking to me in the sweetest of tones, and then—he was gone! And then, and then . . . I found, instead of being here in the palace, I was all alone in a strange, dark forest . . .

BRIGHELLA, *mocking her.* And then you woke, I suppose, and saw goblins dancing round you! I'm not interested in old maids' nightmares!

He goes to the alcove and peers through the curtains.

SMERALDINA. Well, it's your fault if I have nightmares! You had me disgraced in front of the King . . . and now my little Truffaldino has disappeared.

Going to him and pummelling him.

You must find him for me!

BRIGHELLA. I probably shall find him—and sooner than I want to! He's in chains in prison.

SMERALDINA, *screaming more loudly.* Ow!

BRIGHELLA *clasps his hand over her mouth with such force,
she sits down.*

BRIGHELLA. Will you stop that hullabaloo!

SMERALDINA *screams again from where she sits.*

I told you a guard is looking for me to lock me up in prison
too!

SMERALDINA *screams more than ever.* BRIGHELLA *picks up a
cushion and pushes it over her face.*

You're crazy!

BRIGHELLA *runs toward the door, thinks better of it, and
dives out of the window.*

SMERALDINA *sits up, giggling.*

SMERALDINA. Hee! Hee! I'd like to see my surly cousin behind
the bars awhile. But I'll soon get around the guards and
have my Truffaldino out!

She goes to the door. In a loud voice:

Love laughs at locks and bolts!

Exit.

SCENE 5

ANGELA AND DERAMO IN PERIL

Enter DERAMO *and* ANGELA *through the curtains.*

DERAMO.   . . . that is our plan.

ANGELA. My dear Deramo, you may rely on me for its success.

DERAMO. Angela . . .

He takes her hand.

I desire you . . . to use what arts you can to bring about
Tartaglia's downfall . . . but be very wary. He is cunning
and cruel. Take care he does not ensnare you and bear you
off to the altar before he is unmasked for what he is.

Music: TARTAGLIA *theme.*

ANGELA. Quick! Hide! He is coming . . .

DERAMO *goes back behind the curtains.*

ANGELA *reclines on the cushions.*

Pray Heaven I do not fail!

Enter TARTAGLIA *with two* GUARDS.

TARTAGLIA. Ah, my little Angela! Have you got over that humor which so changed your affection for m-me? But, listen,
sweeting . . . I have a surprise for you. I made a secret vow
I would give you a second stag for your wedding day—a
unique one with a white mark—a king stag! He has been
caught and killed. What do you say to that?

ANGELA *gives a faint smile.*

Now, has my little treasure's heart not softened toward her
King and husband-to-be?

ANGELA. Your Majesty, I have been praying Heaven to rid me
of that strange delusion about you which made me so unhappy, and the dislike I felt was beginning to grow less . . .

TARTAGLIA. Oh, s-splendid!

He rubs his hands.

Then, let us prepare for the wedding!

ANGELA.   . . . but when I heard my brother and my father
were imprisoned by your order, while many had been put
in chains, in my unhappiness I had to weep again.

She feigns weeping.

TARTAGLIA. My sun and moon! Don't cry! I was obliged to
imprison them to appease the people who were in revolt on
account of poor Tartaglia's death. But, after a few formal
questions, you may be sure your father and brother will be
freed . . . even if they are guilty.

ANGELA. Is that certain?

TARTAGLIA. C-certain? Are you still not convinced? Well, if
that is all that stands between us and the altar . . .

To one of the GUARDS.

Guard, set Leander and Pantaloon free!

Exit FIRST GUARD.

ANGELA *rises and holds out her hands to* TARTAGLIA.

ANGELA. My dear Deramo, that is the way to my heart! I feel I am beginning to love you already . . .

TARTAGLIA, *excitedly, taking* ANGELA's *hands*. The hour has come! Ask more favors of me. Think of something else. Quickly, what else can I give you?

ANGELA, *feigning tenderness*. Well, my brother, Leander, whom you have just freed from prison, loves Clarissa. Will you make them happy on this happy day?

TARTAGLIA. Is that all?

He goes toward the door.

Why, I will give Leander Clarissa and three castles into the bargain!

Holding out his hand.

Come, Angela!

ANGELA, *feigning more tenderness*. Let me ask just one more boon . . .

TARTAGLIA. Come, my pigeon, ask quickly and let us go.

ANGELA, *in a low voice*. First, send the guard away!

TARTAGLIA, *taken aback*. The guard? . . . Why, of course!

To the GUARD.

Withdraw and don't return till I call.

Exit SECOND GUARD.

Now.

ANGELA. Yesterday morning, as a token of your love and confidence, you told me of a magic secret, whereby you could bring a dead body to life with your spirit, and then change back into your own body. My King, let me see this magic transformation.

TARTAGLIA *turns away and remains silent*.

Are you loath to grant my request? Are you afraid, perhaps, I will not keep my promise?

TARTAGLIA, *dubiously*. No, n-no, of course not. I will grant you this request also, dear one. But . . . my impatience grows. After so many proofs of my affection, show me some proof of yours.

ANGELA. I assure you that, after this last favor, you will see what my love is capable of . . .

ANGELA wonders if she has not gone too far.

TARTAGLIA, *aside.* This may be a trap. But I too can play the fox. Angela . . . the dead stag with the white mark lies between here and the temple. I'll show you on the way. Come.

ANGELA. Oh, my King, do not spoil everything with your haste . . . first let me see this wonder, then I promise I will go to the priest with you.

TARTAGLIA, *beside himself.* Slubberdegullion! I will stand no more dallying! I am King! To the altar!

ANGELA falls to her knees.

ANGELA. Deramo, I implore you!

TARTAGLIA seizes her by the wrists.

TARTAGLIA. Implore nothing! To the altar!

ANGELA. Help! Help! Deramo! Deramo!

DERAMO, *in hiding.* Stop, traitor!

TARTAGLIA, *alarmed, letting go of* ANGELA. What is that voice? I am trapped!

He takes a few steps in the direction of the voice and stops.

The King's voice!

He wheels round toward ANGELA.

You little serpent! You have set a murderer here in ambush to take my life! But I am not to be taken like a rat in a trap!

He draws his sword. ANGELA *rises.*

Tremble for him, and for yourself!

He parts the curtains with the point of his sword and drags out DERAMO.

ANGELA. Heaven defend us!

TARTAGLIA. Who are you, old fool? Answer, you traitor! Who brought you here? Speak, or I'll cleave you in two!

TARTAGLIA raises his sword. ANGELA *utters a cry.*

DERAMO. Malefactor, I am Deramo, your King! If, despite my benefactions, you dare to kill me, be sure Heaven will avenge me!

TARTAGLIA, *lowering his sword and looking closely at him.* Ah!

but I recognize this filthy old man. You are the one I killed
at the hunt yesterday. I should not have left your body in
one piece. So, die again, you old impostor, and into the bot-
tomless pit . . .

TARTAGLIA *follows* DERAMO *around, till he stands on the
left-hand casement step. He catches hold of one of* DERAMO'S
arms and whirls his sword over his head ready to strike.
ANGELA *screams.*

*At this moment, the stage is plunged into darkness, except
for a light on the* PARROT *in the alcove.*

Thunder.

TARTAGLIA *is frozen where he stands with raised sword.*

DERAMO *recoils to the opposite casement opening.*

SCENE 6

PARROT INTO MAGICIAN

In a flash the PARROT *is transformed into a man of tall
stature, with tall hat, dark glasses, a cloak and wand. He is
the magician,* DURANDARTE.

The golden cage, which has burst open, rolls to the front.

DERAMO. A miracle! Durandarte, the magician!

TARTAGLIA. I am betrayed!

DURANDARTE. Tremble, perfidious Minister!

TARTAGLIA. Cursed magician, your enchantment will not stop
my revenge. Ministers, guards, slaves—ho! Your King is set
on by renegades!

DURANDARTE, *calmly.* Shout! Rave! Your voice will not reach
beyond this circle! The Fairy King protects the innocent.
The wicked are punished when they least expect it.

DURANDARTE *slowly lowers his wand, and, in so doing, un-
freezes* TARTAGLIA, *who lowers his arm and drops his sword.*

Treacherous Minister, you sought to usurp the shape and power of the King, and turn the King into a lowly creature, spurned or hunted by all. Know then, that it is the mind which makes the man. Look at this old fellow! But consider his kind deeds . . . and then reflect on your wickedness! His mind shines through his misery! His faithful Angela loves him still. Your wickedness corrodes your looks and makes you an outcast. Let your shapes be changed. Let all the wretchedness of King Deramo, and worse, fall upon you!

Pointing with his wand to TARTAGLIA.

Now tremble!

Pointing with his wand to DERAMO.

Now rejoice!

DURANDARTE *waves his wand.*

Lightning. Thunder.

TARTAGLIA's *legs are covered in rags.* DERAMO's *legs resume their former shape and dress.*

ANGELA. Truffaldino's parrot—a magician!

DERAMO, *to* DURANDARTE. O great friend.

TARTAGLIA. I defy your magic art!

DURANDARTE, *to* TARTAGLIA. Follow your destiny, unworthy soul!

DURANDARTE *waves his wand.*

Lightning. Thunder.

DERAMO *is wearing his royal cloaks. Only his head remains that of the* OLD MAN.

TARTAGLIA *is wearing only a ragged shirt. His head and headdress still resemble that of the true* KING.

ANGELA, *amazed and exulting.* O wonder!

DERAMO. O fortune!

TARTAGLIA. O misery! Enough, sorcerer!

DURANDARTE. Endure your punishment to the end!

To DERAMO.

And you, rejoice, for your destinies will now be fulfilled!

DURANDARTE *waves his wand.*

Lightning. Thunder.

DERAMO *is wearing a jeweled turban, and his features have become youthful once more.*

TARTAGLIA'S *face has become hideous. He has become a cramped and wizened* OLD MAN.

ANGELA, *running to* DERAMO. Deramo, my Deramo!

DERAMO. Angela!

They embrace.

DURANDARTE *comes forward from the alcove.*

DURANDARTE. Come hither, everyone.

All the characters enter.

TARTAGLIA, *dragging himself forward.* Where can I go? Where can I hide myself?

DURANDARTE. Stay here, you evil man. This is where you are to die of shame! You are to be a public show and laughing-stock. Look, everyone!

TARTAGLIA. A curse on the whole lot of you!

The assembled company recoils.

TARTAGLIA *sinks down by the window.*

Aaah! Help! Help! I am dying!

CLARISSA *enters, running.*

CLARISSA. Where is my father?

DURANDARTE. There, my child. His deeds have found him out.

CLARISSA. Oh, my dear father!

TARTAGLIA. Out of my sight!

CLARISSA. It is your child, Clarissa!

TARTAGLIA. Clarissa?

He turns his head toward her.

Clarissa!

CLARISSA, *stroking his head.* I love you! I will not desert you!

TARTAGLIA. Can you touch this head without horror?

CLARISSA. You are my father!

TARTAGLIA, *making an effort to raise himself.* Durandarte! I am avenged! Over and above your justice, there is still . . . love!

He dies.

CLARISSA *utters a cry.*

DERAMO *goes to* CLARISSA *and raises her up.*

CLARISSA *goes to* LEANDER *and weeps in his arms.*

PANTALOON *comes forward.*

PANTALOON, *quizzically.* I really cannot say whether I am more terrified or more curious to know what lies behind this mystery!

DERAMO, *coming forward.* Friends, I can well excuse your astonishment. But I will explain everything in due course. Meanwhile, Leander, take good care of Clarissa. And you, illustrious magician, my old friend, you may dispose of me and of my kingdom!

He goes to DURANDARTE *and takes his hand.* DURANDARTE *bows.*

DURANDARTE. No, King Deramo, I desire nothing. Celebrate your several marriages. Let revelry begin!

Music: Opening ethereally with harpsichord.

The company look about as if hearing music coming from nowhere.

KING DERAMO *takes* ANGELA *by the hand. The court bow. They take leave, and are followed by* PANTALOON, *then* LEANDER *and* CLARISSA (*who gives a last look at* TARTAGLIA); BRIGHELLA *follows.* SMERALDINA *and* TRUFFALDINO *bring up the rear, with fancy steps.* SMERALDINA, *smiling at the public, walks into the left-hand pillar;* TRUFFALDINO *chuckles and leaps out.*

The stage becomes dark again, except for a circle of light on DURANDARTE, *center.*

DURANDARTE *turns once more to* TARTAGLIA's *body, then he turns to the public.*

DURANDARTE. My hour has struck! Durandarte desires no kingdom. His magic lore, his charms and spells,

He turns his back to the audience.

his marvels and wizardry are at an end!

He raises his wand above his head, holding one end in each hand.

I am free!

His wand vanishes.

He removes his hat, turns to the public, and removes his glasses.

But, you, my wise young friends, pardon us for having changed ourselves into animals to entertain you, and give us as our best reward some little sign of your kind humanity!

He bows.

NOTES

THE MANDRAKE (*La Mandragola*), written between 1513 and 1520, is often considered to be the greatest of Italian plays and it occupies an important place in the great studies of Italian literature, such as Francesco de Sanctis' *History of Italian Literature*. In Castiglione's letters is to be found a rather detailed description of a production of another Renaissance comedy (Bernardo Dovizi da Bibbiena's *La Calandria*) which applies, *mutatis mutandis*, to *The Mandrake*. (Perhaps the quickest way, these days, to find this item is by consulting the Viking *Portable Renaissance Reader*.) At least one of the older English critics recognized the merit of Machiavelli's play and gave a highly percipient account of it: this is Lord Macaulay in his essay on Machiavelli. A comment by the present editor will be found in his book *The Dramatic Event*.

Four English versions have preceded the present one in print: the first was by Stark Young (1927); the second by Ashley Dukes (1940); the third by Henry and Anne Paolucci (1957); the fourth by J. R. Hale (1958). The May-Bentley version is first published here.

RUZZANTE RETURNS FROM THE WARS (*Il Reduce*) probably belongs to 1522 or 1523. J. S. Kennard, in his *Italian Theatre*, writes: "Angelo Beolco (Il Ruzzante), Andrea Calmo, and Gigio Artemio Giancarli form the connecting link between the learned and the popular theatre, and facilitate the natural passage from the literary comedy of classic type to the *commedia dell' arte*." Which explains its position, in the present book, between *The Mandrake* and *The Three Cuckolds*. Beolco has played an important part, too, in the modern rediscovery of the older Italian theatre: translated into French by Alfred Mortier, he was introduced to a small but influential French public by Jacques Copeau in the 1920s. Aside from the *Bilora*, which is to be found in Barrett H. Clark's anthology *World Drama*, the *Reduce* seems to be the only one of Beolco's works to have found its way into English. Angela Ingold's version was originally couched in northern English speech and in that form was produced by the Leeds University Italian Society in 1955. For this book it has been Americanized by Mr. Hoffman.

For a note on THE THREE CUCKOLDS, late sixteenth century, see Appendix A.

THE SERVANT OF TWO MASTERS, writes Edward J. Dent, "is one of Goldoni's earliest plays; it was written in 1743 at the request of the actor Sacchi, who suggested the subject and himself played the part of Truffaldino. The Italian theatre of that day was dominated by the improvising actors who wore the traditional masks, and in the original form of this play the comic scenes were left to the actor's own invention. Goldoni wrote them down when he printed the play in 1753, and there can be no doubt that he incorporated a great deal of Sacchi's traditional business. Mozart had a great admiration for *The Servant of Two Masters,* and in 1783 contemplated turning it into a comic opera." The twentieth-century fame of the play is perhaps largely to be attributed to Max Reinhardt, who directed it many times; one of his productions of it was seen in New York. Professor Dent's English version was produced by the Amateur Dramatic Society of Cambridge University in 1928, Michael Redgrave playing Florindo. It is here first printed in the U.S. A note from the Cambridge University Press's edition of the translation appears here as Appendix B.

Of MIRANDOLINA (1752) Lady Gregory wrote: "I translated Goldoni's *La Locandiera,* calling it *Mirandolina,* for the Abbey Theatre, thinking it in key with our country comedies, and it was first produced there in February, 1910. When we were putting it on again I left out two characters, the actresses, as I found the scenes into which they come delayed the action and were not needed. And I gave the whole play at that time an Irish setting, so getting a greater ease in the speaking and in the acting. And even now that it is back again in Italy, the dialogue is in places less bound to the word than to the spirit of the play.

"Many years ago I had the joy of seeing Duse in the ironing scene; and the lovely movements of her hands and the beauty of the voice that called 'Fabrizio!' are still clear in my memory."

Maurice Baring wrote: "Eleanora Duse's *La Locandiera* remains what it was, incomparable and entrancing. Pascal said that had the dimensions of Cleopatra's nose been slightly modified, the history of the world would have been different. Had he seen Madame Duse in this part, he would probably have been grateful that she had nothing to do with affairs of state, for the raising of her eyelid and the magic in her eye when she calls Fabrizio would have wrought still greater havoc than Cleopatra's nose among the great ones of the earth." —*Punch and Judy.*

A fuller description of Eleanora Duse as Mirandolina is to be found in Stark Young's *Immortal Shadows,* and the following sentence from Mr. Young's *The Theatre* constitutes probably the best comment on the play ever made in English: "Goldoni's comedy of *La Locandiera,* usually spoken of by criticisms in English as very slight, takes its admirable depth most of all from the sequence of its parts, the order in which it progresses, the fine, sane, sweet and witty openness of its development by which its relationships and parts are assembled like the parts in a sunlit landscape."

A more literal version of Goldoni's text, as rendered by Merle Pierson, is to be found in Brander Matthews' *Chief European Dramatists.*

Mr. Wildman's version of THE KING STAG, which, in the original, dates back to 1762, is partly based on a French version by Pierre Barbier. A free adaptation, it is designed, not to give the reader a line-for-line account of the Italian, but to provide for the modern theatre an entertainment full of Gozzian delights; and, we are told, it did provide such an entertainment when the Young Vic produced it in 1946 with George Devine as their director. First published here, it is the second of Gozzi's plays to find its way into print in English, the first being Edward J. Dent's translation of *The Blue Monster* (1951). The script of a version of *Turandot* by Isaac Don Levine and Henry Alsberg, produced in New York in the 1920s, seems not to have survived, though there does exist in

English a printed version of *Turandot* which may scarcely claim to be Gozzian: this is *Turandot, Princess of China, A Chinoiserie in Three Acts*, by Karl Vollmoeller, Authorized English Version by Jethro Bithell.

There is a faithful translation of *The King Stag*, as yet unpublished (1958), by Frederick May.

Some technical notes on producing *The King Stag* are to be found in Appendix C.

E.B.

Addendum to the Second Printing, 1962.

Since the first printing appeared four years ago, the following related volumes have appeared:

Goldoni: *Three Comedies*. (London and New York: Oxford University Press, 1961). This volume contains *Mine Hostess*, translated by Clifford Bax; *The Boors*, translated by I. M. Rawson; and *The Fan*, translated by Eleanor and Herbert Farjeon.

Machiavelli: *The Literary Works of*. Edited and translated by J. R. Hale (London and New York: Oxford University Press, 1961.) The plays which this volume contains are: *Mandragola* and *Clizia*.

Machiavelli: *Clizia*. Translated by Oliver Evans (Great Neck, New York: Barron's Educational Series, 1962).

APPENDIX A

The Scenario for THE THREE CUCKOLDS

It is not literally true that *commedia dell' arte* was acted in improvisation after a *scenario*, or scene-by-scene outline of the stage action. Each of the ten or twelve actors of a troupe brought his mask, type, and repertoire to bear on scripts whipped up out of classical tales, academic plays, medieval horrifics, hashed tragedies, or Plautine farces; and each character had the staples of his repertoire jotted down in his own promptbook—Pantalone his catalogues of windy advice to his son and his counsels for friends; Arlecchino his hundreds of *lazzi* (or byplays) on catching flies and eating them with relish, eating an imaginary bunch of cherries, preparing to kill himself and trying different ways for suicide; Isabella her conceits, soliloquies, and *chiusetti* (tag-end rhymed couplets) for occasions of "love reciprocal, rejected, disdainful; friendship, jealousy, leave-taking." Still, the genius of the performance did lie in the "improvisation," since the particular mixture of ingredients for any one afternoon was anticipated only roughly;* the mixture first came to life by way of performance, and ceased for good when the performance was over.

In retirement, players and managers used to edit and publish dialogues, speeches, scenes, sometimes whole plays, more or less, from their own repertoire and that of their company. Of the bare *scenarii* themselves, more than seven hundred are still in existence.

The Three Cuckolds is taken from a *scenario* of the same name, amended and reworked, and it incorporates other features of *commedia* farce which by chance did not find their way into the *scenario's* original bundle of episodes. The literal translation of the *scenario* as printed here is taken from

* But how roughly is "roughly"? Present-day Italian scholars, such as Vito Pandolfi, think that the anticipation was remarkably detailed. [E.B.]

K. M. Lea's *Italian Popular Comedy, 1560–1620, with special reference to the English stage,* Clarendon Press, Oxford, 1934, Vol. 2, pp. 580–84.

THE THREE CUCKOLDS

A Comedy

Dramatis Personae

PANTALONE
FLAMINIA, *his wife*
COVIELLO
CINTIA, *his wife*
ZANNI
FRANCESCHINA, *his wife*
LEANDRO, *a young man*

PROPERTIES: *A washing basket with sheets; chest of lemons; cask; tow; fire; candle; broth; dress for a rogue.*

ACT I

COVIELLO, CINTIA have their scene of reciprocal jealousy. Cintia goes in and leaves Coviello to disclose his passion for Flaminia, the wife of Pantalone; he knocks at her door:

FLAMINIA appears. They have their love scene and in the end she tells him about the chest of lemons. Coviello goes in, Flaminia stays; at this:

PANTALONE is asked to provide her with lemons; he promises to send them in a chest. Flaminia goes in. Pantalone is left to disclose his love for Franceschina, Zanni's wife; he knocks at her door:

FRANCESCHINA hears everything and declares that she favors Pantalone; he departs, she remains; at this:

ZANNI tells his wife to go to work; they have many antics. Franceschina goes in and he stays, saying what a nuisance she is; at this:

COVIELLO asks Zanni to carry him in a chest and explains everything. They go off down the street.

LEANDRO declares his love for Cintia and knocks at her door:

CINTIA hears everything and instructs him to come dressed as a rogue, dumb and disguised. She goes in and he departs to dress up.

PANTALONE can wait no longer and says that at last it is time; he knocks for Franceschina.

FRANCESCHINA leads him into the house and they have their antics over the entrance.

ZANNI with the chest exhorts Coviello not to speak or move; he puts him inside; at this:

LEANDRO as a dumb beggar is forced to shoulder the chest by Zanni, who does not recognize him; at this:

FLAMINIA receives the chest. Zanni enters. Leandro is left and knocks for Cintia.

CINTIA receives him into the house, they have their scene and the act ends.

ACT II

ZANNI blames Flaminia for the trick played on her husband and congratulates himself on the honesty of his wife Franceschina; meanwhile she is heard within, singing and slapping up and down with the washing; then she comes out.

FRANCESCHINA appears with the cask, which she puts over her husband's head, playing the trick of the tart;* at this:

PANTALONE comes out of Franceschina's house, grinning; he goes to knock at his own home. Zanni and Franceschina go in. Pantalone is left calling his wife.

---

* Probably she promises him a tart if he will keep the cask over his head; he bargains and meanwhile the lover slips out. [K.M.L.]

FLAMINIA, with much circumstance, recounts the dream of the eye and makes him hide his eyes from Flaminia; at this:

COVIELLO comes out of Flaminia's house laughing at the trick. He goes to knock at his own. Pantalone and Flaminia go in; Coviello knocks.

CINTIA makes much of Coviello and caresses him and then tells him of the poor beggar she has in the house; at this:

LEANDRO, disguised, comes in with some soup. Coviello scolds and goes into the house with Cintia. Leandro laughs at the hoax and, seeing Zanni approaching, pretends to be dumb again.

ZANNI after several jokes recognizes Leandro and tells him what has been going on in Pantalone's house. Leandro tells him what has happened at Coviello's and goes in, laughing. Zanni stays; at this:

PANTALONE learns from Zanni the jest of the rogue. Pantalone tells him the jest of the cask and Zanni in the end tells about the lemon chest and goes in. Pantalone is left; at this:

COVIELLO is told of the hoax of the rogue; they have their scene together shouting "Cuckold" at each other.

ACT III

FRANCESCHINA, to borrow a buck basket, knocks for

CINTIA, who promises to give it her with the washing and takes her into the house.

PANTALONE wishes to return to Franceschina, who had pleased him; at this:

FRANCESCHINA comes with the basket and the clothes. Pantalone explains his intentions and she makes him get into the basket and covers him with clothes; at this:

ZANNI, aware of all that is going on and knowing there is someone in the basket, has many antics about throwing the clothes into the copper and boiling them. He carries in the basket and, coming out again, tells Franceschina that he is going into the country. She is delighted and goes into the house. Zanni goes down the street.

COVIELLO after his former success wishes to try again, he knocks for

FLAMINIA, who hears his wish and receives him once more and leads him into the house.

LEANDRO, CINTIA do the same; Cintia embraces him and takes him into the house again.

ZANNI comes to make sure about his wife; he draws near to the door and hears caresses going on; he knocks in a fury.

FRANCESCHINA, hearing that Zanni wants to burn down the house, makes him carry out the basket of clothes before he sets fire to the place. With an uproar

PANTALONE comes out among the clothes in the basket; at this

ALL THE COUPLES, arm in arm, rush to the alarm of fire in the room. Leandro explains what each has done to the other and delivers over to each his proper wife, with whom he is at last content. They go in and the comedy ends.

Intentionally, none of the dialogue in this adaptation is taken from the extant collections. The dialogue herein simply expands the comedy's situations in the spirit of the originals (though its matter is wholly traditional). Nothing is clearer from the collections than that *commedia* dialogue and its accompanying mime could be theatrically superb. Arlecchino's recorded monologues and *lazzi* are hilarious. And there was a Dottore Gratiano, played by an old Bolognese merchant, who, when he did scenes with Salvator Rosa's Pascariello, caused "laughter so violent that it was pronounced physically dangerous." But dialogue originally in dialect, playing on current idiom and phrasing (and supported by a convention of gesture whose history is too rapid and subtle ever to be recovered from any period), translated into translator's English, is merely a joke's memorial, not a joke. The *commedia* canon used faithfully and literally might be a bit better than dull on the printed page—and readers of translated comedies have learned to be kind—but it would be painfully unyielding in performance. Anything that does not yield to performance is an anomaly in *commedia dell' arte*.

L.K.

THE SERVANT OF TWO MASTERS, Directorial Notes

The improvised Comedy of Masks, the history of which goes back to the days of ancient Rome, was frequently coarse and obscene. In the early eighteenth century, as Goldoni himself says, there was an English theatre and a French theatre, but no real Italian theatre. The opera had become the most popular entertainment of the cultivated classes, and even the opera stood badly in need of reform until Apostolo Zeno and Metastasio gave it real literary distinction. Goldoni made it his mission to give an artistic form to the spoken comedy. The four traditional masks which appear in his plays are Pantalone, the Doctor, Brighella and Arlecchino. Pantalone is the old Venetian merchant, wearing the dress of the sixteenth century. By tradition he was merely senile and lascivious; Goldoni made him a model of respectability, while never losing sight of his comic character. The Doctor represents the old man of the educated classes; he is a Doctor of Law of the University of Bologna, pompous and pedantic, much given to Latin quotations. He plays a small part in Goldoni's plays. Brighella and Harlequin come from Bergamo and represent the two types of servant, knave and fool. Truffaldino is also from Bergamo and is much the same person as Harlequin.

Goldoni is at his best when he lays his scene in his native Venice. His heroes and heroines are conventional figures, often of little interest, but he gives a vivid presentation of types from humbler life, porters, waiters, fisherfolk and gondoliers. The trend of the age was toward sentimental comedy, and this becomes more and more noticeable in Goldoni's later plays, especially those written after 1762 for the *Théâtre Italien* in Paris. The masks disappear and the scene is laid in more aristocratic circles. The earlier plays, written for Venice, deal with middle-class family life; Goldoni's Venice is the Venice of the remoter streets, not the gay international city of pleasure, shown us in *Volpone* and in the Memoirs of Casanova. Goldoni's plays are conventional in construction, trivial in incident, undistinguished in dialogue and strictly moral in intention; yet when they are seen on the stage, especially if acted by a Venetian company, no one could fail to enjoy their delightful humor. Goldoni's puritanism was in fact of an entirely negative type; he simply ignored the coarser and rougher jests because, like Mozart's Don Alfonso, he saw every little event of daily life from a comic point of view.

The four Mask characters, Pantalone, the Doctor, Brighella, and Truffaldino, ought to wear their traditional costumes. There are many pictures of these available, but it must be remembered that the minor details of them varied considerably at different periods.

Pantalone, who is always tall and thin, with a pointed gray beard, is dressed entirely in red; he wears a close-fitting doublet (never an eighteenth-century long coat), breeches, stockings, and red oriental slippers turning up at the toes. Over this dress he wears a long furred gown rather like an alderman's. On his head he wears a loose red cap like that worn by Handel and other men of his time when not wearing wigs. This costume dates originally from about 1500 or earlier and bears no resemblance at all to any dress of the eighteenth century.

The Doctor is usually short and fat, indeed rather gross in appearance, generally without a beard, though sometimes with a small mustache and "imperial"; he is dressed in black with a close-fitting short coat with white ruffled collar and cuffs, and a black cloak like an academical gown. He generally has a large round black hat with a very wide brim, which is not turned up. As with Pantalone, his dress does not belong to the eighteenth century.

Brighella is generally represented in white or a very light color; he has a loose coat like a modern jacket, but buttoned up with a turned-up collar, and loose trousers showing the ankles, with a belt outside his coat. His dress is decorated with short horizontal rows of braid like much exaggerated buttonholes, and his trousers have four of these too, on the outsides, between the knee and the ankle. (There may perhaps be some connection between these and the useless buttons and holes on men's sleeves of today.) He also has a cloak and a loose cap.

Truffaldino's dress is the same as Harlequin's, but it may

be preferable to give him the earlier and more primitive form of it, a baggy coat and ankle-length trousers of coarse sacking irregularly patched, with a very wide-brimmed soft hat. One side of it is turned up straight and a rabbit's tail stuck in it. He carries the traditional lath or wooden sword (originally a rake). Truffaldino is short and tubby, with a very swarthy face.

The other characters wear ordinary dress of the period. The porters should be ragged odd-job men, preferably barefooted.

Masks are not recommended for a modern English performance, as most actors find them a hindrance, and their unfamiliarity makes them bewildering to an audience of today. The black mask of Harlequin and the other "zanies" originally represented merely the dirty face of a charcoal burner or chimney sweep.

The local Italian dialects cannot be represented in English, and the use of British dialects would be quite misleading. But it should be at least suggested that the Venetian characters are homely middle-class people. Pantalone, as a Venetian, is a quick and voluble talker; the Doctor, a Bolognese, pompous and pedantic, takes his time, but sometimes talks Pantalone down by sheer weight of legal language.

Brighella is traditionally something of a ruffian and a knave, though always a cheerful and amusing one; in this play there is little to suggest that character, though he evidently enjoys intrigue and is ready to oblige anybody for the usual consideration.

He and Truffaldino have the common Venetian habit of dropping the final vowel of proper names—Pantalon', Pasqual', Truffaldin'; in all these cases the accent falls on the last printed syllable, exactly as when the names are pronounced correctly.

Silvio and Clarice are very young—not more than eighteen —and very ignorant of life. Clarice has been kept very close at home and seems to have derived her style from novels. Silvio has also been very strictly brought up, but is most anxious to show himself a grown-up "man of the world." Florindo and Beatrice, on the other hand, come from a slightly higher social class; they are completely at their ease, and talk literary Italian. In this English version their language is purposely made a little stilted.

Smeraldina is not strictly a Mask character, but like Brighella and Truffaldino, she comes from the country near Bergamo and is therefore rustic and almost uncouth in manner. She is very outspoken and has a violent temper; she must on no account be made into a smart parlormaid or comic-opera *soubrette*.

This play offers many opportunities for traditional comic business called *lazzi* (probably from *le azioni,* the actions), and all of these should be made the most of. The play opens with a moment of seriousness; the formal betrothal before witnesses, although purely domestic, must have a certain gravity, as it is almost the equivalent of a legal civil marriage. After it is over, the company relax, and the entrance of Truffaldino at once starts the atmosphere of farce. In Scene 2 the business with the porter may give the actors a free hand; the same applies to Truffaldino's sealing of the letter with chewed bread. The quarrel between Pantalone and the Doctor in Act II is another traditional scene. Other occasions for exaggerated comic business occur when Brighella and Truffaldino plan the arrangement of the dinner table, and when the dinner is actually served. It will be found effective to make the first waiter quite an old man.

Truffaldino's dumb show with Smeraldina is another traditional *lazzo* which calls for elaboration; the beating of Truffaldino is an obvious opportunity. The third act has many resemblances to comic opera (no doubt it was this that attracted Mozart) in the formal symmetry of Truffaldino's dialogues with his two separate "masters," and in the obvious operatic caricature of the mock suicides and the recognition scene. The last scene is almost a Mozartian *ensemble*. This "musical" quality of speech is very characteristic of Goldoni; he constantly requires his actors to take up their cues in a regular rhythm just as if they were singing a duet.

Pasquale is a purely imaginary person, but from the first moment that he is named it must be made clear to the audience that he is going to be one of the most important characters in the play.

E.J.D.

APPENDIX C

THE KING STAG, *Technical Notes*

ACT I, SCENE 1

The Parrot is made on a wire frame with an opening in the back through which a hand can be inserted. Inside is a glove with strings attached to the fingers by which the movements of the head and beak can be manipulated. The head is on a spring.

The Parrot's Voice: An actor behind the scenes imitates a parrot's voice. It is essential he should articulate clearly. Cigolotti should appear to be a ventriloquist.

The Parrot in the Cage: The parrot can move when placed in his cage by means of the following device. His perch is fixed to a wheel concealed in a false bottom to the cage. A string runs round the wheel and the ends hang loose. When the cage is set down near the curtain, the actor behind the curtain pulls the strings through, under the curtain, and holds them ready to pull when the parrot speaks. Two wires project underneath the parrot. These are inserted in two holes in the perch—thus ensuring the turning of the parrot in the cage.

ACT I, SCENE 8

The Laughing Bust: When the privy chamber is opened, in front of the right-hand wing stands a pedestal with a thin neck—no actor could possibly be concealed in it. Behind the bust, in the open wing, is a small trap door which can be opened from behind. An actor opens it and places his head inside under cover of the cloth which Deramo removes before interviewing Clarissa. Deramo replaces the cloth when the bust laughs immoderately at Smeraldina (at the moment indicated in the text)—ostensibly to prevent Smeraldina noticing it.

When Deramo removes the cloth, after Smeraldina's exit and before Angela's entry, a mask, resembling the actor's whitened face, fills the aperture in the bust.

To attract the attention of the audience to the bust, a spotlight picks it out whenever Deramo looks at it to observe its reactions.

The Breaking of the Bust: The top shell of the bust is detachable. Deramo pretends to strike it with his sword, a stick is passed through the trap door at the back and pushes it off the pedestal. It falls in two pieces—the shell and the mask. A flashpan at the top of the pedestal, under the bust, is set off at this moment. The flash and smoke conceal the maneuver.

ACT II, SCENE 3

The Parrot flies away: Cigolotti brings on the parrot in his cage with wires already attached for flying.

ACT II, SCENE 6

Transformations: King into Stag, Tartaglia into King, King Stag into Old Man.

Deramo recites the spell over the stag with a white mark on its forehead. He sinks down and dies, while the king stag comes to life. Tartaglia begins to recite the spell when hunting horns sound and a shot is heard. He picks up his harquebus and runs off. When the huntsmen have passed, a second actor, dressed like Tartaglia, enters, recites the magic words, and dies. Deramo rises and is similarly interrupted by the returning huntsmen; he also runs off with his harquebus. When the huntsmen have gone, it is Tartaglia, dressed and masked like the King, who returns. He drags off the body of his double. Tartaglia preserves his stutter and forceful manner, even when King to all appearances.

When the actor playing Deramo goes off right, he quickly changes into the clothes and mask of the Old Man, in which guise he re-enters across the stream, that is, from the opposite side. He speaks like a peasant until he is brought to life again

by the king stag reciting the spell. In fact, Deramo, as the Old
Man lying dead, speaks the words of the charm, while the king
stag moves his head as if saying them himself.

The Parrot walking into Truffaldino's basket trap: The trap
is a simple inverted basket, hung by a hook from the rocks
and held up by a stick to which is attached a string which
Truffaldino pulls at the appropriate moment so that it falls over
the parrot.

In the face of the rock is a concealed opening from below.
The actor who manipulates the parrot with his hand stands on
a box, putting his hand through the opening. He makes the
parrot walk down into the trap, and continues to manipulate
its head when it speaks to Truffaldino from inside the trap.
Truffaldino eventually pulls the parrot off the actor's hand and
places it in his golden cage.

Carrying off the King Stag: While Truffaldino is speaking
to the audience, the two peasants pretend to tie the stag by
its feet to a pole. In fact, the actor playing the king stag clasps
the pole with his hands from inside the material of his costume
above the hoofs. He crosses his feet over the other end of the
pole.

The Transformation of the Parrot into Magician: In the
blackout which follows the spotlight on the parrot's cage in
the alcove, the cage is removed and a cage which is burst open
thrown on the floor. The magician, Durandarte, stands in the
alcove and is dimly lit.

The gauze curtains on either wing are draped up to frame
Tartaglia as King on the right side and Deramo as the Old Man
on the opposite side. (This is the position to which Deramo
recoils when Angela screams.)

*The Transformation of Tartaglia and Deramo in three
stages:* After the first wave of Durandarte's wand, accom-

panied by lightning in the alcove, the wings are in darkness, Deramo strips off the lower half of his Old Man's cloak, so that his legs appear dressed as the King. A second actor replaces Tartaglia with rags over his legs, but otherwise still dressed as the King.

After the second wave of the wand, with lightning as in the first change, the actor playing Tartaglia resumes his position, completely clothed in rags but still with the mask and headdress of the King. A second actor replaces Deramo. He is dressed as the King, except for his Old Man's mask and hair.

After the third wave of the wand, with lightning as in the first two changes, the actor playing Deramo resumes his position, complete with his original mask and King's headdress. Tartaglia removes his King's mask and headdress and puts on the wig and mask of a repulsive Old Man. He is crabbed and bent.

The Vanishing of the Wand is done as a conjuror's trick.

C.W.

ANCHOR BOOKS

DRAMA

AN ANTHOLOGY OF GERMAN EXPRESSIONIST DRAMA: A Prelude to the Absurd—Walter H. Sokel, ed., A365

AN APPROACH TO SHAKESPEARE, in two volumes—D. A. Traversi, A74a, b

THE BIRTH OF TRAGEDY AND THE GENEALOGY OF MORALS—Friedrich Nietzsche; Francis Golffing, trans., A81

BRECHT: THE MAN AND HIS WORK—Martin Esslin, revised edition, A245

BRAND—Henrik Ibsen; Michael Meyer, trans., intro. by W. H. Auden, A215a

THE CLASSIC THEATRE: Volume I: Six Italian Plays—Eric Bentley, ed., A155a

THE CLASSIC THEATRE: Volume II: Five German Plays—Eric Bentley, ed., A155b

THE CLASSIC THEATRE: Volume III: Six Spanish Plays—Eric Bentley, ed., A155c

THE CLASSIC THEATRE: Volume IV: Six French Plays—Eric Bentley, ed., A155d

COMEDY—Henri Bergson; George Meredith, A87

A COMPANION TO SHAKESPEARE STUDIES—H. Granville-Barker and G. B. Harrison, ed., A191

FIVE COMEDIES OF ARISTOPHANES—Benjamin Bickley Rogers, trans.; Andrew Chiappe, ed., A57

FIVE PLAYS OF STRINDBERG—Elizabeth Sprigge, trans., A219

GHOSTS AND THREE OTHER PLAYS—Henrik Ibsen; Michael Meyer, trans., A215e

GOETHE'S FAUST—Walter Kaufmann, trans., bilingual edition, A328

HAMLET AND OEDIPUS—Ernest Jones, A31

HEDDA GABLER AND THREE OTHER PLAYS—Henrik Ibsen; Michael Meyer, trans., A215c

INFERNO, ALONE AND OTHER WRITINGS—August Strindberg, new translations, Evert Sprinchorn, ed., A492c

MIDDLE ENGLISH ANTHOLOGY—Ann S. Haskell, AO10

THE MODERN THEATRE, Volume 1, Eric Bentley, ed., A48a

THE MODERN THEATRE, Volume 2, Eric Bentley, ed., A48b

THE MODERN THEATRE, Volume 5, Eric Bentley, ed., A48c

THE MODERN THEATRE, Volume 5, Eric Bentley, ed., A48e

THE PEOPLED WOUND, The Work of Harold Pinter—Martin Esslin, A739

PEER GYNT—Henrik Ibsen; Michael Meyer, trans., A215d

REFLECTIONS: Essays on the Modern Theatre—Martin Esslin, A771

SHAKESPEARE OUR CONTEMPORARY—Jan Kott; Boleslaw Taborski, trans., A499

SIX PLAYS OF STRINDBERG—Elizabeth Sprigge, trans., A54

4Ab

DRAMA (cont'd)

THEATRE EXPERIMENT: An Anthology of American Plays—Michael Benedikt, ed., A636
THE THEATRE OF THE ABSURD—Martin Esslin, revised edition, A279
TRAGEDY AND PHILOSOPHY—Walter Kaufmann, A689

ANCHOR BOOKS

FICTION

ANCHOR BOOKS

CLASSICS AND MYTHOLOGY